Lecture Notes in Computer Science 13857

The series Lecture Notes in Computer Science (LNCS), including its subseries Lecture Notes in Artificial Intelligence (LNAI) and Lecture Notes in Bioinformatics (LNBI), has established itself as a medium for the publication of new developments in computer science and information technology research, teaching, and education.

LNCS enjoys close cooperation with the computer science R & D community, the series counts many renowned academics among its volume editors and paper authors, and collaborates with prestigious societies. Its mission is to serve this international community by providing an invaluable service, mainly focused on the publication of conference and workshop proceedings and postproceedings. LNCS commenced publication in 1973.

Slim Kallel · Mohamed Jmaiel ·
Mohammad Zulkernine · Ahmed Hadj Kacem ·
Frédéric Cuppens · Nora Cuppens
Editors

Risks and Security of Internet and Systems

17th International Conference, CRiSIS 2022
Sousse, Tunisia, December 7–9, 2022
Revised Selected Papers

 Springer

Editors
Slim Kallel ⓘD
University of Sfax
Sfax, Tunisia

Mohammad Zulkernine
Queen's University
Kingston, ON, Canada

Frédéric Cuppens ⓘD
Polytechnique Montréal
Montréal, QC, Canada

Mohamed Jmaiel ⓘD
University of Sfax
Sfax, Tunisia

Ahmed Hadj Kacem ⓘD
University of Sfax
Sfax, Tunisia

Nora Cuppens ⓘD
Polytechnique Montréal
Montréal, QC, Canada

ISSN 0302-9743 ISSN 1611-3349 (electronic)
Lecture Notes in Computer Science
ISBN 978-3-031-31107-9 ISBN 978-3-031-31108-6 (eBook)
https://doi.org/10.1007/978-3-031-31108-6

This Springer imprint is published by the registered company Springer Nature Switzerland AG
The registered company address is: Gewerbestrasse 11, 6330 Cham, Switzerland

Preface

This volume contains the papers presented at the 17th International Conference on Risks and Security of Internet and Systems (CRiSIS 2022), which was organized in Soussse Tunisia, December 7–9, 2022. It continued a tradition of successful conferences: Bourges (2005), Marrakech (2007), Tozeur (2008), Toulouse (2009), Montréal (2010), Timisoara (2011), Cork (2012), La Rochelle (2013), Trento (2014), Mytilene (2015), Roscoff (2016), Dinard (2017), Arcachon (2018), Hammamet (2019), Paris (2020), and Ames (2021).

The CRiSIS conference constitutes an open forum for the exchange of state-of-the-art knowledge on security issues in Internet-related applications, networks, and systems. Following the tradition of the previous events, the program was composed of high-quality contributed papers. The program call for papers looked for original and significant research contributions to the following topics:

- Access control and delegation
- AI and machine learning-based security approaches
- Blockchain and distributed ledger technologies
- Cryptography, biometrics, watermarking
- Distributed systems security and safety
- Modeling and verifying secure systems
- Security of Internet of Things
- Security of smart cities

In response to this call for papers, 39 papers were submitted. Each paper was single-blind reviewed by at least three reviewers, and judged according to scientific and presentation quality, originality, and relevance to the conference topics. The Program Committee selected 14 regular papers and 4 short papers. The program was completed with excellent invited talks given by Benjamin C. M. Fung (McGill University, Canada), Dajin Wang (Montclair State University, USA), and Layth Sliman (Paris 2 Panthéon-Assas University, France). Finally, the conference included one tutorial given by Lamia Chaari (University of Sfax, Tunisia).

We would like to express our appreciation to the authors of the submitted papers, the Program Committee members, and the external referees. We owe special thanks to the Organizing Committee for the hard work they did locally in Sousse.

December 2022

Slim Kallel
Mohamed Jmaiel
Mohammad Zulkernine
Ahmed Hadj Kacem
Frédéric Cuppens
Nora Cuppens-Boulahia

Organization

General Chairs

Ahmed Hadj Kacem   University of Sfax, Tunisia
Frédéric Cuppens   Polytechnique Montréal, Canada
Nora Cuppens-Boulahia   Polytechnique Montréal, Canada

Program Committee Chairs

Mohamed Jmaiel   University of Sfax, Tunisia
Mohammad Zulkernine   Queen's University, Canada

Publicity Chair

Saoussen Cheikhrouhou   University of Sfax, Tunisia

Publication Chair

Slim Kallel   University of Sfax, Tunisia

Local Organizing Members

Ismail Bouassida   University of Sfax, Tunisia
Riadh Ben Halima   University of Sfax, Tunisia
Slim Kallel   University of Sfax, Tunisia
Nesrine Khabou   University of Sfax, Tunisia
Bechir Zalila   University of Sfax, Tunisia

Program Committee

Takoua Abdellatif   University of Carthage, Tunisia
Saed Alrabaee   United Arab Emirates University, UAE
Esma Aïmeur   University of Montreal, Canada

Additional Reviewers

Afef Mdhaffar
Stavros Simou
Mariam Lahami
Ghofrane Fersi
Michail Pantelelis
Aikaterini-Georgia Mavroeidi
Amal Abid
Rim Fekih

Contents

Context Correlation for Automated Dynamic Android App Analysis to Improve Impact Rating of Privacy and Security Flaws

Kris Heid$^{(\boxtimes)}$ and Jens Heider

Fraunhofer SIT, Rheinstr. 75, 64295 Darmstadt, Germany
{kris.heid,jens.heider}@sit.fraunhofer.de

Abstract. Privacy and security flaws in apps are commonly detected by static and dynamic analysis approaches. However, the realistic impact rating for detected flaws is often limited. Static approaches lack runtime information and dynamic analysis miss program structure information. We aim to build a dynamic analysis environment and rate the flaw impact based on the data flow context. We correlate the traced API call chains with data sources and sinks of processed information. This way, the actual runtime information is used and program structures for significant data flows can be reconstructed. Therefore, this publication proposes a method for collecting execution traces based on automated function hooking and mechanisms to create and analyze data flow graphs from these traces. We demonstrate the scalability of our privacy and security analysis by automatically analyzing and evaluating the top 1000 free apps from Google Play. Manual app analysis and damn vulnerable app projects prove the high quality results of our automated approach during evaluation.

Keywords: automated dynamic analysis · data flow graph · privacy · security · android · context correlation

1 Introduction

Smartphones are more and more integrated into our everyday private as well as business life. Many people rather own a smartphone than a personal computer, since everything can be done with a smartphone nowadays. Many companies offer their services in dedicated apps whereas only a website is available for usage on a classic personal computer. Running a program/app on the device instead of calling a website is often more comfortable to the user. However, apps can have a much deeper access on the smartphone compared to a website. This inherently brings privacy and security concerns onto the table. Smartphones are extremely valuable targets since they store much personal information. Additionally, these devices are always online and accompany the user everywhere.

It is nowadays well known that most apps contain libraries to profile users and evaluate or maybe sell such data. The terms and conditions and privacy

S. Kallel et al. (Eds.): CRiSIS 2022, LNCS 13857, pp. 1–17, 2023.
https://doi.org/10.1007/978-3-031-31108-6_1

policy should reveal which information is collected and where such information goes. But is this text understandable and more important is it actually correct?! Also, security issues in apps are common even though (hopefully) not purposely put into the app.

Common people only have weak measures to control the behavior of an app, such as the permission system. However, it is unclear for a user, whether an app for example requesting access to contacts does this to only display them or to also upload them to a third party server.

Our motivation is to deliver such privacy and security related data on large scale to users. To deliver valuable information to users, it is not sufficient to protocol access to relevant resources. Just like in the example above, it is more relevant, what is done with such resources/data. This is the point where our novel context correlation comes into play. We observe data sources and data sinks of the smartphone as well as security and privacy related data processing in between. Tracing such data flows in a static analysis is quite common and well researched. However, creating and correlating such data dependencies for a dynamic analysis environment is relatively new. Static and dynamic analysis approaches both have their strengths and weaknesses, and we try to bring the data dependency graph from static analysis into the dynamic analysis world.

Our proposed automated dynamic analysis environment is able to:

1. Install and launch an app on an Android smartphone or emulator
2. Interact with an app and handle login fields as well as context specific input (for example an address for a navigation app)
3. Protocol relevant Android API calls and network traffic
4. Evaluate protocolled data and automatically generate privacy and security issues with predefined detection rules.

We do an automated analysis of the top 1000 free apps from Google Play to demonstrate that our approach works well.

The remainder of this publication is structured as follows: Sect. 2 gives an overview of related work and their shortcomings in this area. Section 3 illustrates our analysis environment and Sect. 4 highlights the context correlation approach. Section 5 shows evaluation results and how well context correlation works in practice for the top 1000 apps. This section also proves the reported issue quality through a manual crosscheck and a check against damn vulnerable app projects. Section 6 concludes our work and highlights our future plans.

2   Related Work

Static analysis methods for the data flow analysis from sources to sinks is already well researched. A well known publication that gained wide attention in 2014 is FlowDroid [1]. FlowDroid was one of the first tools to achieve full context and data flow sensitivity and correlate privacy leaks and malicious app behavior. This concept has been picked up, improved and varied over the past years with for example DroidSafe [5], AppContext [10], Klieber et al. [7], Yavuz [11] and many more. Data flow analysis in a static context is very convenient since good techniques exist to trace and model data flow and analyze variable dependencies. In contrast, dynamic analysis doesn't have access to such information. Dynamic environments typically rely on tracking a limited set of (operating system) API methods, and observe the app's interaction.

TaintDroid [4] was one of the first and most recognized publications in the area of dynamic analysis. TaintDroid used a modified java virtual machine for taint tracking sensitive private information. Private data is tagged and the data flow of the jvm-variable is traced. However, since Android 5 translates byte-code to ARM binary-code, this method became obsolete. TaintMan [12] and ARTist [2] use dynamic taint tracking on Android 5's new ART runtime to re-enable prior techniques. CopperDroid [8] discovered the dependability of Android specific properties which frequently changed, and thus proposes higher abstraction to especially analyze malware behavior. DroidTrace [13] is a ptrace based system also designed for malware tracing. In summary, malware analysis is besides tracking sensitive private data the main driver behind dynamic analysis. Malware detection oftentimes identifies malware by a sequence of API calls/syscalls, whereas privacy protection rather focuses on the data flow from source to sink.

For analyzing the vulnerability and with such the security of an app, it is necessary to correlate data flow with (multiple) critical API calls. An attempt of a combined static and dynamic security analysis has been proposed by Tang et al. [9]. However, the most of the security analysis is done during the static code analysis, and the dynamic analysis is only limited to a few API methods without data-flow dependency. Zhou [14] proposes in a position paper a pipeline to detect privacy leaks through data flow from sources to sinks in a dynamic environment. The idea doesn't cover security aspects, but comes close to our concepts. However, the implementation and evaluation of this tool remains open in their publication.

2.1 Contribution

In conclusion, there are many publications targeting malware detection in a dynamic environment, plenty privacy analysis environments, but slim to none security analysis environments. To the best of our knowledge, this work is the first dynamic analysis environment linking data flow through hooked system APIs. We did not find any other work, which is able to provide private data to an app and trace private data through hashing or encryption functions to a data sink solely with a dynamic analysis.

3 Dynamic Analysis Environment

The purpose of the analysis environment is firstly to execute the app and provide its UI with input, which means clicking buttons, filling out text fields, swiping and more. During this process, we observe the app's background behavior with hooks to the Android API. In this publication we only briefly describe our environment in the following and in Fig. 1 due to page limitations. A more detailed description can be obtained through our previous publication [6].

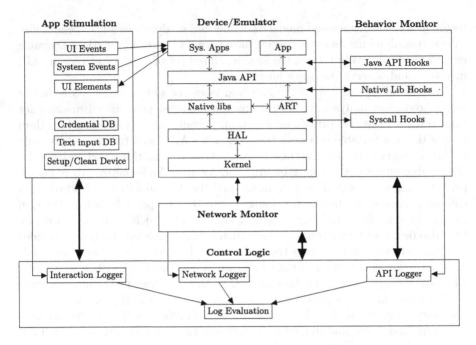

Fig. 1. Tool Composition for a Dynamic Analyzer

App Stimulation: Contains the automated UI and background interaction. It is able to enter privacy sensitive data, such as personal information, login credentials and context aware input such as a specific address for navigation, the user's name and age and much more. We chose the Appium[1] framework to read the currently shown UI elements and evaluate the context. If for example text input elements with the labels: username, password and a login button (or variations) are found, appropriate input data will be provided.

Behavior Monitor: Hooks system API methods of interest and thus traces the app's interaction with the device or emulator. Frida[2] is used to monitor usages of the Android API. Each Android API method hook logs information such as the function name and argument signature. Also, function argument and return values are logged. In case of complex objects, a hash as given by the .hashCode() function is used to identify instances.

Network Monitor: Is a proxy to monitor and decrypt network traffic. We chose mitmproxy [3] since it has a convenient Python API to programmatically control it. Most other proxy tools lack such an interface.

Control Logic: Orchestrates device setup and teardown. It also collects all generated data during the app interaction such as network traffic, UI entered information and execution traces. In the last step the *log evaluation* sub module analyzes the collected data and generates issues if security or privacy

---

[1] http://appium.io/.
[2] https://frida.re.

flaws have been discovered. This step is the main contribution of this work and will be explained in detail in the next section.

4   Context Correlation and Issue Generation

We create a graph in order to correlate the app context and generate security and privacy issues. In short: Recorded API calls of the *Behavior Monitor* are linked together in a graph. Edges model data dependencies for arguments and return values and object reuse (different method calls on the same object). Network traffic flows are also put into the graph and argument and return value elements of the API calls are linked to it. Then, privacy sensitive data sources (data entered into the UI) are collected and data dependencies are also linked to existing graph nodes. Data sinks are a defined set of nodes (network traffic, API methods) without outgoing edges.

Privacy and security analysis passes of our tool operate on the graph to annotate information and findings. After all passes finished, annotated information on connected graph nodes are correlated. This correlation allows more detailed insights on security issues. This step also reduces the number of generated issues by covering multiple issues in a single one and remove duplicates.

As an example, one could think of an app which encrypts private data with an insecure legacy encryption algorithm (DES) and send it over an unprotected network connection (http). Without correlation, an insecure encryption and an unrelated unprotected network access would be reported. With correlation, insecurely encrypted private data send over an unprotected network connection will be reported. This gives the user a way better understanding and ability to judge the issue's criticality.

After this brief overview, the following sections describe our approach in more detail.

4.1   Privacy Sensitive Data Sources

We have based our privacy sensitive data sources on the definition from Flow-Droid [1] and extended it with commonly used properties found in today's Android versions. We currently track sensitive data as described in the following. Thereby, we do not detect access to these methods by API hooks since data values can often be retrieved via multiple methods. We just read all values of interest and store them to later on detect them in the graph.

Call History: The list of incoming, outgoing and missed calls.
SMS: All incoming and outgoing messages (SMS) stored on the phone.
Contacts: Contact names, numbers and e-mail addresses stored in the phone's contact DB
Calendar Entries: Entries stored in the calendar DB with a unique date, time and comment.

Device Properties: There exist some device properties which are often used for fingerprinting/device identification such as Wifi/Bluetooth MAC, serial number, IMEI, build version, brand, device, manufacturer, GSM operator, hardware SKU/platform, unique Android ID, advertisement ID and installed apps.

The aforementioned values are (where possible) generated to unique values before app interaction. For each collected raw value, also other common representations, such as base64 and hexadecimal aliases are calculated in order to later on find the values in alternative representations.

4.2   Data Sinks

We define data sinks as data locations, were (private) data is stored accessibly to others. This could be a transmission to a server, but also improper storage on the phone where another application could pick up the data. We currently support the following data sinks:

Network. Outbound network traffic is a potential data sink. All network traffic is recorded by a proxy, which can later on be searched for significant data.

Filesystem. The whole filesystem is a data sink. However, there are filesystem locations accessible by the respective app only, and other locations accessible by all installed apps. The latter being of course more concerning. We are able to identify which file has been read/written/modified including databases and Android's Key storage as well as what has been modified in file.

Intent. We monitor all intents, which are used to pass data among apps.

LogCat. Personal information could also be leaked through LogCat. Other apps are able to access an app's LogCat, under certain conditions.

Potential other, currently unimplemented, data sinks would be outgoing voice calls or SMS, Bluetooth and NFC. We left out voice call and SMS since it is not possible for an app to do such on latest Android versions, without user interaction in system settings. Bluetooth and NFC has been omitted, due to the lack of fitting communication partners in our test environment.

4.3   Graph Generation

The created graph in this step is a directed graph which represents data flow, as well as method calls as edges between the nodes. Thus, it's a combination of a data flow graph and a call graph. Nodes in this graph are logged API calls, network data or data sources such as the provided private data described in Sect. 4.1. API calls or network data can be declared as data sinks.

Listing 1.1. Graph generation pseudocode

```
1   foreach node in [apiCalls, personalInformationSources, networkTransmissions] :
2       graph.add(node)
3
4   foreach startNode in graph.apiCallNodes():
5       //get all nodes with newer timestamp until new object with same hash appears
6       newerNodes = newerNodesUntilObjHashRedefine()
7       foreach laterNode in newerNodes:
8           if startNode.instance() == laterNode.argument()
9               || startNode.instance() == laterNode.instance()
10              || startNode.returnValue() == laterNode.argument()
11              || startNode.returnValue() == laterNode.instance() :
12              connect(startNode, laterNode)
13
14  foreach node in graph.apiCallNodes():
15      if isEncryptionOrHashOperation(node):
16          cipherSourceNode = ciphertextAsSourceNode(node)
17          graph.add(cipherSourceNode)
18          connect(cipherSourceNode, node.findFirstEncryptionParent())
19
20  foreach sourceNode in graph.personalInformationSourceNodes():
21      foreach apiCallNode in graph.apiCallNodes():
22          if sourceNode.plain() == apiCallNode.argument()
23              || matchesAlternativeEncoding(sourceNode.plain(), apiCallNode.argument()):
24                  connect(sourceNode, apiCallNode)
25      foreach cipherSourceNode in graph.cipherSourceNodes():
26          if cipherSourceNode.contains(sourceNode):
27              connect(sourceNode, cipherSourceNode)
28      foreach netNode in graph.networkTransmissions():
29          if netNode.isInContentOrHeader(sourceNode.plain())
30              || netNode.isInContentOrHeaderInAlternativeEncoding(sourceNode.plain()):
31                  connect(sourceNode, netNode)
```

The graph is generated by the simplified pseudocode described in Listing 1.1 and it is described in the following steps:

1. Add all logged API calls and network transfers to the graph, which are at first completely unconnected. Each node contains a timestamp of its respective recorded API call.
2. For each node → Collect all newer nodes until no more nodes are available or another node has the same Object hash as the current node. For all collected nodes → Try to make a connection with the current node. Connections hold a source and a target tag. Source tags are:

   inst: The instance of the object is used in another API call

   ret: The return value of the method is used in another API call

priv. data: Predefined privacy sensitive data is used in another API call

   The according target tags are:

   inst: A method is called on this object's instance

   arg: An object or value is used as an argument into the respective method

content: An object or value is found in the content of the node which is mostly used for network transmissions.

Thus, a source and target combination declares how the two API calls are related. Complex object instances are identified by their hash code (java's hashCode() method). Primitive data type values are used as is.

Table 1. Observed API calls

ID	Method	Args. Sig	Arguements	Obj. hash	ret. type	ret. obj
A1	SecretKeySpec.init	byte[], String	[23,33,56,...], DES	18f3a	-	-
A2	Cipher.createCipher	String, Provider	DES/CBC/ PKCS5Padding, null	-	Cipher	Cipher@48c1db9
A3	Cipher.init	int,Key,SecureRandom	1, SecretKeySpec@18f3a, MySecureRnd@c47915f	48c1db9	void	-
A4	Cipher.update	byte[]	[4,45,23,...]	48c1db9	byte[]	null
A5	Cipher.doFinal	byte[], int	[0,0,0,...], 0	48c1db9	int	8

3. Encryption, signature and hashing functions consist of multiple API calls to first initialize the operation and later execute the operation with data. While algorithm misconfiguration happens in the first part and data dependency happens in the last part. Encryption source nodes are added to the graph to link misconfigured algorithms with the processed (privacy sensitive) data.

4. Add all source nodes to the graph and calculate for each source value the alias representation such as base64, hexadecimal. Each data source is associated with a protection level (Low/Med./High), indicating the value's data leakage severity.

5. For all source nodes → Iterate over all other nodes → Create a connection, if the source node's data or alias can be found in another node's API call method argument or network transmission content.

4.4   Example Graph

An example call graph, generated from recorded API calls in Table 1 and network traffic is shown in Fig. 2. For example: Table 1 ID *A2* `Cipher.createCipher()` returns an object instance with the hash code `48c1db9` on which the method `init()`, `update()` and `doFinal()` is called. In Fig. 2 this is represented by the nodes and edges A2→A3→A4→A5. Also, private data S1 is used as an argument to node A4 (`update()`) which will then encrypt the argument. During graph generation, encryption/signature/hashing chains consisting of an initialization function with multiple update function calls, which successively fill in the data to the cryptographic operation, are identified. The node S1 (GPS location data) is linked to its encrypted representation in node S4, which is linked to A3, the initialization function of the encryption/signature/hashing chain. This content relation between data sources and initialization functions binds the encrypted content to the node representing the encryption parameters to ease the correlation later on. The recorded network traffic is searched for data as defined by source nodes S1, S2,... including return values of encryption/signature/hashing chains. The ciphertext returned by A5 is then found in the network traffic of node N1 and a link is created. In the next step, the graph can be traversed by different analyzers to create privacy and security related issues.

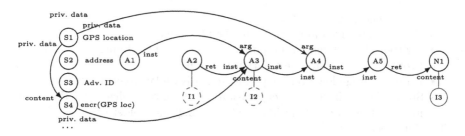

Fig. 2. Generated graph and generated issues **with** (blue) / **without**(- - - dashed) correlation and graph dependency. Legend: A=API call, N=Network Transmission, S=private data source, I=Issue

4.5   Graph Analysis: Issue Creation

We have implemented different analysis passes to find different privacy and security related issues. Some analysis passes just require for one specific API call. For example Table 1 A2: `Cipher.createCipher("DES/CBC/PKCS5Padding,null)` can directly be declared as insecure due to the used DES cipher algorithm, as its 56-bit keys can nowadays be recovered by brute forcing quite efficiently. Other analysis passes require looking at several API calls, like for example reusing cryptographic salt, which is insecure. Different API methods connected via different dependency edges have to be analyzed if they reuse the same salt.

The graph is enriched in analysis passes with discovered properties. Such properties do not necessarily trigger the creation of a reported issue but can also contain later on used information for other analysis passes. However, severe flaws generate reported issues, which are also attached on the respective graph node(s). The issues on connected nodes can be combined later on in the context correlation phase, to form an enriched single issue.

As a first proof of concept, the analysis passes span five categories with a total of 19 security and privacy related checks, which are constantly further extended with more detection patterns:

- AdTracker:
  - Analyze network endpoints for known AdTracker domains
- Cryptography checks:
  - Own (mostly insecure) random number generator implementations
  - Insecure hashing, encryption and signature algorithms (such as DES, MD5, etc.)
  - Long enough key length (like at least 128 for AES)
  - Insecure cryptographic configurations (like ECB mode or RSA without padding)
  - Zero initialization vectors on AES/CBC
  - Reuse of initialization vectors
  - Usage of constant salt or seed
  - Low iteration count for key derivation functions
  - Trust-all trust managers
  - Permissive host name checks

- Filesystem checks:
  - Privacy sensitive data written to the filesystem
  - Written file locations to be publicly accessible by all apps
  - Proper password storage location (KeyChain)
  - Proper storage location for public and private keys/certificates
  - Stored data is in the correct location: JPEG in the /sdcard/DCIM folder, mp3s in the /sdcard/music or /sdcard/ringtones folder etc.
- LogCat checks:
  - Privacy sensitive data in LogCat messages
- Network checks:
  - Insecure connections, like http
  - Privacy sensitive data has been submitted via the network

Whenever one of the above checks finds an issue, a detailed issue report is created. This report is attached to the respective nodes in the graph. The report contains information like: issue type (privacy/security), a CWE if applicable, source (private data source), destination (data sink), protection (AES, https), data type (name, address,...), data encoding (plain, base64), severity, textual description. However, not all issue fields are filled, since such information is often not fully available at the time of this issue creation. Properties found and attached to graph nodes in later analysis passes can also influence or enrich fields of connected nodes. This is why an issue correlation pass runs when all other passes completed.

4.6   Issue Correlation Pass

The goal of this step is to enrich issue information and associate related issues. This gives deeper insights on what the app does in the background. This step is given as simplified pseudocode in Listing 1.2. All graph nodes with an associated issue are collected. For these nodes, all parent nodes (incoming connections in the directed graph) and parents of parents are collected and the existing values for source, data type and data encoding are merged. All children nodes (outgoing connections) are collected to update the destination (sink) of the issue. After the issues have been correlated, all issues have to be collected, while sorting out duplicates and issues already covered by other issues through the correlation step.

Example: Improved Issue Quality. The improved issue quality through this correlation step and the usage of the graph's dependencies, is highlighted in the following example, extracted from Table 1 and Fig. 2. We construct the issues that would be created with and without the graph and the issue correlation to demonstrate enriched issue context. The extractable flaws from Table 1 and Fig. 2 **without** a graph and correlation are: usage of insecure DES encryption

Listing 1.2. Issue correlation on graph (pseudocode)

```
1    foreach node in graph.allNodesWithIssues():
2        if node.issue().source() == null:
3            foreach parent in node.getParents():
4                if parent.isSourceNode():
5                    node.issue().mergeSource(parent)
6                    node.issue().mergeDataType(parent)
7                    node.issue().mergeDataEncoding(parent)
8                    node.issue().setRelated(parent.issue())
9
10       if node.issue().destination() == null:
11           foreach child in node.getChildren()
12               if child.issue().hasDestination():
13                   node.issue().mergeDestination(child)
14                   node.issue().setRelated(child.issue())
15
16   Set issues = new Set()
17   foreach node in graph.allNodesWithIssues():
18       foreach issue in issues:
19           if issue.equalsNeglectTimeAndUID(node.issue())
20               && !issue.parentsAndChildren().contains(node):
21               issues.add(node.issue())
22
23   print(issues)
```

Table 2. Issues created **without** dependency graph and correlation

ID	type	CWE	source	dest	protection	data type	data enc	severity	textual description
1	security	327	dev. props	-	DES	-	-	medium	DES is a weak algorithm...
2	security	327	–	–	–	–	–	medium	Self implemented random...

Table 3. Issues created **with** dependency graph and correlation

ID	type	CWE	source	dest	protection	data type	data enc	severity	related	textual description
1	security	327	dev. props	web.com	DES	GPS location	-	high	2,3	DES is a weak...
2	security	327	–	web.com	DES	–	–	medium	1,3	Self impl. random ...
3	security	327	dev. props	web.com	DES	GPS location	plain	high	1,2	Sending private...

and an own random number generator implementation. In detail, the issues are shown in Table 2 and in the graph in Fig. 2 as nodes I1 and I2. Without a dependency graph and correlation, one would not find the private data which is insecurely encrypted as well as the ciphertext of the private data in the network transmission.

The described graph approach is able to gather more information by using the created dependencies and the issue correlation. Node A3 with issue I2 attached can be enriched by searching parent nodes for sources and thus finding the encrypted GPS location as data source. Also, issue I1 is found in the node A3's parents and set as related. By searching node A3's child nodes, one finds the network transmission as destination to enrich issue I2 and also issue I3 can be set as related. The same process is applied to issues I1 and I3 where respective source, destination and related fields are enriched. Thus, without the graph and issue correlation, the app would be judged as: "The app uses a self implemented random number generator and a weak encryption algorithm". However, applying graph dependencies and issue correlation, we are able to relate the issues and give a much stronger judgment: "The app encrypts the user's GPS location with a weak encryption algorithm and additionally uses a self implemented random number generator for this encryption. The resulting ciphertext then is sent to a network server."

In conclusion, the judgment without graph and correlation information trivializes or doesn't fully detect the app's behavior, with such information the behavior is better described and from a security and privacy perspective far from uncritical.

5   Evaluation

We have analyzed the top 1000 free apps in Google Play (according to 42Matters[3]). With this larger scaled analysis, we want to demonstrate that our analysis environment described in Sects. 3 and 4 works well and scales. We also want to show the benefit of our proposed correlation step and that this is applicable on real world apps and gives the analyst a real benefit. Four Pixel 4a running Android 11 were used in our test environment. On average, it took 27min to conduct the dynamic analysis per app, including 10min app stimulation (UI interaction) and 15min automated collected data evaluation.

5.1   Overview and Statistics

From all 1000 tested apps, we have discovered issues on 912 apps, with a total of 26348 issues. Most apps hold less than 15 issues, whereas the maximum number of discovered issues was 663 for a single app. This app heavily reused initialization vectors. From the total of 26348 issues the issues fell into the categories:

Ad Tracker usage	2468	9%
Improper file system storage usage	6167	23%
Transmission of privacy sensitive data through network	8561	32%
Weak or vulnerable cryptography usage	9290	36%

---

[3] https://42matters.com.

The following CWEs where discovered in the issues:

CWE 921 (sensitive data storage without access control)	30	<1%
CWE 295 (improper certificate validation)	55	<1%
CWE 319 (clear text sensitive information transmission)	113	<1%
CWE 940 (improper verification of communication channel)	281	1%
CWE 312 (clear text sensitive information storage)	5940	23%
CWE 327 (broken cryptographic algorithm)	9235	35%
CWE 359 (private data exposure)	10832	41%

The most issues (36%) were found with cryptographic algorithms. Also, many exposures of privacy sensitive information were discovered. All CWEs that our analysis is able to detect were also discovered in the real world apps.

We try to judge the severity of the issue in our vulnerability and privacy analysis. We classified 93% of all incidents as low severity and 7% of high severity. The 4557 high severity issues consisted of the following CWEs:

CWE 295 (improper certificate validation)	55	3%
CWE 319 (clear text sensitive information transmission)	113	7%
CWE 940 (improper verification of communication channel)	281	16%
CWE 327 (broken cryptographic algorithm)	1272	74%

Figure 3 shows the detected privacy sensitive data which has been detected as data sources for issues. The build-ID is most often subject to issues, also the Google advertisement ID and installed apps are often issue data sources. Such information is often used for fingerprinting. Also, the user's location (GPS position and city) is often submitted, which is understandable for navigation apps, but also other apps submit the user's exact location, where we cannot see a direct necessity regarding the app's functionality. Other interesting submitted private data is the user's age, which is often requested during registration and names of contacts in the address book.

5.2   Deep Manual Issue Inspection

We did a static manual analysis of apps containing the highest critical issues in order to verify the findings of the automated dynamic analysis. Critical issues are the ones with private data transmission over an unprotected communication channel. In total, six apps were discovered in this highest category. App developers were informed about the discovered weaknesses beforehand.

dating.app.chat.flirt.wgbcv (159200) Basic dating and chat app

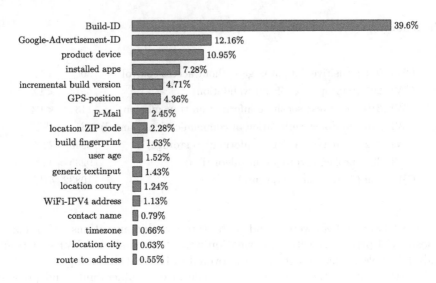

Fig. 3. Used private data (data sources) in issues

automatic: Private, UI entered data transmitted via unprotected network
manual: A Cordova app, running a single JavaScript which communicates only via HTTP with the server. Intercepting the traffic allows modification of profile details, chat messages and many more. The only (weak) authentication mechanism is the Android ID.

com.atpc (481) YouTube music downloader
automatic: Private, UI entered data transmitted via unprotected network
manual: Search queries are transmitted for auto complete suggestions to http://suggestqueries.google.com via POST. We judge the finding as lower criticality, since search queries can be manipulated or intercepted, of which the user should be aware of being sent to the internet and thus are not private. Anyways, it would be easy to request queries via HTTPS

tunein.player (265323) Radio app
automatic: Private, device properties transmitted via unprotected network
manual: The Android ID, build ID, screen resolution etc. are unprotected transmitted to http://b.scorecardresearch.com. The website is used for tracking user behavior. We judge this issue as not that critical since it is usual behavior of ad trackers even though it would be better to use HTTPS for this communication.

de.eos.uptrade.android.fahrinfo.berlin (1001210) Berlin public transport. Buy tickets, see routes & departures. *(Issue already fixed in the latest release)*
automatic: Insufficient certificate check in protected communication.
manual: The app uses a custom host name certificate checker which allows all host names. Allow all checker can be enabled in the program code and it is enabled by default. We acknowledge the high criticality of this issue, since it is possible to buy tickets via the app. Attackers could loot credit card information or steal bought tickets.

com.alibaba.intl.android.apps.poseidon (74201) Alibaba B2B Trading platform

automatic: Insufficient certificate check in protected communication.

manual: The app uses different self implemented host name certificate checker of which some allow all host names, others insufficiently check host names and others are wrappers to system checkers. Due to complexity and obfuscation we can't tell in detail where which checker is used. We observed the allow-all checker to be only used for delivering images. However, using this number of custom host name verifiers highly increases the chances of insecure implementations.

com.wondershare.filmorago (646) Video cutting studio

automatic: Insufficient certificate check in protected communication.

manual: In the static manual analysis, the issue is verifiable. We were not able to identify which content is loaded without a proper certificate check, due to obfuscation. However, we observed a transmission of a fingerprint via http POST without proper certificate checking.

In summary, one can say that the automated analysis discovered all severe issues correctly. The manual static analysis revealed the same issues as the automated analysis. Nevertheless, in some cases we lowered the issue's criticality after manual inspection. This shows, that automated analysis gives good results on a broad number of apps, but educated security experts are able to judge the practical criticality on a finer grained level.

5.3 Damn Vulnerable App

The previous section analyzed vulnerabilities in real world apps. However, it is hard to argue that an app where the automated analysis did not find an issue, really has no issue. Therefore, we chose three different projects for damn vulnerable apps to evaluate if our environment detects known vulnerabilities. During our search for vulnerable app projects we discovered that many projects are nowadays abandoned, not buildable or unsuitable for the intended use case of an automated analysis. Finally, we found three vulnerable app projects which are usable for an automated privacy and security analysis: AndroGoat[4], Pivaa[5], MSTG-Hacking-Playground[6]. The selected apps each contain a button which exhibits a vulnerability or privacy issue on click. This allows us to build a test case which clicks a button, analyzes the app behavior and checks it against the expected issue. The results of these tests are shown in Table 4. The tables contain a vulnerability description in the first column, the second column indicates if our automated analysis environment contains checks for this vulnerability as listed in Sect. 4.5. We are aware, that we have not implemented checks for every available vulnerability on Android and oftentimes such checks are not possible in an automated environment. The last column of the tables indicate if our

---

[4] https://github.com/satishpatnayak/AndroGoat.
[5] https://github.com/htbridge/pivaa.
[6] https://github.com/OWASP/MSTG-Hacking-Playground.

Table 4. Provided and detected vulnerabilities by damn vulnerable app projects

AndroGoat vulnerabilities	I	D	Pivaa vulnerabilities	I	D	MSTG-Hacking-Playground	I	D
Root Detection	✓	✓	Weak Initialization Vector	✓	✓	Bad Encryption	✓	✓
Emulator Detection	-	-	Possible MITM Attack	✓	✓	Keychain Password Extraction	-	-
Insecure Storage Shared Prefs	✓	✓	Remote URL in WebView	-	-	Private Internal Data Storage	✓	✓
Insecure Storage SQLite	✓	✓	Object deserialization found	-	-	Private External Data Storage	✓	✓
Insecure Storage Temp File	✓	✓	User input in SQL queries	-	-	Shared Pref. Private Data	✓	✓
Insecure Storage SD Card	✓	✓	Missing tapjacking protection	-	-	Private Data SQLite	✓	✓
Keyboard Cache	-	-	Enabled Application Backup	-	-	Private Data Logging	✓	✓
Insecure Logging	✓	✓	Enabled Debug Mode	-	-	Private Data to Server	✓	✓
Input Validations	-	-	Weak encryption	✓	✓	Keyboard Cache	-	-
Unprotected Android Components	-	-	Hardcoded encryption keys	-	-	Disable Clipboard EditText	-	-
Hard coding issues	-	-	Dynamic load of code	-	-	Memory Dump	-	-
Network intercepting HTTP	✓	✓	Public accessible files	✓	✓	Webview Remote/Local	-	-
Network intercepting HTTPS	✓	✓	Usage of HTTP protocol	✓	✓	SQL Injection	-	-
Network intercepting Cert. Pin.	✓	✓	Weak hashing algorithms	✓	✓	Content Provider Injection	-	-
Misconfigured Network Security	-	-	Predictable RND Gen.	-	-	Code Injection	-	-
Android Debuggable	-	-	Unprotected Content Provider	-	-	Network intercepting HTTPS	✓	✓
Android allowBackup	-	-	Exported Broadcast Receiver	-	-	SSL Pinning	✓	✓
Custom URL Scheme	-	-	Exported Service	-	-			
Broken Cryptography	✓	✓	JS enabled in a WebView	-	-			
			setPluginState in WebView	-	-			
			Temporary file creation	✓	✓			
			Hardcoded data	-	-			
Note:			Untrusted CA acceptance	✓	✓			
			Banned API functions	-	-			
I = Check **I**mplemented in analysis			Self-signed CA in WebView	-	-			
D = Analysis **D**etected Issue			Path Traversal	-	-			
			Cleartext SQLite database	-	-			

environment was able to detect the app's vulnerability successfully. Fortunately, all app vulnerabilities that we have implemented checks for were also discovered. This means that our automated analysis environment has a high detection ratio on real world apps regarding the common flaws documented by the known vulnerable apps.

6 Conclusion and Future Work

This publication introduced a new method to correlate the context in an automated dynamic analysis and with this step achieve more expressive issue reports. The evaluation highlighted the approach's scalability and the high quality of the reported issues. Through the correlation step, the automatically generated reports deliver a comprehensible description of the flaws and most important, the relation of the flaws. The detection rate for known vulnerabilities in vulnerable demo app projects was 100% for all implemented checks. As future work we are planning on extending analysis passes as new vulnerabilities appear. As future work, we are would like to deliver issue reports to interested users and developers to increase the overall security of Android apps.

Acknowledgements. The project underlying this report was funded by the German Federal Ministry of Education and Research under grant number 16SV8520. The author is responsible for the content of this publication.

References

1. Arzt, S., et al.: Flowdroid: Precise context, flow, field, object-sensitive and lifecycle-aware taint analysis for android apps. SIGPLAN Not. **49**, 2594299 (2014)
2. Backes, M., Bugiel, S., Schranz, O., Von Styp-Rekowsky, P., Weisgerber, S.: Artist: the android runtime instrumentation and security toolkit. In: IEEE European Symposium on Security and Privacy (EuroS P) (2017)
3. Cortesi, A., Hils, M., Kriechbaumer, T., contributors: mitmproxy: a free and open source interactive HTTPS proxy (2010-). https://mitmproxy.org/
4. Enck, W., et al.: TaintDroid: an information-flow tracking system for realtime privacy monitoring on smartphones. ACM Trans. Comput. Syst. **57**, 393–407 (2014)
5. Gordon, M., deokhwan, K., Perkins, J., Gilham, L., Nguyen, N., Rinard, M.: Information-flow analysis of android applications in droidsafe (2015)
6. Heid, K., Heider, J.: Automated, dynamic android app vulnerability and privacy leak analysis: design considerations, required components and available tools. In: European Interdisciplinary Cybersecurity Conference. EICC, ACM (2021)
7. Klieber, W., Flynn, L., Bhosale, A., Jia, L., Bauer, L.: Android taint flow analysis for app sets. In: Proceedings of the 3rd ACM SIGPLAN International Workshop on the State of the Art in Java Program Analysis. SOAP 2014 (2014)
8. Tam, K., Khan, S., Fattori, A., Cavallaro, L.: CopperDroid: automatic reconstruction of android malware behaviors (2015)
9. Tang, J., Li, R., Wang, K., Gu, X., Xu, Z.: A novel hybrid method to analyze security vulnerabilities in android applications. Tsinghua Science and Technology (2020)
10. Yang, W., Xiao, X., Andow, B., Li, S., Xie, T., Enck, W.: AppContext: differentiating malicious and benign mobile app behaviors using context. In: 37th IEEE International Conference on Software Engineering (2015)
11. Yavuz, T., Brant, C.: Security analysis of IoT frameworks using static taint analysis. In: ACM Conference on Data and Application Security and Privacy (2022)
12. You, W., Liang, B., Shi, W., Wang, P., Zhang, X.: TaintMan: an art-compatible dynamic taint analysis framework on unmodified and non-rooted android devices. IEEE Trans. Depend. Sec. Comput. **17**, 209–222 (2020)
13. Zheng, M., Sun, M., Lui, J.C.: DroidTrace: a ptrace based android dynamic analysis system with forward execution capability. In: International Wireless Communications and Mobile Computing Conference (IWCMC) (2014)
14. Zhou, Y.: An automated pipeline for privacy leak analysis of android applications. In: International Conference on Automated Software Engineering (ASE) (2021)

Errors in the CICIDS2017 Dataset and the Significant Differences in Detection Performances It Makes

Maxime Lanvin[2]([✉]), Pierre-François Gimenez[2], Yufei Han[1],
Frédéric Majorczyk[3], Ludovic Mé[1], and Éric Totel[4]

[1] Inria, Univ. Rennes, IRISA, Rennes, France
{yufei.han,ludovic.me}@inria.fr
[2] CentraleSupélec, Univ. Rennes, IRISA, Rennes, France
{maxime.lanvin,pierre-francois.gimenez}@centralesupelec.fr
[3] DGA-MI, Univ. Rennes, IRISA, Rennes, France
frederic.majorczyk@intradef.gouv.fr
[4] Samovar, Télécom SudParis, Institut Polytechnique de Paris, Palaiseau, France
eric.totel@telecom-sudparis.eu

Abstract. Among the difficulties encountered in building datasets to evaluate intrusion detection tools, a tricky part is the process of labelling the events into malicious and benign classes. The labelling correctness is paramount for the quality of the evaluation of intrusion detection systems but is often considered as the ground truth by practitioners and is rarely verified. Another difficulty lies in the correct capture of the network packets. If it is not the case, the characteristics of the network flows generated from the capture could be modified and lead to false results. In this paper, we present several flaws we identified in the labelling of the CICIDS2017 dataset and in the traffic capture, such as packet misorder, packet duplication and attack that were performed but not correctly labelled. Finally, we assess the impact of these different corrections on the evaluation of supervised intrusion detection approaches.

Keywords: intrusion detection · dataset labelling · machine learning

1 Introduction

Information technologies revolutionized our communication, collaboration, production, and consumption. Since they are now so profoundly connected with critical systems and crucial data, they are regularly targeted by malicious users that seek to break information confidentiality, integrity or availability. Many security mechanisms have been proposed against such attacks, notably Network Intrusion Detection Systems (NIDS) that aim at identifying attacks by monitoring network traffic in the target system. This detection involves the analysis of network traffic, generally by looking for traces of known attacks. Unfortunately, NIDS

This work has been partly realised thanks to a doctoral grant from Creach Labs (DGA, Brittany Region).

are prone to false positives and false negatives that can significantly impact cost and performance. For this reason, their performance must be carefully evaluated. This evaluation relies extensively on the use of benchmark datasets of network traffic. These datasets consist of two parts: the network data (either raw network packets or a more high-level network flow description) and the labels, i.e., the class (benign or attack) in which each packet or flow belongs.

Due to privacy and confidentiality reasons, there are only a few public datasets of real traffic for evaluating NIDS [12]. To circumvent those constraints, other datasets are generally obtained by generating network traffic in a testbed. One of these datasets is CICIDS2017 [14]. Though currently considered to be of good quality and widely used, it has nevertheless been criticized. Engelen et al. [4] notably pointed out some flaws in CICFlowMeter, the tool used to create flow descriptions from raw traffic capture, as well as issues with labels of some network flows that should not be labelled as attacks (network flows without a payload).

We discovered several new problems in CICIDS2017: most notably, several port scan attacks were not properly labelled, and a non-negligible part of the traffic capture was duplicated, leading to feature extraction and labelling issues. In addition to providing corrected traffic captures and labels, we took advantage of this opportunity to investigate why some references of the literature [11] exhibited high recall and precision values even though the dataset has serious labelling issues. We thus present in this paper three contributions:

- we first release a fixed version of the CICIDS2017 dataset for both labels and network captures,
- we propose a patch for CICFlowMeter that avoids processing malformed input data,
- we evaluate the consequences of the different dataset corrections on the evaluation of several popular intrusion detection models.

The rest is organized as follows. Section 2 presents some related works on network datasets and intrusion detection models. Section 3 highlights the identified errors of labelling and how to fix them. Finally, we measured the impact of the corrections on the evaluation of supervised approaches in Sect. 4.

2   Related Works

2.1   Datasets

Several datasets have been proposed to evaluate the performances of intrusion detection tools. DARPA98 [8] was one of the first datasets provided to the academic community. Several datasets like KDD99 or NSLKDD [15] were then derived from this first dataset. Even though they are still widely used by the research community, these datasets have been heavily criticized [5,16] and are generally considered obsolete. In 2015, the UNSW-NB15 dataset [10] was proposed to offer modern traffic to evaluate NIDSes. This dataset is not well fitted for anomaly-based intrusion detection as the experiment duration is only about 30 h, and there is no period of time free of attacks. In 2018, the Canadian Institue for Cybersecurity (CIC) provided the CICIDS2017 dataset [14] and, together with the Communications Security Establishment, the CSE-CIC-IDS2018 [3].

CICIDS2017 uses a network architecture with machines using several common Operating Systems (OS), namely GNU/Linux, macOS and Windows, along with a firewall, switches and routers. The traffic is emulated through a testbed architecture. This architecture is divided into a victim network with four machines and an attacker network with fifteen machines. The traffic was collected on work hours during five days, from Monday to Friday. Only the first day of the week is free from attack. During the four remaining days, a large variety of attacks was conducted. The attacks in the datasets are brute force attacks (FTP and SSH), Web attacks like XSS and SQL injection, Deny of Service (DoS) attacks and its distributed version (DDoS), port scan, botnet communications and infiltration. The CSE-CIC-IDS2018 includes the same attacks, but the network architecture is much larger and more complex. The network traffic is captured for ten days instead of only five in CICIDS2017.

In CICIDS2017 and CSE-CIC-IDS2018, the authors provided the raw network captures as pcap files and the network flow descriptions as CSV files. These network flow descriptions contain high-level descriptions of a network flow between a source (that initiated the communication) and a destination. The descriptions include various network statistics, notably source IP, destination IP, source port, destination port, protocol, packet number and flow duration. These flows are bidirectional, meaning that each one contains information on both sides of the communication, from source to destination and from destination to source (in contrast, for example, to the NetFlow format proposed by Cisco). The translation from network traffic to network flow descriptions is performed by the CICFlowMeter tool[1].

2.2   Machine Learning Use on CICDS2017

Most papers that use these datasets rely on machine learning models to learn and detect attacks. In that case, the datasets are generally split in two: one part is used for learning the model (called the "train set"), and the other part is used for evaluation (called the "test set"). The popular models [7], [11], [9] for these datasets include decision trees, k nearest neighbors, naive Bayes classifier, Random Forest [1], SVM [2], and multilayer perceptron [6]. These methods are used in a supervised learning setting, where the train set is labelled and contains both benign and malicious traffic. For example, Maseet et al. [9] obtain very high performances on CICIDS2017: out of the seven experimented supervised methods, five of them have an F1-Score, a recall and a precision higher than 0.99. In almost all these works, researchers based the learning and the evaluation on the network flow descriptions and not the raw network captures.

2.3   Previous Criticism on CICIDS2017

In 2021, Engelen et al. [4] revealed several issues they found in the CICIDS2017 intrusion detection dataset. They found several flaws in the CICFlowMeter tool and that some attacks in the dataset were not well executed and thus ineffective.

---

[1] https://github.com/ahlashkari/CICFlowMeter.

About the first issue, CICFlowMeter wrongly splits TCP connections because of a wrong implementation of the TCP connection termination. This phenomenon has two consequences. The first one is to create a lot of erroneous network flows since it splits a unique network connection into multiple ones. The second consequence is that the direction of the network flow description can be inverted. In that case, all the forward and backward data are swapped, including the IP addresses, which is damageable when it comes to labelling the dataset since the network flows are labelled based on their source and destination IP addresses. Engelen et al. released a fixed version of CICFlowMeter that avoids many labelling issues. In the rest of the article, we will only use this updated tool, not the original one.

The authors also found that some attacks were conducted without sending malicious payload. This is an issue because the attacks become ineffective, so the maliciousness of these packets is debatable. To overcome this issue, they decided to create another class of labels to account for these attack attempts.

In 2022, Rosay et al. [13] presented other issues related to CICFlowMeter, such as feature duplication, miscalculations and wrong protocol detection, as well as label issues for several attacks. However, their handling of TCP termination is not perfect and misses some packets leading to distorted statistics. For this reason, we work with Engelen et al. flow descriptions.

3 Errors in the CICIDS2017 Dataset and the CICFlowMeter Tool, and Their Fixes

Pursuing the work of Engelen et al., we found four different issues in the CICIDS2017 dataset: a case where CICFlowMeter failed to properly create correct flow descriptions, incoherent timestamps, some duplication in the network captures, and an attack that is omitted from the labels.

The first two issues have consequences on the network flow descriptions and lead to an inversion of the source and the destination of the network flow descriptions that may impact labels. The third issue has only an impact on the network flow descriptions. The last one has an impact on the labels directly.

To explain why the first two issues may impact the labels, we must explain the labelling process we used. It must be noted that we do not have insights into how the authors of CICIDS2017 labelled those network flow descriptions after they generated the network flow descriptions from the network capture with the CICFlowMeter tool. However, Engelen et al. provide an automated script to label the network flows as attacks using their source IP address, destination IP address and timestamp. Indeed, the documentation of the CICIDS2017 dataset provides the time periods and the IP addresses concerned by the attacks. We used the same process to label the network flows. As this process takes into account the source and destination, an inversion of those IP addresses may lead to errors in the labels of the network flows.

Those four issues are presented in the next subsections. The fixed version is available on the repository https://gitlab.inria.fr/mlanvin/crisis2022.

3.1   CICFlowMeter Issue with Misordered Packets

CICFlowMeter is a tool that extracts network flow descriptions from pcap files that contain network captures. The network flow descriptions generated by CICFlowMeter are bidirectional and distinguish a source (the machine that initiates the communication) and a destination. As a reminder, the initial TCP handshake consists in exchanging three messages (SYN from source to destination, SYN-ACK from destination to source, and ACK from source to destination) to establish a connection. We identified a remaining flaw in CICFlowMeter that occurs when pcap files are not sorted by timestamps, as it happens in the original dataset of CICIDS2017. In that case, the tool reads the network packets in the order of the network capture files, but the SYN-ACK packet can sometimes be stored before the SYN packet in the pcap file, even though, according to the timestamp, the SYN packet did occur before the SYN-ACK one.

```
16:01:11.009724 IP 192.168.10.50.http > 172.16.0.1.20823: Flags [S.]
16:01:11.009723 IP 172.16.0.1.20823 > 192.168.10.50.http: Flags [S]
16:01:11.023740 IP 172.16.0.1.20823 > 192.168.10.50.http: Flags [.]
16:01:11.023744 IP 172.16.0.1.20823 > 192.168.10.50.http: Flags [P.]
```

Listing 1: Misordered packets from CICIDS2017. The timestamp is the leftmost column, and the flags are the rightmost column. Flags [S] mean SYN, [.] mean ACK and [S.] means SYN-ACK.

Table 1. Flow description of Listing 1. CICFlowMeter inverted source and destination.

Src IP	Src Port	Dst IP	Dst Port	Protocol	Timestamp
192.168.10.50	80	172.16.0.1	20823	6	07/07/2017 16:01:11

As an example, the Listing 1 illustrates this phenomenon with an extract of one network connection of the pcap files of CICIDS2017. We can observe that the first packet in the network capture is a SYN-ACK even if its timestamp is not the earliest. CICFlowMeter uses the first received packet to infer the source and destination. Therefore, the source and destination are exchanged in the resulting network flow description provided in the CSV files, cf. Table 1. Table 2 shows the number of misordered frames in the network capture per day (the number of frames can be considered as very close to the number of packets in our case). The figures show that Wednesday and Friday are the two days with the maximum number of misordered packets, with about twice as many misordered packets as the other days. We know Dos/DDoS attacks are performed on these two days, so our hypothesis is that the packet misordering seems to be related to the kind of attack that is performed. Since a high number of packets characterizes these attacks, there might be a race condition during the packet capture and store.

A solution to this misbehaviour is sorting the pcap files before processing them with CICFlowMeter. The tool *reordercap*[2] can perform such an operation. The version of CICFlowMeter[3] proposed by Engelen et al. now includes our patch that verifies the packets' order in the network capture to avoid this issue.

Table 2. Numbers of misordered frames in the different pcap files

Pcap files	#Misordered frames	#Frames	Proportion(%)
Monday-WorkingHours.pcap	3234	11709971	0.028
Tuesday-WorkingHours.pcap	3721	11551954	0.032
Wednesday-WorkingHours.pcap	12654	13788878	0.092
Thursday-WorkingHours.pcap	3655	9322025	0.039
Friday-WorkingHours.pcap	7094	9997874	0.071

3.2 Incoherent Timestamps

Another issue we found in the CICIDS2017 network captures is that the timestamps can be incoherent with the protocol. For example, in Listing 2, the packet SYN-ACK has a lower timestamp than the packet SYN, even though, according to the TCP protocol, such configuration should not happen. This produces the inverted flow description of the Table 3 for the same reason as in the previous subsection.

```
14:48:12.894976 IP 192.168.10.3.88 > 192.168.10.8.49173: Flags [S.]
14:48:12.895030 IP 192.168.10.8.49173 > 192.168.10.3.88: Flags [S]
14:48:12.895032 IP 192.168.10.8.49173 > 192.168.10.3.88: Flags [.]
14:48:12.895095 IP 192.168.10.3.88 > 192.168.10.8.49173: Flags [.]
```

Listing 2: Excerpt of a network connection from CICIDS2017 with ordered packets in the pcap file but with a disordered logic. The timestamp is the leftmost column, and the flags are the rightmost column. Flags [S] mean SYN, [.] mean ACK and [S.] means SYN-ACK

We have no hypothesis on what produced this issue, and it is difficult to fix automatically. For this reason, we did not fix it. However, such incoherent timestamps can cause CICFlowMeter to invert source and destination because, in this case, it considers the sender of the SYN-ACK packet to be the source.

---

[2] https://www.wireshark.org/docs/man-pages/reordercap.html.
[3] https://github.com/GintsEngelen/CICFlowMeter.

Table 3. Extracted flow description from the misordered packets presented on Listing 2. CICFlowMeter inverted source and destination.

Src IP	Src Port	Dst IP	Dst Port	Protocol	Timestamp
192.168.10.3	88	192.168.10.8	49173	6	06/07/2017 14:48:12

3.3 Dealing with Data Duplication

Observing the network captures, we found many duplicated packets in the data. Listing 3 contains an example of such duplicated packets. We can see the repetition of the SYN and RST packets: the time interval between two identical packets is only a few microseconds. Besides, their content is the same.

We cannot be sure of the cause of that phenomenon as we do not have enough detailed information on the network capture. As the time interval between two identical packets is very small and as UDP and ICMP packets are duplicated, we can rule out the hypothesis that this behaviour is normal due to the TCP retransmission mechanism. For now, our main hypothesis is that the port mirroring on the main switch of the CICIDS2017 testbed was not configured correctly. We did not analyze the network capture entirely, but we only saw duplicated packets between the testbed's internal hosts. That could be explained by the fact that all the ports of the switch connected to internal hosts are configured to mirror incoming *and* outcoming packets to the mirror port. That hypothesis is reinforced by the fact that broadcast packets to the internal subnetwork are duplicated 13 times, which corresponds to the number of internal machines.

We corrected this issue with the tool *editcap*[4] that can find and remove duplicated packets within a given time window. Using this tool with a time window of $500\mu s$, we measured how many packets were duplicated during the whole week of the CICIDS2017 dataset. The Table 5 reports the number of duplicated packets per day. On average, more than 497000 packets are duplicated per day, representing 4.5% of the packets per day. The duplication modifies the network flow description that is extracted by the tool CICFlowMeter. For example, the traffic shown in Listing 3 is transformed by CICFlowMeter into the flow description shown in Table 4. Its numbers of forward and backward packets are two because of the duplication, even though only one forward and one backward packets were actually exchanged in the network. As our experiment will show in Sect. 4, this duplication has serious impacts on the performances of the classifiers.

Table 4. Excerpt of the flow description of Listing 3

Src IP	Src Port	Dst IP	Dst Port	Total Fwd Pkts	Total Bwd Pkts
192.168.10.8	3632	192.168.10.9	28316	2	2

---

[4] https://www.wireshark.org/docs/man-pages/editcap.html.

```
15:45:30.347074 IP 192.168.10.8.distcc > 192.168.10.9.28316: Flags [S],
seq 2582752148, win 8192, options [mss 1460,nop,nop,sackOK], length 0
15:45:30.347078 IP 192.168.10.8.distcc > 192.168.10.9.28316: Flags [S],
seq 2582752148, win 8192, options [mss 1460,nop,nop,sackOK], length 0
15:45:30.347258 IP 192.168.10.9.28316 > 192.168.10.8.distcc: Flags [R.],
seq 0, ack 2582752149, win 0, length 0
15:45:30.347261 IP 192.168.10.9.28316 > 192.168.10.8.distcc: Flags [R.],
seq 0, ack 2582752149, win 0, length 0
```

Listing 3: Example of duplicated network packets CICIDS2017

Table 5. Number and proportion of duplicated packets per day.

Day	Number of duplicated packets	Total number of packets	Proportion of duplicated packets
Monday	514,241	11,709,971	4.39%
Tuesday	482,553	11,551,954	4.18%
Wednesday	480,209	13,788,878	3.48%
Thursday	556,013	9,322,025	5.96%
Friday	466,448	9,997,874	4.67%

3.4   Attack Omission: Labelling Issues and Correction

While using CICIDS2017 to evaluate machine learning models, we noticed an excessive number of false positives when processing Thursday's traffic. According to CICIDS2017 documentation, there is an infiltration step where the victim is meant first to download a malicious file or use an infected USB flash memory from 2:19 PM to 3:45 PM and then the infected machine is meant to perform a port scan afterwards. In the original CSV files, only 36 network flows are labelled as part of the infiltration. However, by analyzing the network flows corresponding to our false positives, we found some common network characteristics that led us to find a port scan that was not correctly labelled. We estimate that several tens of thousands of network flows are related to this port scan.

This preliminary experiment was done manually. However, manually labelling tens of thousands of network flows related to these attacks would have been too expensive and prone to error, so we decided to use an automated method. We could have used a rough method and labelled all the traffic between the infected machine and the other machines during the period of the infiltration attack. This is for example the method used by Engelen et al. [4] to label attacks. However, such a method would have introduced labelling errors as there is also benign traffic between the infected machine and the other machines. We estimate that this rough method would label about 7,000 benign flows as attacks out of the 80,000 total flows between the infected machine and the others, so close to 10% of wrong labels. We thus decided to deduce from the port scan attack what network characteristics we could use to label the network flows correctly.

Table 6. Number of emitted and received packets and associated number of network flows for the traffic between 192.168.10.8 and all the machines belonging to the subdomain 192.168.10.0/24 from 2:15 PM to 3:50 PM on Thursday.

With duplication			Without duplication		
Fwd Packet	Bwd packets	Count	Fwd Packet	Bwd packets	Count
2	0	31436	1	1	38228
2	2	30042	1	0	31138
1	1	13840	5	4	315
1	2	1099	1	6	191

We know that the attacks take place on Thursday between 2:15 PM and 3:50 PM and that the infected machine's IP address is 192.168.10.8. Due to some source/destination inversion that is difficult to fix (see Subsect. 3.2), we will look into every network flow with this IP address either as the source or destination IP address. Our labelling method is refined by taking into account the number of *forward* (from source to destination) and *backward* (from destination to source) packets characteristics.

There are multiple ways of performing a port scan, but the general idea is that the attacker will probe a port with a packet and deduce from the behaviour of the scanned machine whether the port is open or not. There are two typical situations: the scanned machine either replies by emitting one packet or does not reply, depending on the port's status, the kind of scan and the network configuration. With certain port scan techniques like SYN scan, the attacker expects an answer from the scanned machine to infer the port's status, and with others like Null, FIN, or Xmas scans, an opened port will be revealed by the absence of response[5]. An absence of response from the scanned machine can also be observed if the dedicated firewall or the host-based firewall filters the packet. With these considerations in mind, we can propose patterns to filter the network flows based on the number of forward or backward packets: we expect attacks to have one emitted packet and either one or zero received packets.

The Table 6 presents the top four patterns that gather the maximum number of network flows from and to the victim, either with or without the duplicated packets. On the right part of the table, when there is no duplication, the patterns "1 forward - 1 backward" and "1 forward - 0 backward" are indeed the most frequent patterns, and other patterns are negligible (the patterns "5 forward - 4 backward" and "1 forward - 6 backward" are mostly not related to the port scan according to the manually inspected examples). There are also about a hundred occurrences of the patterns "2 forward - 2 backward" and "2 forward - 0 backward" that we believe are also part of the port scan. There are port scans that use protocol quirks and whose flow is not properly reconstructed by CICFlowMeter. These incorrectly reconstructed flows include ICMP reconnaissance by Nmap,

---

[5] https://nmap.org/book/man-port-scanning-techniques.html.

ACK scans and UDP scans. So, for the dataset without duplication, we use the patterns "1 forward - 1 backward", "1 forward - 0 backward" and "2 forward - 2 backward" and "2 forward - 0 backward".

When taking duplicated packets into account (left part of the table), the expected pattern "1 forward - 1 backward" was only the third most frequent pattern. Indeed, the first two patterns, "2 forward - 0 backward" and "2 forward - 2 backward" are the duplicated equivalent of the expected pattern ("1 forward - 1 backward" and "1 forward - 0 backward") but seen twice, i.e., with two emitted and/or received packets instead of just one. This is the consequence of the duplication problem described in Subsect. 3.3.

In addition to the duplication phenomenon, sometimes timestamps are shifted between the two observations of the same network flow. When these two effects combine, it can produce some unexpected behaviours where a simple SYN and RST connection is duplicated into SYN - RST - SYN - RST packets, and then transformed into SYN - RST - RST - SYN packets due to timestamp errors. In this case, there are one emitted packet (a SYN packet) and two received packets (two RST packets), so a "1 forward - 2 backward" pattern. The last SYN packet triggers the creation of a new flow having the pattern "1 forward - 0 backward". So, for the dataset with duplication, we use the same patterns as for the dataset with duplication (that are still valid because not all packets are duplicated), and we add the "2 forward - 2 backward", "2 forward - 0 backward", "1 forward - 2 backward" patterns.

Besides, we manually exclude the network flows associated with legitimate protocols (DNS, LDAP, NTP, and NETBIOS-NS) that are present in the network traffic. Our heuristic could have mislabeled them.

To summarize, we labelled every network flow as a port scan attack if the flow happened on Thursday between 2:15 PM and 3:50 PM, if it comes from or to IP 192.168.10.8, if its protocol is neither DNS, LDAP, NTP or NETBIOS-NS, and if its numbers of forward and backward packets respect the patterns mentioned earlier.

We applied this filter and counted the numbers of network flows related to port scan per IP address. We counted about $4,060$ port scans for all six Ubuntu machines, about $5,300$ for the Windows 7 machine, about $6,900$ for the Mac machine, about $8,000$ for the two Windows 10 machines and about $12,000$ for the Window 8.1 machine. The number of ports that are scanned by a default Nmap scan is about one thousand. Since the number of identified flows for half of the machines is around four thousand, our hypothesis is that they are four scan attacks of the network.

4   Assessment of the Consequences on Intrusion Detection Models Performances

Finding and fixing these issues in CICIDS2017 is a great opportunity to examine the current experimental evaluation performed on this dataset and assess its consequences on the performances. More specifically, we would like to answer the following research questions:

- **Q1**: How does the pcap ordering fix affect the performances of these models?
- **Q2**: How does the correct labelling of the port scan affect the performances of these models?
- **Q3**: How does the flow deduplication affect the performances of these models?
- **Q4**: How could previous articles obtain very high performances with machine learning algorithms in the presence of these issues?

In this section, we first describe our experimental evaluation protocol, evaluate several supervised classification models, namely decision trees, random forest, naive Bayes and support-vector machine classifiers, and finally answer the four research questions we defined.

4.1 Experimental Evaluation Protocol

To answer the research questions raised previously, we build several train sets and test sets based on the network captures files with different corrections to assess their effect. The corrections include the reordering of the pcap file before applying CICFlowMeter (denoted as **R** for the rest of the article). If the pcap file isn't reordered, then the labels provided by [4] are used. Our second correction is the addition of the new port scan labels denoted as **P**. We will also assess the impact of the duplicated network packets, and we denote the presence of duplicated packets by **D**.

As we described in Sect. 3.1, the labelling script proposed by [4] sets three kinds of labels: "benign", "malicious" and "attempted". To simplify the experiments and the analysis of their results, we decided to label these attempts as benign. We also ran our experiments by labelling them as attacks: the differences were slight and did not impact our conclusions. The train and test set configurations are detailed in Table 7. We distinguish three sets of experiments. The goal of the first set (**RD** and **RPD**) is to observe the effect of the reordering of the pcap file by comparing with **D** and **PD** and answer **Q1**. The second set (**RD** and **RPD**) is built to assess the impact of the port scan addition on the labels provided by Engelen et al. and answer **Q2**. The last set of experiments (**R** and **RP**) consists in assessing the removal of the duplicated packets in the network capture and answering question **Q3**. It must be noted that we think the correct version of the dataset is the one noted **RP**, i.e. with the port scan correctly labelled, the reordering of the packets and without duplication.

We evaluated four supervised models: a naive Bayes classifier, a support-vector machine (SVM), a decision tree and a random forest. We chose these supervised models since they obtained the best performances for intrusion detection given the survey [11]. A benchmark on CICIDS2017 [9] also highlighted the good performances of the decision tree and naive Bayes models on the dataset. We used the scikit-learn library implementation for all these models. We used standard configuration for the different models except for tree-based models, for which we limited their maximum depth to 15 to prevent overfitting.

We adopted a particular strategy for splitting the dataset into train and test sets to conduct a fair study. Indeed, we did not want to put mislabelled flows in

Table 7. Experimental configurations depending on capture and labelling corrections

Sets name	Reordered (**R**)	Scan Port added (**P**)	Has Duplicates (**D**)
D			✓
PD		✓	✓
RD	✓		✓
RPD	✓	✓	✓
R	✓		
RP	✓	✓	

the train set. Otherwise, if the train set were mislabelled, the supervised methods would certainly have poor performances on the test set.

To train the models on consistent data, the train set only includes correctly labelled flows but not any flow that Engelen et al. classified as "attempts". More precisely, we first collected about 65% of each attack, except for the newly discovered port scan attack. This means that the attack types (except the new port scan attack) are present in the training data with about the same proportion as in the dataset. Then, we added as many benign flows as to have a balanced dataset with as many benign examples as malicious examples. This dataset depends on the applied correction, so there are several train sets. However, each one of the three sets of experiments shares a common train set.

From the raw features provided by CICFlowMeter we drop features with constant values: `Fwd URG Flags`, `Bwd URG Flags`, `URG Flag Count`. We also drop `Flow ID` that is unique to each flow. Besides, we drop `Src IP`, `Dst IP`, `Timestamp` since they could make the models learn shortcuts such as identifying malicious IP addresses or attack campaign periods. The `Src Port` feature is removed since it is random and could lead to overfitting. Flow descriptions containing NaN values are dropped. Finally, we normalize the data by centering and scaling each feature as it is necessary for SVM.

To assess the impact of the labelling corrections, we rely on classic metrics used in intrusion detection: the numbers of True Positives (attacks correctly detected), True Negatives (benign traffic correctly identified), False Positives (alarms caused by benign traffic) and False Negative (attacks not detected). More specifically, we use the True Positive Rate (TPR, or recall), which is the proportion of attacks that are correctly detected, and the False Positive Rate (FPR), which is the proportion of benign traffic that generates false alarms. We could not use the classic area under the ROC (Receiver Operating Characteristic) curve as it is not easily obtainable on ordinal models such as decision trees.

4.2   Experiments Results

The Figs. 1 and 2 show respectively the TPR and the FPR obtained by the models for the different labelling corrections.

Q1 : How does the pcap ordering fix affect the performances of these models? This experiment relies on train and test sets **D** and **RD**, as well as **PD** and

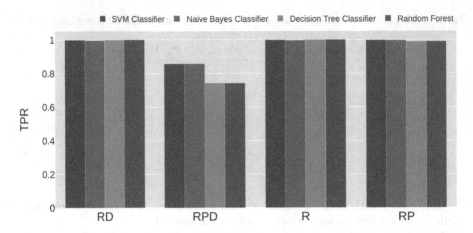

Fig. 1. TPR of the different supervised models given the different experimental configurations.

RPD. The reordering affects the creation or deletion of only about four thousand network flows, which is less than 0.2% of the total count for the whole week. We also measured a bit more than four thousand network flows with the source and destination that are swapped after reordering. This also represents about 0.2%, which is only a small percentage of the total number of network flows. Reordering the pcap files fixes the source/destination inversion issue and produces more accurate labelling. With the reordering, all the metrics are slightly better, but the differences are so slight (the mean change on all metrics is less than 0.1%) that we decided not to include them on the charts for the sake of brevity.

Q2: How does the correct labelling of the port scan affect the performances of these models? This experiment relies on train and test sets **RD** (no port scan label) and **RPD** (with port scan label). We can consider two cases, depending on the labels of the considered dataset used as the ground truth for computing the metrics. With **RD** labels, the port scan attack flows that are detected are counted as false positives because the port scan is not labelled (even if the port scan is really present in the network data). With **RPD** labels, the port scan attack flows that are detected are counted as true positives because the port scan is labelled. Once the port scan attack is correctly labelled, we observe in the Fig. 1 that the tested supervised models lose, on average, about 20% of recall. It means that these models do not correctly detect a vast proportion of the newly labelled attack. Since the FPR from all models is reduced by about 3% for all models after correctly labelling this attack, we can understand that these models detected at least some part of the port scan.

The drop of the recall is very surprising because there is already a correctly labelled port scan attack in the train set, so the models should be able to detect this new attack correctly. This question is discussed along with **Q3**.

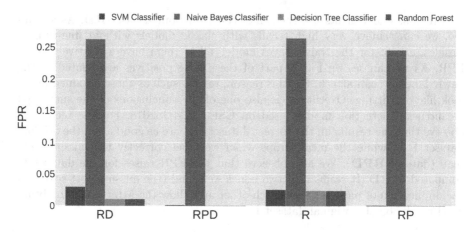

Fig. 2. FPR of the different supervised models given the different experimental configurations.

Q3: How do the duplicated packets affect the performances of these models? This experiment relies on train and test sets **RD** and **R**, as well as **PRD** and **RP**. The Fig. 1 shows that without duplication, the models are able to detect the new relabelled port scan attack correctly: we can see that the recall goes from about 80% on **RPD** to close to 100% on **RP**. In other words, the duplication issue prevented the models from identifying this attack correctly. The duplication has little effect on other attack detection: the recall is about the same between **RD** and **R**. The TPR change a little (upward or downward depending on the model) between **RD** and **R**, but it seems difficult to draw any conclusion.

To explain that effect on the recall, we analysed the explanation of the decision tree prediction for the two port scan attacks with and without duplication. The decision paths are similar, with some differences on the decision related to the following features: `Flow IAT Min`, `Flow IAT Mean`, `Bwd Packets/s` and `Flow Packets/s`. The duplication directly impacts these features because, as we saw in Subsect. 3.3, the duplication causes two packets in both ways instead of having one emitted packet and one received packet. Therefore the backward number of packets per second is doubled as well as the number of packets per second. For the two other features, the Inter-Arrival Time (IAT) is modified since the duplication makes duplicated packets very close in time. This reduces a lot the minimum and the mean IAT values. So, the duplication of the packets disturbs significantly the flows extracted by CICFlowMeter.

So, with duplication, the models do not detect the port scan attack correctly because it mostly consists of flows with duplicated packets that do not match the behaviours learned on the other correctly labelled port scan, which do not have duplicated packets. Without duplication, the newly labelled scan port matches the learned attack behaviour.

Q4: How could previous articles obtain very high performances with machine learning algorithms in presence of these issues?

Previous experiments use the same scenario as our dataset **RD**. As we can see, we can achieve very high recalls with classic models without fine-tuning. Besides, except for the Naive Bayes model, all of them have a relatively small FPR. As we can see on Fig. 2, part of these false positives are related to the newly labelled scan attack. For this reason, results such as those obtained by [9] look like overfitting. Overfitting is also one of the conclusions of the survey [7] on intrusion detection models used on CSE-CIC-IDS2018. For the recall, we observe that the results on the correct dataset **RP** are as good as on the original dataset **RD**, while the recall drops when we label correctly the missing port scan (dataset **RPD**). We also observe that the FPR raises for the dataset **R** compared to **RD**. It seems that two issues we found (the missing port scan and the duplication of packets) offset each other and allow the ML models to obtain good results on the original dataset **RD**.

5   Conclusion

CICIDS2017 is often used to evaluate the performances of NIDS. However, it has several flaws in both its traffic captures and its labelling. First, the tool CICFlowMeter misbehaves when packets are misordered in the traffic capture, which leads to source/destination inversion and wrong feature values in the network flows. Second, the traffic capture contains incoherent timestamps. Third, about 5% of the packets are duplicated, modifying the network characteristics of the flows used for detection. Finally, the infiltration step contains a port scan attack that was not labelled as such either in the original authors' CSV files or in the revision of the labels provided by [4]. Once the dataset was fixed and relabelled according to these modifications, we measured the intrusion detection performances of several supervised models that are often used. The newly labelled port scan attack is not entirely detected by the models, leading to a loss of recall of about 20%. However, we get back to good performances on the new port scan attack by removing duplicated packets. We allow us to conclude that previous work could not obtain a precision close to 100% without overfitting. Finally, the security community could benefit from merging our corrections with the features calculations and protocol handling of [13].

Through this article, we highlighted the importance of the quality of the network intrusion detection datasets to evaluate the NIDS accurately. A good quality comes from a clean labelling process, and an accurate network captures management to prevent packet duplication, for instance. Without these prerequisites, the evaluation is distorted, and the models learnt on the dataset may be unfit for realistic network characteristics.

We would advise dataset authors to provide as many details as possible on their labelling strategy, how they perform attacks, their network infrastructure and post-processing steps on the provided data. For future work, we want to improve detection explainability to understand false positives better and help analyse the corresponding alarms. This would allow to detect such data and labelling mistakes more easily.

References

1. Breiman, L.: Random forests. Mach. Learn. **45**(1), 5–32 (2001)
2. Cortes, C., Vapnik, V.: Support-vector networks. Mach. Learn. **20**(3), 273–297 (1995)
3. CSE-CIC: A realistic cyber defense dataset (CSE-CIC-IDS2018) (2018). https://registry.opendata.aws/cse-cic-ids2018
4. Engelen, G., Rimmer, V., Joosen, W.: Troubleshooting an intrusion detection dataset: the CICIDS2017 case study. In: SPW, pp. 7–12 (2021). https://doi.org/10.1109/SPW53761.2021.00009
5. Kumar, V., Das, A.K., Sinha, D.: Statistical analysis of the UNSW-NB15 dataset for intrusion detection. In: Das, A.K., Nayak, J., Naik, B., Pati, S.K., Pelusi, D. (eds.) Computational Intelligence in Pattern Recognition. AISC, vol. 999, pp. 279–294. Springer, Singapore (2020). https://doi.org/10.1007/978-981-13-9042-5_24
6. LeCun, Y., Bengio, Y., Hinton, G.: Deep learning. Nature **521**(7553), 436–444 (2015)
7. Leevy, J.L., Khoshgoftaar, T.M.: A survey and analysis of intrusion detection models based on CSE-CIC-IDS2018 big data. J. Big Data **7**(1), 1–19 (2020). https://doi.org/10.1186/s40537-020-00382-x
8. Lippmann, R., et al.: Evaluating intrusion detection systems: the 1998 DARPA off-line intrusion detection evaluation. In: Proceedings DARPA Information Survivability Conference and Exposition. DISCEX2000, vol. 2, pp. 12–26 (2000)
9. Maseer, Z.K., Yusof, R., Bahaman, N., Mostafa, S.A., Foozy, C.F.M.: Benchmarking of machine learning for anomaly based intrusion detection systems in the cicids2017 dataset. IEEE Access **9**, 22351–22370 (2021)
10. Moustafa, N., Slay, J.: UNSW-NB15: a comprehensive data set for network intrusion detection systems. In: MilCIS, pp. 1–6 (2015). https://doi.org/10.1109/MilCIS.2015.7348942
11. Panigrahi, R., et al.: Performance assessment of supervised classifiers for designing intrusion detection systems: a comprehensive review and recommendations for future research. Mathematics **9**(6), 690 (2021)
12. Ring, M., Wunderlich, S., Scheuring, D., Landes, D., Hotho, A.: A survey of network-based intrusion detection data sets. Comput. Secur. **86**, 147–167 (2019)
13. Rosay, A., Cheval, E., Carlier, F., Leroux, P.: Network intrusion detection: a comprehensive analysis of CIC-ids2017. In: ICISSP (2022)
14. Sharafaldin, I., Lashkari, A.H., Ghorbani, A.A.: Toward generating a new intrusion detection dataset and intrusion traffic characterization. In: ICISSP (2018)
15. Tavallaee, M., Bagheri, E., Lu, W., Ghorbani, A.A.: A detailed analysis of the KDD cup 99 data set. In: 2009 IEEE Symposium on Computational Intelligence for Security and Defense Applications, pp. 1–6 (2009)
16. Wang, Y., Yang, K., Jing, X., Jin, H.L.: Problems of KDD cup 99 dataset existed and data preprocessing. In: Applied Mechanics and Materials, vol. 667, pp. 218–225. Trans Tech Publications (2014)

A Comparative Study of Attribute Selection Algorithms on Intrusion Detection System in UAVs: A Case Study of UKM-IDS20 Dataset

Ahmed Burhan Mohammed[1]([✉]) [ID], Lamia Chaari Fourati[2] [ID], and Ahmed M. Fakhrudeen[3] [ID]

[1] National School of Electronics and Telecommunications of Sfax, Lecturer at University of Kirkuk, Kirkuk, Iraq
ahmedlogic79@uokirkuk.edu.iq
[2] Digital Research Center of Sfax (CRNS); Laboratory of Signals, systeMs, aRtificial Intelligence and neTworkS (SM@RTS, Sfax University, Sfax, Tunisia
lamiachaari1@gmail.com
[3] Software department, College of Computer Science and Information Technology, University of Kirkuk, Kirkuk, Iraq
dr.ahmed.fakhrudeen@uokikrkuk.edu.iq

Abstract. Security issues of unmanned aerial vehicles (UAVs) have received great attention. A new dataset named UKM-IDS20 has been recently developed for intrusion detection in UAVs to distinguish between abnormal and normal behaviors. The feature selection process in datasets is essential in improving IDSs performance. Decreasing features reduces the complexity of the storage and executive load. This paper investigates the influence of feature selection IDS for UAV networks. To achieve our goal, we propose the IGC-MLP algorithm. In the beginning, the algorithm utilized feature selection algorithms to determine the optimal features. Then, the resulting features are applied to the multilayer perception classification model. We evaluate our algorithm in two scenarios (15 and 20 features). The evaluation demonstrates that our model achieves better accuracy (99.93%). Consequently, reducing the number of features reduces memory size and CPU time needed for intrusion detection.

Keywords: Attribute Selection · Unmanned Aerial Vehicles · Deep Learning · Intrusion Detection System · Neural Network · IDS · MLP

1 Introduction

The process of selecting a particular attribute is performed in two steps. While the first step concerns which subset is created, the second step deals with the order [1], [2]. More specifically, in the first step, a subset is created and compares the candidate group by the searches updated with the selected group until the desired results are reached. The new candidate sub-group is better than ever based on a particular assessment. Therefore, this group is called the best group, and this process continues until the end state is achieved. Next, the second step works on arranging the attributes and what specific characteristics are used to find the importance of those attributes. [3] Two types of

S. Kallel et al. (Eds.): CRiSIS 2022, LNCS 13857, pp. 34–46, 2023.
https://doi.org/10.1007/978-3-031-31108-6_3

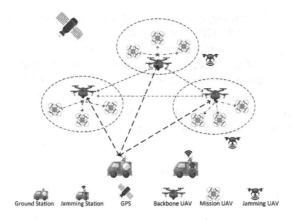

Ground Station   Jamming Station   GPS   Backbone UAV   Mission UAV   Jamming UAV

Fig. 1. UAV Communication

algorithms have been implemented in the literature for attributes selection: 1) Filter approaches algorithm and 2) Wrapper approaches [4] (Fig. 1).

Security issues of unmanned aerial vehicles (UAVs) have received significant attention. For intelligent IDS development, the UAV domain shows particular challenges. For example, dataset availability, control configurations, UAV platforms, and communication protocols. The IDS is required to help the UAVs to determine attacks as their attacks increase. In a specific environment, the IDS continuously oversees the actions, such as system calls of a particular operating, Syslog records, and network traffic. The monitoring aims to detect whether these actions are symptoms of a specific attack or a legitimate use [4]. Intrusion detection can be classified into two categories: Anomaly-based Intrusion Detection or Signature-based Intrusion Detection [5]. In anomaly detection, statistical models and heuristic rules are elaborated according to abnormal and normal activities. These activities are utilized to classify the behavior, whether it is as malicious or benign [6]. To improve the detection performance, artificial intelligence methods are also used to detect new attacks [7]. On the other hand, Signature-based Intrusion Detection aims to determine and classify (or misuse detection) the attack according to predefined patterns. It is also called misuse detection. Even though keeping good levels of false alarm rates, the intrusion can be performed in several ways. This behavior effectively deals with well-known Distributed Denial of Service (DDoS) attacks. However, the available methods are not efficient when a new attack occurs.

This paper studies the attribute selection algorithms' impact on IDS in UAVs. This study utilizes a very recent dataset (named UKM-IDS20) [8]. Therefore, we propose an algorithm comprised of two parts. Firstly, a statistical signature characterizes the traffic and then selects an estimator model to reconstruct the attack traffic. Furthermore, this procedure is robust and does not correspond with any particular attack. Moreover, any attack that does not follow the initial model follows these steps: Detection, Analyzing, and Managing. Accordingly, the performance and security of the network will be improved [5].

In the literature, flexible signature-based network intrusion detection systems (NIDS)) has been proposed to overcome this disadvantage. Secondly, the selected features are applied to the multilayer perception (MLP) classification model. Therefore, we named our algorithm IGC-MPL. Two feature groups (15 and 20) are chosen for the evaluation. Finally, the evaluation metrics of this study are accuracy, F-measure, and recall. The remainder of this research is organized as follows. Some previous works on IDS-based UAVs are reviewed in Sect. 2. The feature dataset UKM-IDS20 and the adopted feature selection algorithms are described in Sect. 3. Section 4 presents and evaluates the proposed algorithm to study UAV performance. Conclusion Finally, the conclusion and future direction are drawn in Sect. 5.

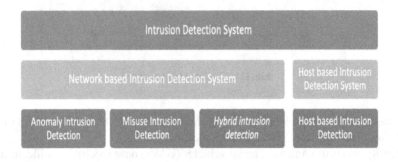

Fig. 2. Categories of IDS.

2   Literature Review

As mentioned earlier, the detection methods of IDSs are categorized into: Anomaly detection and misused detection. According to the literature, both types have certain drawbacks. Furthermore, intrusion detection could be Host-based Intrusion Detection or Network Detection System. In Hybrid Intrusion Detection, Host-based Intrusion Detection Systems and Network Intrusion Detection systems (i.e., Anomaly Detection Systems (ADS)) are combined [8] (see Fig. 2).

In the cyber security field, Artificial Intelligence (AI) techniques are implemented in IDSs. In an autonomous system, a manually generated test is a basic form of testing [9]. AI deals with and studies a human tester creating scenarios; accordingly, its performance is evaluated [10]. Therefore, datasets have been proposed for comparing and evaluating different NIDSs [11]. Each data point in labeled data is dedicated to a class of attack or normal. The number of false alarms and correct detection is utilized as an evaluation metric. However, for anomaly-based intrusion detection, the lack of available public datasets is one of the crucial challenges [12]. Therefore, over the last few years, this challenge has attracted many scientific and industrial communities to create several intrusion detection datasets, such as UNSW-NB15 [13], CIDDS-001 [14], and CI- CIDS 2017 [15]. However, to keep track of the latest continuous development, there is no common index of exiting datasets. GPS Spoofing and Jamming are widespread attacks on the UAVs; however, performing these tests can be challenging in several areas. The dataset contains a log from a benign flight and one where the UAV

Table 1. IDS Dataset Comparison.

Dataset	Developed year	Traffic Type	References
DARPA 1998	1998	Emulated	[27]
KDD '99	1999	Emulated	[19]
UNSW-NB15	2015	Emulated	[13]
CSE-CIC-IDS2018	2018	Real	[2]
ECU-IoFT	2022	Real	[29]

Table 2. IDS Dataset with attack categories.

Dataset	Attack Categories
DARPA 1998	Probe, DoS, R2L and U2R
KDD '99	Probe, DoS, R2L and U2R
UNSW-NB15	Fuzzers, Analysis, Backdoor, DoS, Exploits, Generic, Shellcode, Worms, and Reconnaissance
CSE-CIC-IDS2018	DoS, Heartbleed, Brute-Force, Botent, DDoS, infiltration, and Web attacks
ECU-IoFT	API Exploit, Wi-Fi Cracking, and DE authentication
UAV attacks	GPS spoofing and jamming and Benign Flight

experiences GPS spoofing and jamming [16]. The most popular datasets and their main attacks are summarized in Tables 1 and 2, respectively.

As a subsection of artificial neural networks (ANNs), deep learning has been implemented in different areas, where the ANNs have a deep architecture that spans multiple hidden layers [17]. In determining the indications of an attack, the iterative process is not easy for a human to perform, such as network traffic, parsing logs, and documents demand a reverse-engineered code [18]. To harness their discriminative capabilities, several kinds of machine learning models were developed [19]. Deep learning has recently been paid more attention. It studies data and its behavior through multiple discriminative or generative algorithms [20]. To improve the anticipation of neural networks, stacking many hidden layers together has been implemented. Consequently, complex patterns in the data can be identified more accurately [21].

Implementing the engineering-based machine learning models faces significant challenges: 1) To improve the efficiency of the learning models and 2) To manipulate huge numbers of features [22]. For this purpose, the feature selection (FS) method is an efficient way to tackle these challenges [23]. Accordingly, with the FS, irrelevant or redundant features are reduced (eliminated). As a direct consequence, prediction performance is improved, and cost-effective performance is achieved [24]. Before classification begins, as a critical preprocessing, FS removes some features that have not a significant impact. This process may increase the classification performance. Thus, FS is an essential step, especially in vast search data. It's worth mentioning that, due to feature interaction, the complexity of FS heightens as the features' number increases.

According to several factors, the FS algorithms are categorized into supervised, semi-supervised, and unsupervised models. The factors are: output type, search strategies, evaluation criterion, learning methods, and training data. [25] Based on learning methods, models are classified into embedded, wrapper, and filter methods [3]. The algorithms of ranker-based FS are classified into two principles. Firstly, based on the effect of the feature on data analysis or classification. Secondly, based on the most impact on the algorithm performance (e.g., accuracy) that was assigned subset creation (i.e., uses desired features to develop a ranking list based on its score) [26].

3   Dataset and Methods

3.1   Dataset

According to [27], the UKM-IDS20 dataset was created in fourteen days. In the first week, normal connection records were established. Network simulation attacks are recorded in the second 7 days. It is essential to mention that attack activities were separately simulated. The TShark tool has collected raw packets from the network. [28] During two weeks, data of 586 MB was recorded from the captured packets. Table 3 illustrates the UKM-IDS20 dataset features.

Table 3. UKM-IDS20 dataset features

Feature	Name	Feature	Name	Feature	Name
ftr.1	dur	ftr.17	src_ttl	ftr.33	fst_src_sqc
ftr.2	Trnspt	ftr.18	dst_ttl	ftr.34	fst_dst_sqc
ftr.3	srvs	ftr.19	pkts_dirctn	ftr.35	src_re
ftr.4	flag_n	ftr.20	src_byts	ftr.36	dst_re
ftr.5	flag_arst	ftr.21	dst_byts	ftr.37	src_fast_re
ftr.6	flag_uc	ftr.22	src_avg_byts	ftr.38	dst_fast_re
ftr.7	flag_sign	ftr.23	dst_avg_byts	ftr.39	ovrlp_count
ftr.8	flag_synrst	ftr.24	strt_t	ftr.40	long_frag_count
ftr.9	flag_a	ftr.25	end_t	ftr.41	dns_ratio
ftr.10	flag_othr	ftr.26	dst_host_count	ftr.42	avg_rr
ftr.11	src_pkts	ftr.27	host_dst _count	ftr.43	http_rqsts_count
ftr.12	src_pkts	ftr.28	rtt_first_ack	ftr.44	http_redirct_count
ftr.13	urg_bits	ftr.29	rtt_avg	ftr.45	http_clnt_error_count
ftr.14	push_pkts	ftr.30	avg_t_sent	ftr.46	http_srv_error_count
ftr.15	no_lnkd	ftr.31	avg_t_got	ftr.47	Class name
ftr.16	arp	ftr.32	repeated	ftr.48	Class binary

To provide the ability to extract attributes that are related to time series, the time separation was applied. Not all the collected data was handled manually during each capturing time. The developers generated some data from the network's services (for example, ADDS). [24] The generated traffic (captured and recorded in the dataset) by services is real because of utilizing genuine testbed software [8]. While Table 4 outlines the types of attacks in UKM-IDS20 dataset, Table 5 summarizes the training and testing sets for the connection records of each type in the dataset.

Table 4. Types of Attacks in UKM-IDS20 dataset.

No.	Type of attacks	Instances
1.	Normal	8909
2.	TCP flood	588
3.	Port scanning	597
4.	ARP poisoning	592
5.	UDP data flood	553
6.	Mass HTTP requests	601
7.	Metasploit exploits	547
8.	BeEF HTTP exploits	500

Table 5. Classification of connections' records in the UKM-IDS20 dataset.

Type	Normal	ARP poisoning	DoS			Scans	Exploits		Total
			UDP data flood	Mass HTTP requests	TCP flood		Metasploit exploits	BeEF HTTP exploits	
Training set	7,140	476	461	461	467	474	441	404	10,308
Testing set	1,769	116	140	140	121	123	106	96	2,579

3.2 Attribute Selection Algorithms

The datasets used in identifiers contain many features representing the features of internet traffic flows. Meanwhile, the features are divided into two parts of great importance in the detection process and little importance in the detection process. Thus, selecting more effective features can increase the accuracy and speed of IDs by using algorithms. [14] Feature selection is applied to understand data better and select a subset of important features and is formulated as a multi-goal problem. This work uses three types of algorithms specialized in selecting features [29].

1. InfoGainAttributeEval (Information Gain Attribute Evaluation (IGAE)): Evaluates the worth of an attribute by measuring the information gained with respect to the class. It is calculated as follows: InfoGain(Class,Attribute) = H(Class) - H(Class—Attribute).

2. GainRatioAttributeEval (Gain Ratio Attribute Evaluation (GRAE)): Similarly, this type evaluates an attribute's worth by measuring the gain ratio with respect to the class. It can be determined as follows. GainR(Class, Attribute) = (H(Class) - H(Class—Attribute))/H(Attribute).

3. CorrelationAttributeEval (Correlation Attribute Evaluation (CAE)): Evaluates the worth of an attribute by measuring the correlation (Pearson's) [30] between it and the class. Nominal attributes are considered on a value-by-value basis by treating each value as an indicator. An overall correlation for a nominal attribute is arrived at via a weighted average.

3.3   Creating MLP Model

Artificial Neural Networks (ANNs) are structures inspired by the workings of the brain. [31] These networks can estimate model functionality and handle linear/nonlinear functions by learning from data relationships and propagating into unseen situations. One of the most famous of these artificial neural networks (ANNs) [32] is Perception multi-layered (MLP), which has the advantage. This powerful modeling tool performs a supervised training procedure using model data with known outputs. This procedure creates a nonlinear function model that makes it possible to predict output data from specific input data.

4   Modeling

In this paper, we utilize the attribute selection algorithms (InfoGainAttributeEval, GainRatioAttributeEval, and CorrelationAttributeEval) with MLP to create our algorithm (IGC-MLP), where the letters of IGC are the first letter of the algorithm. The pseudocode of the IGC-MLP is shown in Theorem 1.

Our algorithm aims to improve the efficiency of classifiers and achieve more accurate classification of data compared to cases where all features are applied. As mentioned earlier, UKM-IDS20 includes 48 features. The benefits of choosing features include understanding the data, reducing the required storage space, and reducing operating costs. In the dataset, the search space size is significantly increased with the number of features 48. In practice, global search technologies are not feasible to come up with an adequate solution and face the problem of existence for penetration.

Theorem 1. *The IGC-MLP algorithm*
> *Input: Dtrain train dataset, Dtest test dataset, Fi (i= 1,2...,n) (the number of feature) Output: S feature subset*
>
> *Two kind of working applied in the strategy (first with 15 Feature and second with 20 features) Initialize feature set as empty, S=0.*
>
> *//Add feature Calculate and threshold Fij of each feature; Calculate total number of features. Assuming the number of features after adding is N1, initialize N1=0. for t = 1 : K if feature is impacted then S = S ADD Fij; //add to feature subset (using three algorithms for feature selection as IGC) N1 = N1 + 1; –end End*
>
> *Train classifier by the features in S.*

// Creating classification model; (applying MLP Neural Network) // Classify the test data by the model, and the classification accuracy is Cadd.

// Remove feature FFi (i= 1,2...,n) represents the features of feature S subset after selecting features. tempC = Cadd; for p = 1 : N1 tempS = S - FFi; // Train classifier by the features in tempS, and get a classification model; Classify // the test data by the model, and the classification accuracy is Ct. if Ct ¿ tempC; //Remove feature tempC = Ct; //Update threshold of accuracy –end end

5   Performance Evaluation

We utilized the UKM-IDS20 dataset to perform our evaluations and considered benchmarks within Network Intrusion Detection System (NIDS) research. Furthermore, using these datasets assists in drawing comparisons with existing methods and research. This paper evaluates the following metrics: Accuracy, Precision, Recall, False Alarm, and F-score [21]. They are calculated according to the number of detections divided into TP, TN, FP, and FN. Very briefly, TP, TN, FP, and FN are the number of true positive, true negative, false positive, and false negative detections, respectively. IGC-MLP algorithm is evaluated in two feature patterns: 15 features and 20 features. The classification algorithm is then applied by creating a model based on the training data set using MLP. Then, the model is applied to the examination data set. Lastly, the true and false ratios of the classification are calculated to determine the model's accuracy and time consumption.

5.1   Scenario 1: 15 Feature

Fig. 3 shows the output result of the selection algorithms. As the number of features in the dataset increase, the algorithms start selecting according to their perspectives. After selecting the best-influenced features, the classification algorithms were applied to these results to reach the best results that effectively affect the dependence on these attributes to reach the final result of intrusion detection. Figure 4 depicts the training model with neural network MLP.

5.2   Scenario 2: 20 Feature

Similarly, however, for the 20 features scenario, Fig. 5 shows the output result of the selection algorithms. As the number of features in the dataset increase, the algorithms start selecting according to their perspectives. After selecting the best-influenced features, the classification algorithms were applied to these results to reach the best results.

After conducting the outcomes of the scenarios, we calculated the evaluation metrics as follows: Recall, F-Measure, Correctly Classified Instances, Total Number of Instances, and Accuracy. Table 6 and Fig. 6 summarize the measurements. For instance, in scenario 1, Recall and F-measure are the same as in training and Test. However, scenario 2 is not similar, where training reached 0.999 while testing reached 0.995. Additionally, the Table 5 demonstrates that correctly classified instances and the total number of instances are almost similar. Lastly, the accuracy of scenario 2 became 99.93,

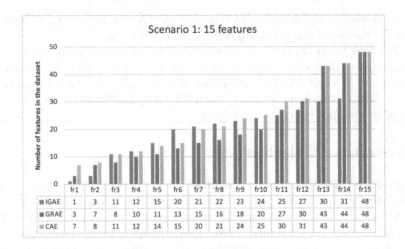

Fig. 3. 15 Features selected by applying IGC-MLP.

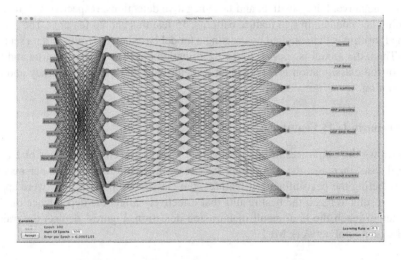

Fig. 4. 15 Features training model with MLP.

Table 6. Comparison of the performances between two scenarios.

Evaluation metrics	Scenario 1 (15 features)		Scenario 2 (20 features)	
	Training	Testing	Training	Testing
Recall	0.998	0.998	0.999	0.995
F-Measure	0.998	0.998	0.999	0.995
Correctly Classified Instances	10289	2458	10301	2451
Total Number of Instances	10308	2463	10308	2463
Accuracy	82.99%	80.99%	99.93%	99.51%

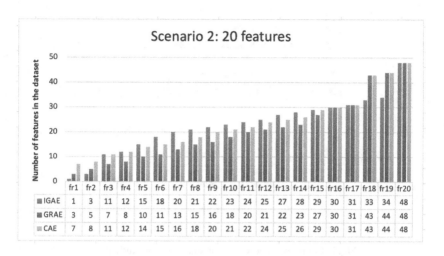

Fig. 5. 20 Features selected by applying IGC-MLP.

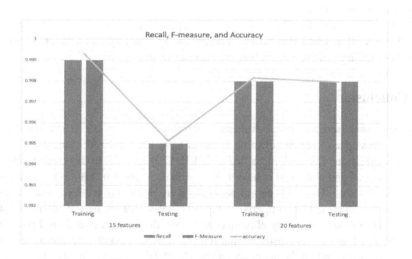

Fig. 6. Recall, F-measure, and Accuracy outcomes.

Table 7. Comparison of the performances between current study with pervious study in [8].

Dataset	Accuracy of Our Study	Accuracy of Study [8]
Training	99.93	96.46
Tersting	99.51	94.66

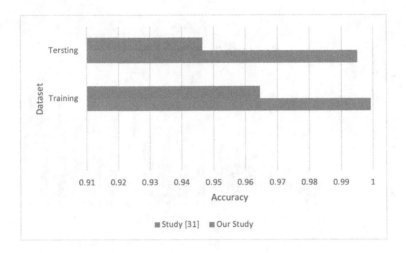

Fig. 7. Comparison between our study and the study [8].

whereas it is 82.99. Consequently, the findings demonstrated that IGC-MLP is very reliable for intrusion detection.

Lastly, Table 7 and Fig. 7 demonstrate the superiority of our work in compare with HOE-DANN [8] in terms of accuracy of detection. Specifically, our work outperformed [8] in both training and testing, where the increasing was 3.

6   Conclusion

This paper proposed a features evaluation algorithm (IGC-MLP), where three types of algorithms specialized in selecting features have been utilized. A new dataset for intrusion detection was applied (called UKM-IDS20) for IDS to distinguish between network normal and abnormal behavior. Two scenarios (pattern features) were chosen, 20 and 15 features. The MLP neural networks were applied to achieve better classification for the attacks. The comparisons between the scenarios are conducted in terms of Recall, F-measure, correctly classified instances, the total number of instances, and accuracy. The findings demonstrated that IGC-MLP is very reliable for intrusion detection. Results indicate that the accuracy can reach 99.93% greater. This is because it can accurately detect attacks using fewer features. Instead of classifying groups into normal versus intrusion activities, In the future, we plan to extend our work to consider more groups so that the algorithm can classify diverse types of intrusion within the datasets of IDS.

References

1. Condomines, J.-P., Zhang, R., Larrieu, N.: Network intrusion detection system for UAV ad-hoc communication: from methodology design to real test validation. Ad Hoc Netw. **90**, 101759 (2019)

2. Oliveira, N., Praca, I., Maia, E., Sousa, O.: Intelligent cyber attack detection and classification for network-based intrusion detection systems. Appl. Sci. **11**(4), 1674 (2021)
3. Balogun, A.O., et al.: A novel rank aggregation-based hybrid multifilter wrapper feature selection method in software defect prediction. In: Computational Intelligence and Neuroscience, 2021 (2021)
4. Bangui, H., Buhnova, B.: Recent advances in machine-learning driven intrusion detection in transportation: survey. Procedia Comput. Sci. **184**, 877–886 (2021)
5. Choudhary, G., Sharma, V., You, I., Yim, K., Chen, I.-R., Cho, J.-H.: Intrusion detection systems for networked unmanned aerial vehicles: a survey. In: 2018 14th International Wireless Communications & Mobile Computing Conference (IWCMC), pp. 560–565 (2018)
6. Yadav, V., Rahul, M., Yadav, R.: A new efficient method for the detection of intrusion in 5g and beyond networks using ml (2021)
7. Reza Fotohi and Somayyeh Firoozi Bari: A novel countermeasure technique to protect WSN against denial-of-sleep attacks using firefly and hopfield neural network (HNN) algorithms. J. Supercomput. **76**(9), 6860–6886 (2020)
8. Al-Daweri, M.S., Abdullah, S., Ariffin, K.A.Z.: An adaptive method and a new dataset UKM-ids20, for the network intrusion detection system. Comput. Commun. **180**, 57–76 (2021)
9. Ravi, N., Ramachandran, G.: A robust intrusion detection system using machine learning techniques for manet. Int. J. Knowl.-Based Intell. Eng. Syst. **24**(3), 253–260 (2020)
10. Li, X., Zhongyuan, H., Mengfan, X., Wang, Y., Ma, J.: Transfer learning based intrusion detection scheme for internet of vehicles. Inf. Sci. **547**, 119–135 (2021)
11. Sedjelmaci, H., Senouci, S.M., Ansari, N.: Intrusion detection and ejection framework against lethal attacks in UAV-aided networks: a Bayesian game-theoretic methodology. IEEE Trans. Intell. Transp. Syst. **18**(5), 1143–1153 (2016)
12. Małowidzki, M., Berezinski, P., Mazur, M.: Network intrusion detection: half a kingdom for a good dataset. In: Proceedings of NATO STO SAS-139 Workshop, Portugal (2015)
13. Moustafa, N., Slay, J.: Unsw-nb15: a comprehensive data set for network intrusion detection systems (unsw-nb15 network data set). In: 2015 Military Communications and Information Systems Conference (MilCIS), pp. 1–6. IEEE (2015)
14. Anomaly-based intrusion detection system through feature selection analysis and building hybrid efficient model. J. Comput. Sci. 25, 152–160 (2018)
15. Ring, M., Wunderlich, S., Scheuring, D., Landes, D., Hotho, A.: A survey of network-based intrusion detection data sets. Comput. Secur. **86**, 147–167 (2019)
16. Zhang, J., Zulkernine, M., Haque, A.: Random-forests-based network intrusion detection systems. IEEE Trans. Syst. Man Cybern. Part C (Appl. Rev.) **38**(5), 649–659 (2008)
17. Mohammed, A.: Anomalous network packet detection. Master's thesis (2015)
18. Whelan, J., Sangarapillai, T., Minawi, O., Almehmadi, A., El-Khatib, K.: Novelty-based intrusion detection of sensor attacks on unmanned aerial vehicles. In: Proceedings of the 16th ACM Symposium on QoS and Security for Wireless and Mobile Networks, pp. 23–28 (2020)
19. Koroniotis, N., Moustafa, N., Sitnikova, E.: A new network forensic framework based on deep learning for internet of things networks: a particle deep framework. Futur. Gener. Comput. Syst. **110**, 91–106 (2020)
20. Mokbal, F.M.M., Wang, D., Osman, M., Yang, P., Alsamhi, S.H.: An efficient intrusion detection framework based on embedding feature selection and ensemble learning technique. Int. Arab J. Inf. Technol. **19**(2), 237–248 (2022)
21. Aversano, L., Bernardi, M.L., Cimitile, M., Pecori, R., Veltri, L.: Effective anomaly detection using deep learning in IoT systems. In: Wireless Communications and Mobile Computing (2021)

22. Samaras, S., et al.: Deep learning on multi sensor data for counter UAV applications-a systematic review. Sensors **19**(22), 4837 (2019)
23. Shone, N., Ngoc, T.N., Phai, V.D., Shi, Q.: A deep learning approach to network intrusion detection. IEEE Trans. Emerg. Top. Comput. Intell. **2**(1), 41–50 (2018)
24. Sarkar, S.S., Sheikh, K.H., Mahanty, A., Mali, K., Ghosh, A., Sarkar, R.: A harmony search-based wrapper-filter feature selection approach for microstructural image classification. Int. Mat. Manuf. Innovat. **10**(1), 1–19 (2021)
25. Yang, J., Li, T., Liang, G., Wang, Y.P., Gao, T.Y., Zhu, F.D.: Spam transaction attack detection model based on GRU and WGAN-div. Comput. Commun. **161**, 172–182 (2020)
26. Kumari, A., Gupta, R., Tanwar, S., Kumar, N.: A taxonomy of blockchain-enabled softwarization for secure UAV network. Comput. Commun. **161**, 304–323 (2020)
27. Abdulhadi, H.M.T., Talabani, H.S.: Comparative study of supervised machine learning algorithms on thoracic surgery patients based on ranker feature algorithms. UHD J. Sci. Technol. **5**(2), 66–74 (2021)
28. Aicha Idriss Hentati and Lamia Chaari Fourati: Comprehensive survey of UAVs communication networks. Comput. Stand. Interf. **72**, 103451 (2020)
29. Ahmed, M., Cox, D., Simpson, B., Aloufi, A.: Ecu-ioft: a dataset for analysing cyber-attacks on internet of flying things. Appl. Sci. **12**(4), 1990 (2022)
30. Zaidi, S., Atiquzzaman, M., Calafate, C.T.: Internet of flying things (IoFT): a survey. Comput. Commun. **165**, 53–74 (2021)
31. Mohammed, T.A., Mohammed, A.B.: Security architectures for sensitive data in cloud computing. New York, NY, USA. Association for Computing Machinery (2020)
32. El-Rewini, Z., Sadatsharan, K., Sugunaraj, N., Selvaraj, D.F., Plathottam, S.J., Ranganathan, P.: Cybersecurity attacks in vehicular sensors. IEEE Sensors J. **20**(22), 13752–13767 (2020)

PRIAH: Private Alerts in Healthcare

Abdel Mlak Said[1]($\boxtimes$) (ID), Aymen Yahyaoui[1,2] (ID), and Takoua Abdellatif[1,3] (ID)

[1] SERCOM Lab, University of Carthage, Carthage 1054, Tunisia
maliksaid@outlook.fr
[2] Military Academy of Fondouk Jedid, Nabeul 8012, Tunisia
[3] ENISO, University of Sousse, Sousse 4023, Tunisia

Abstract. Privacy is today a mandatory property to implement in modern systems and particularly in Healthcare systems where patients' personal data is exchanged between different persons and services. Many solutions are currently implemented for privacy preservation, mainly for EHR (Electronic Health Record) data exchange and storage. Nevertheless, when dealing with electronic alerts about the patient's emergent health state, current systems still suffer from scalability issues. Indeed, privacy implementation generally requires cryptography and interception techniques which slow down alert arrival to its destinations. In this work, we propose a Big data-based system called PRIAH which stands for PRIvate Alerts in Healthcare. In this system, all alerts contain no identification indications about the patient's identity, so that only authorized users can access patients' private data. The originality of PRIAH consists in the optimal integration of three subsystems for ensuring private alerts: A machine learning-based component for alert detection, a pseudonymization system for privacy implementation, and a Big data streaming system for scalability. The system evaluation shows that the integration of the three sub-systems has no significant overhead compared to Big data non-secure systems.

Keywords: Big Data · Internet of Things · Privacy · Data Processing · Machine Learning · Alerts · Pseudonymization · Healthcare

1 Introduction

In Healthcare systems, multiple sensors or IoT (Internet of Things) devices are deployed to collect data that monitors users' activities, state, and environment and make automated decisions to protect patients' well-being [1]. These decisions can take place at the edge of the network for minimal latency or may be sent to Big data [2] systems on the server-side for storage and future diagnosis (Fig. 1).

Nevertheless, patients encounter concerns about the protection of their data that can easily be spread to non-authorized persons and organizations without their consent. Indeed, according to a recent IBM's Cost of a Data Breach report [3], the average Healthcare data breach costs its victims $7.13 million, the highest

© The Author(s), under exclusive license to Springer Nature Switzerland AG 2023
S. Kallel et al. (Eds.): CRiSIS 2022, LNCS 13857, pp. 47–61, 2023.
https://doi.org/10.1007/978-3-031-31108-6_4

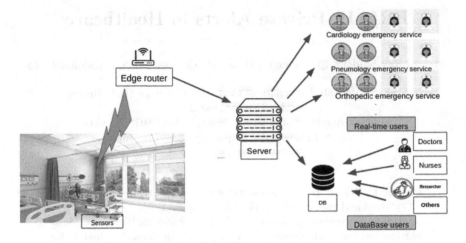

Fig. 1. Smart hospital architecture.

cost in 2020 across all industries. That is almost double the global average cost. Of these incidents, 80% resulted in the exposure of customers' personally identifiable information. These incidents are likely to occur in emergencies where the priority is given to saving patients regardless of their privacy constraints. Another reason that explains why privacy is rarely implemented in Healthcare real-time alerts is the technical implementation overhead. Indeed, privacy code is generally based on data interception and encryption techniques [4] that generally slow down the alert dissemination to destinations.

On another side, recent Big data streaming technology comes with interesting solutions to process big volumes of data in real-time [5]. But, there are generally no standard solutions for privacy-preserving, and recent works [6] cannot be applied directly to Healthcare systems that deal with emergency alerts since the focus is mainly put on protecting EHR storage and safeguarding Healthcare information dissemination and processing [7].

In this paper, we propose an extension of a Big data-based system for Healthcare alert processing called PRIAH which stands for PRIvate Alerts in Healthcare. The main contribution of PRIAH compared to state-of-the-art works is the efficient integration of the following three sub-systems to ensure a scalable alert dissemination while preserving patients' privacy:

- Alert identification and dissemination sub-system: PRIAH identifies alerts using machine learning techniques that discriminate abnormal patients' state from normal information messages. A message labeling distinguishes alerts from normal messages and a Big data publish/subscribe message broker allows disseminating alerts to their destinations.
- Privacy preservation sub-system: Following an edge-cloud architecture, alerts are identified and pseudonymized at the edge to avoid sending private data over the network. Furthermore, privacy is respected for monitoring data, stor-

age data, and alerts so that accessing to data is allowed only with patient consent. Only a trusted security component allows revealing the patients' identities.
- Real-time notifications and scalability: We rely on a Big data streaming system for collecting, disseminating, and processing alerts in real-time. Alert detection and privacy-preserving components are integrated in the Big data system and rely on the scalability features of Big data streaming technology to have no significant overhead on the overall system performance.

The proposed system is applied to a smart hospital use case and can be generalized to other kinds of Healthcare systems. The rest of the paper is structured as follows. Section 2 presents background details about the main treated concepts. Section 3 presents related works. Section 4 describes the proposed solution, including a high-level architecture and its components. Section 5 displays the main results and evaluation. Section 6 concludes the paper and refers to future work.

2   Background

The background section introduces fundamental fields concerning the contribution of this work.

2.1   Smart Hospital Ecosystem

In smart hospital architecture, data is collected from sensors, treated on the edge-server side, and finally consulted by end-users. We describe hereafter the main system components.

- Health sensors: Wearable sensors are an example of patient devices that present different monitoring functions (e.g., heart rate, blood oxygen saturation, and sleep patterns). These sensors measure health parameters and vital signs wherever patients or their caregivers need them [8].
- Edge router: Also known as the border router, which is a specialized router residing at the edge or boundary of a network. This node ensures the connectivity of its network with wider networks [9]. The border router is a special node characterized by more computational ability. It is used in analysis tasks and reduces calculations from the server-side for more accurate and faster results.
- Server: Allows data storage and processing in real time.
- Users: We distinguish two kinds of users. First, real-time users are nurses and doctors from emergency services that need to handle urgent interventions. Second, database users are doctors, nurses, researchers who need access to data stored in the database.

Collected data contains multiple information depending on sensors, but all sensors convene on specific information which is: device-id, data-category, data-value, patient-name, and time. In this work, we used the format of data described in Fig. 2.

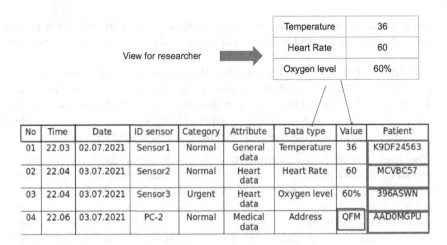

Fig. 2. Format of a pseudonymized packet and a view.

2.2 Privacy-preserving Strategies

Many privacy-preserving techniques have been developed. De-identification method is an operation of hiding the data or some data fields, this operation can be reversible or irreversible where it is possible to keep information about that data point for analytical reasons. Many techniques often mentioned when confidentiality and privacy of data are required:

- Correspondence table are generally table made up of two columns: the Value represents the input value of real data, and pseudonym which represents the associated post-processing value.
- Anonymization refers to the removal of information that could lead to an individual being identified, either on the basis of the removed information or in combination with other information.

In this work, we focus on data anonymization. A well-known technique is pseudonymization which has gained additional attention, where it is referenced as both a security and data protection by design mechanism [10].

General Data Protection Regulation (GDPR), which is a European law that targets personal data protection of citizens, defines pseudonymization as the processing of personal data in such a way that the data can no longer be attributed to a specific data subject without the use of additional information [11].

The pseudonymization permits data handlers to use personal data more liberally without fear of infringing on the rights of data subjects since the de-identified data is held separately from the "additional information". This technique will improve the system security since allowed persons will have the ability to reverse the operation and get clear data. In principle, a pseudonymization function maps identifiers to pseudonyms. Encryption is considered a robust pseudonymization technique. The block cipher is used to encrypt the patient identifier using a secret key, which is both the pseudonymization secret and the recovery secret. For example, the name of the patient is encrypted with a key in his EHR so that only his doctor or other medical staff have this key to decrypt the message and identify the patient.

2.3   Alert Detection and Edge Computing Paradigm

Since different sensors in the smart hospital generate multiple and several types of data and since data flow needs high-speed computing, edge computing is presented as a solution for ensuring minimal latency in IoT systems. Recent works propose the placement of an alert or anomaly detection module on edge for better resource utilization and optimization [12].

The anomaly detection module identifies the abnormal behavior of the system by determining the ordinary behavior and by using it as a baseline. In Healthcare systems, patients have been treated in various situations and any deviation from the ordinary behavior of the human body is considered an alert and should notify emergency service to intervene and act in real-time. Therefore, a machine-learning algorithm OC-SVM (One-Class Support Vector Machine) is used to deal with outliers detection. One-class SVM is a variation of the SVM that can be used in an unsupervised setting for anomaly detection [13]. While the regular SVM finds a max-margin hyperplane that separates the positive examples from the negative ones for classification. The One-Class SVM finds a hyper-plane that separates the given data-set from the origin such that the hyperplane is as close to the data points as possible. OC-SVM mode is trained in only one class, referred to as the normal class. The model learns all the features and patterns of the normal class. When a new observation is introduced to the model, then based on its learning, the OC-SVM detects if the new observation deviates from the normal behavior then it classifies it as an anomaly.

In our previous work [1], we have shown that implementing anomaly detection component at the edge level improves the overall system reliability by providing accurate e-health decision making. For this reason, this approach is adopted in this current work.

2.4   Big Data and Streaming Processing

Big data streaming systems are essential tools to manage many data flows or data streams. A building block is Big data **Message Brokers**, which are nodes that manage topics, store events, and perform processing. Multiple brokers can be used over several nodes to allow higher performance. Furthermore, applying the publish/subscribe communication pattern, brokers allow dispatching messages following a set of topics. In our context, we have at least two topics: normal data indicating the patient's monitoring information and alerts indicating an emergency. **Producers** are nodes that send streams of data to topics in the broker. **Consumers** are nodes and users that are allowed to read streams of data from topics in the broker. Healthcare team members are consumers of the messages sent about patients' health.

In our context, Real-time processing enables Healthcare systems to capture events, process them very quickly and extracts insights or perform operations on the data in real or near real-time. Those events and alerts related to patients' emergency health states hold personal information of patients that should be protected [14]. Unlike classical batch processing which implies the processing of static data, streaming processing involves processing dynamic or continuous data. For processing, we used Apache Kafka which is a processing framework that aims to provide a unified, real-time, low-latency system for handling the data streams [15].

3 Related Work

Related works can be divided into three major fields: Alert identification and dissemination, Privacy preservation implementation and Real-time alerts and notifications.

3.1 Alert Identification and Dissemination

Many researchers aim to deploy and integrate alert detection to identify anomalies that exhibit deviations from normal patterns. In [16], authors employed and evaluated five machine learning algorithms to detect anomalies in heart rate data. An overview of health monitoring based on IoT technologies is presented in [24], where authors also introduce WISE a health monitoring system framework, which enables the real-time monitoring of the patients. Authors in [18] propose an IoT-based heart attack detection and alert system. It compares measured heart rates data with normal rates, and if there is a large difference, then an alert is identified. This system is continuous, safe, and accurate in monitoring heart rates. In our previous work [1], we have presented an efficient anomaly detection system for smart hospitals, which combines two modules: event detection to detect patient health anomalies and intrusion detection for network anomalies. Both modules work together to ensure efficient monitoring. In our work, we adapt the anomaly detection component we developed so far to develop the alert detection system for PRIAH.

3.2 Privacy Preservation

There are different proposed solutions to protect data in the e-health databases or EHR (Electronic Health Record) such as [7]. The authors combine pseudonyms, anonymity, ABAC (Attribute-based access control), and RBAC (Rule-based access control) techniques to achieve security and privacy in medical records. Authors in [19] propose a pseudonymization approach that preserves the patient's privacy and data confidentiality in EHR. It allows (direct care) primary use of medical records by authorized Healthcare providers and privacy-preserving (non-direct care) secondary use by researchers. In [20], authors implemented the AT&T scheme for managing the access control mechanism of patients' data using encryption. In [21], an encryption-based solution is proposed in IoT sensors. Homomorphic strategy and DES algorithm are the main features of this solution. This solution in [22] ensures content privacy by encrypting the data exchanged using symmetric keys, that are in turn encrypted according to the proposed L-IBE encryption scheme. Those solutions focus on improving and optimizing cryptographic algorithms to secure data and preserve its privacy.

While these work only consider EHR privacy mainly for secure storage, in our work, we additionally focus on protecting privacy in alerts, which raises scalability and real-time challenges.

3.3   Real-Time Processing of Alerts

In the context of real-time processing, several works concentrate on monitoring systems. An e-health framework for patient monitoring based on the Internet of Things (IoT) and Fog computing is presented in [23]. In this system, data is collected and sent to the cloud server through a specific REST API by the JSON data model, allowing communication with health care providers (administrators and doctors), where they can receive recommendations, notifications, and alerts. The work in [24] introduces Big data architecture for a real-time network intrusion detection system for IoT streaming data. It uses different machine learning algorithms, where results show high detection accuracy and considerable throughput achieved based on Apache Flink. This work only focuses on anomalies that may be related to sensor failures or network intrusions. In other works [25], authors present a scalable solution based on a privacy-preserving predictive clinical decision scheme called PCD, that could predict diseases while protecting the privacy of patients. They use a homomorphic encryption scheme to encrypt data and RNN model for prediction. For scalability and performance evaluation, authors only focus on the accuracy and time efficiency of the RNN model and do not consider the overall system evaluation, especially the end-to-end alert dissemination delay which is critical in e-health systems in emergency cases.

Compared to related work, the contribution of PRIAH consists in ensuring in a single system the three properties (1) the accuracy of alerts detection, (2) the patients' privacy preservation, and (3) the real-time dissemination and processing of alerts. Alert detection and privacy implementation modules can be enhanced or adapted to the Healthcare context. Nevertheless, we believe that the proposed architecture can be reused in different Healthcare contexts.

4   PRIAH Approach

Figure 3 describes the PRIAH architecture and its main components, where we implement an alert detection component and a pseudonymization module in multiple edge routers. The edge router is located in different patients' rooms. If the alert detection component detects an anomaly, it produces an alert to the emergency service. These alerts as well as normal data are consumed by the database module for future exploitation by database users.

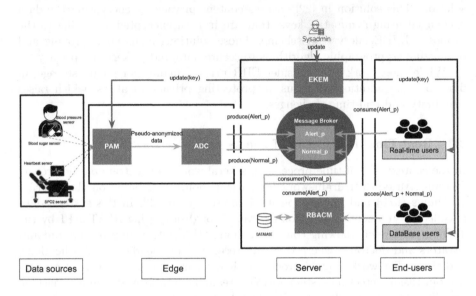

Fig. 3. PRIAH architecture.

4.1 PRIAH Components at the Edge

PRIAH have two key component that's reside on the edge, which is a specialized router with more computational resources.

4.1.1 Pseudonymization Module PAM

The PAM acts as an encryption engine. The received packets from different sensor nodes are treated at PAM level. This latter extracts and encrypts personal information in the collected data (Boxes with red shape in Fig. 2) as follows:

– It extracts the personal information from the patient name field in the packet or if the data type reveals information about patients such as address.
– It uses different pseudonymization techniques. This module replaces personal information with a pseudonym.

4.1.2   Alert Detection Component (ADC)

ADC detects anomalies related to the patient's health status by generating alerts for emergency services. For that, it produces two different topics, the first is related to alert (Alert_p), and the second is related to normal data for storage (Normal_p). These two types of messages are sent to the message broker in the server. The received data from PAM is classified based on machine learning algorithm. For the choice of machine learning algorithm, we rely on previous work [1], where OC-SVM algorithm have shown high detection rate. Compared to rule-based processing, machine learning algorithms can detect any abnormal behavior in the health states of patients, since a model is built to recognize normal states, and any deviation from such pattern is detected as abnormal data. The alert detection phase occurs after extracting the attribute and the data value from the packet. The attribute presents the class of machine learning algorithms.

4.2   PRIAH Components at the Server Side

Centralized components are located in the server side to communicate with other edge nodes. We rely on a publish/subscribe broker where edge component produce data and end users consume data after treatment.

4.2.1   Message Broker

The message broker plays an important role in the PRIAH solution linking all system components, exchanging different information. Therefore, the ADC after receiving the pseudonymized message, produces the alert (Alert_p) and the normal data (Normal_p). The Database consumes those parameters for future diagnosis. Meanwhile, real-time users consume direct alerts (Alert_p) for emergency intervention.

4.2.2   Rule Based Access Control Module RBACM

Views in the database are referred to as "virtual tables". A view also has rows and columns, just as they are in a real table in the database. The creation of the view can be done by selecting fields from one or more tables present in the database. A view can either have all the rows of a table or specific rows based on certain conditions. This will restrict access to a table, yet allow users to access non-confidential data via views. Afterwards, data is consumed in a pseudonymized format and stored in the database. Data is extracted as views following the user access right. For example, it is possible to restrict access to the sensor table that contains the ID of sensors but allow access to a view containing the data type and value (Fig. 2). Every database user has a specific role, and for each role, users have access to a specific view. Note that in all cases and independently of the views, the personal data that can reveal the patient's identity, like his name,

ID, and localization, is pseudonymized. Similarly, as real-time users, database users have a decryption key which allows them to consult personal information if needed. For example, doctors may need access to all fields of their patients' personal information.

Access control is based on an authentication mechanism. The user first asks for his authorization from the server, and requests data from the database, then she/he asks for his login and password for authentication. Next, she/he consults the corresponding view depending on his right.

4.2.3 Encryption Key Exchange Module EKEM

Since the PAM changes personal information into a pseudonym, it requires a periodic update of the encryption key. This update can be done automatically or the system administrator can intervene for the update. The EKEM acts as a synchronization engine. It sends the encryption key to different components. The system administrator only updates the encryption algorithm, the shared key, and related parameters. The synchronization is then performed and keys are exchanged. In our system, Diffie-Hellman (DH) key exchange method is used. The principle is that each part of the system has a public key that is visible to everyone and a private key that only the holder can see. Combining those two keys enables secure exchange of the new encryption keys.

4.3 System Administrator

The system administrator has two main tasks. She/he is in charge of updating encryption keys with the EKEM, and she/he defines access roles and security policies for database users through the RBACM component as well.

4.4 End-Users

In smart hospital infrastructure, there are two distinct types of end-users:

4.4.1 Real-Time Users

In emergency and crisis cases, the emergency services, called "real-time users" too, receive urgent data about patients, so that they can intervene and save lives. Different emergency services are available depending on data attributes. For example, with a heart attack, the cardiology emergency service is the one to intervene. Others real-time users have access to alerts but without any personal information for statistics.

4.4.2 Database Users

Database users can be doctors, researchers, nurses, and other Healthcare providers that consult data they are authorized to.

- Researchers are allowed to consult specific fields but not personal data fields. For that, they don't have the decryption key.

- Doctors have access to all their patient's data.
- Administrative services in the hospital have access to personal information such as names, locations, and addresses.
- Doctor may need an external consultation from another doctor or consultant (advisor) to diagnose his patient's disease or to submit treatment suggestions (after getting patient consent to seek specialist advice). The advisor can consult the patient's data permanently and continuously, and does not need his personal information. He only needs certain fields of the patient's data. So, he will only access to certain field through RBACM.
- Patients can decide if one of their relatives can have full access to their data. For example, if the patient suffers from a difficult disease, so, in this case, a relative can replace the patient.

5 Implementation and Results

In this section, two main parts are presented. The first part deals with the simulation process to implement the proposed system. The second part describes the used data-set and the evaluation of the alert detection component. The last part presents the performance of the system.

5.1 Implementation

In this section, we present the major tools and algorithm used to implement the system architecture.

5.1.1 Simulation Setup:
The simulation parameters for the system performance evaluation are shown in Table 1. Using Apache Kafka as Big data technologies allow us to increase the number of sensors, and therefore the amount of data.

Table 1. Simulation parameters

Parameter	Value
Working environment	Laptop with 8 GB of ram and 1.60 GHz × 8 of processor
Programming language	Python 3.6.9
Message broker	Kafka 2.8
Encryption	AES in CBC mode with a 128-bit key for encryption; using PKCS7 padding
Database	Mysql
Message format	String

5.1.2   Pseudonymization Implementation:
Since both EKEM and PAM holds a public key, with Diffie-Hellman (DH) key exchange method, the PAM can securely receive the pseudonymization key.

The PAM extract personal data (Fig. 2) from the received packet, then encrypt this field and re-inserted in the packet to be delivered to the ADM.

For that, we used python library cryptography.fernet to encrypt the data.

5.1.3   Alert Detection Implementation:
A one-class SVM with non-linear kernel (RBF) with parameters (nu = 0.1, kernel = "rbf" and gamma = 0.1) [28] is implemented in ADC. As a programming language, Python v3.6 is used, and the machine learning library scikit-learn is considered to implement One-class SVM.

5.2   Evaluation

For the evaluation, we focus on evaluating the alert detection component and the end-to-end latency of system.

5.2.1   Evaluation of Alert Detection:
To evaluate the efficiency of ADC, the performance of the proposed system was evaluated based on the Anomaly Detection Rate (ADR) metric, which identifies the rate of abnormal events and observations in a period [1]. A data-set containing 3000 instances of normal human body data (temperature and heart rate) is used for training the OC-SVM algorithm [26]. The simulation shows that:

- Using a data-set of heart failure from kaggle [27], results show an ADR of 100% for detecting abnormal behavior of heart failure.
- In a scenario of fever illness simulated by increasing the value of temperature and heart rate, results show an ADR of 78% for abnormal data detection.

5.2.2   System Performance:
For the performance evaluation, the end-to-end latency from consumer to producer is calculated for PRIAH against a system without privacy implementation. The end-to-end delay refers to the time taken for a message to be transmitted across a network from source to destination. In our scenario, we calculate the time between the edge router until the end-users passing by the Kafka broker. We do not take into account the communication delay between the edge and the server and between the server and the end-users.

Figures 4, 5 presents the simulation evaluations of PRIAH:

- The first evaluation consists of calculating the end-to-end delay of 1 message with multiple pseudonymization techniques: Per substitution, AES and DES encryption compared to a nominal behavior of the system without pseudonymization. Results (Fig. 4) show that the end-to-end delay increases by about 20% of overall time (2 milliseconds) for the substitution mode and about 30% of overall time (3 milliseconds) for AES and DES encryption. This evaluation allows having an estimation of the encryption time compared to the overall PRIAH processing time measured in the second evaluation.

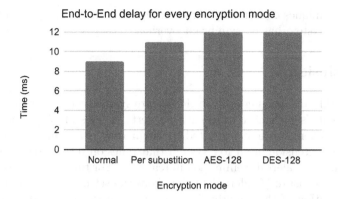

Fig. 4. End-to-end latency for every encryption mode.

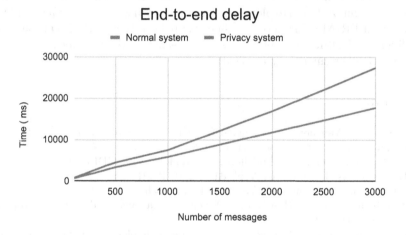

Fig. 5. End-to-end latency.

- The second scenario consists of simulating a producer that sends data across the Kafka Broker to the consumer. While varying the number of sent messages from 100 to 3000 messages, the end-to-end latency is calculated for each system. Results (Fig. 5) show that after 3000 messages the end-to-end delay with the privacy framework increased by 15% of overall time compared to the normal system (from 17000 ms to 27000 ms).

Figure 5 shows the simulation process where PRIAH end-to-end latency is slightly higher than the normal system, which presents an acceptable time overhead. Furthermore, these two evaluations show that PRIAH time is mainly spent in the cryptography operations used for pseudonymization. The interception functionalities at the edge for message classification and at the Kafka Broker level for message dispatching are not costly compared to the pseudonymization processing delay. This means that with PRIAH system architecture and with improved techniques of pseudonymization, introducing the privacy feature in an IoT e-health system has no significant overhead.

6   Conclusion

Privacy is still a challenging topic in Healthcare systems where personal information of patients is exchanged especially for alerts, while scalability and real-time processing challenges are incremented to the privacy requirement. In this work, PRIAH is an extension of an IoT system that relies on recent Big data technology for Healthcare alert dissemination in real-time. For that, a set of components are inserted to ensure (1) alert detection from the set of collected data and (2) pseudonymization of these alerts. The system ensures that alerts, stored data, and any information related to private patient life are communicated to Healthcare services or third-party services only following the patient consent. For future work, we are interested in exploring other pseudonymization techniques and testing them in PRIAH. Furthermore, since we believe that PRIAH can be reused for different Healthcare other than smart hospitals, we are interested in using PRIAH for other emergency applications.

References

1. Said, A.M., Yahyaoui, A., Abdellatif, T.: Efficient anomaly detection for smart hospital IoT systems. Sensors **21**(4), 1026 (2021)
2. Rhahla, M., Allegue, S., Abdellatif, T.: Guidelines for GDPR compliance in Big Data systems. J. Inf. Secur. Appl. **61**, 102896 (2021)
3. https://www.ibm.com/se-en/security/data-breach
4. Tawalbeh, L., et al.: IoT privacy and security: challenges and solutions. Appl. Sci. **10**(12), 4102 (2020)
5. Casado, R., Younas, M.: Emerging trends and technologies in big data processing. Concurr. Comput. Pract. Exp. **27**(8), 2078–2091 (2015)
6. Chenthara, S., et al.: Security and privacy-preserving challenges of e-health solutions in cloud computing. IEEE access **7**, 74361–74382 (2019)
7. Al-Zubaidie, M., Zhang, Z., Zhang, J.: PAX: using pseudonymization and anonymization to protect patients' identities and data in the healthcare system. Int. J. Environ. Res. Public Health **16**(9), 1490 (2019)
8. Kadhim, K.T., et al.: An overview of patient's health status monitoring system based on Internet of Things (IoT). Wirel. Personal Commun. **114**(3), 2235–2262 (2020)
9. Yahyaoui, A., et al.: READ-IoT: reliable event and anomaly detection framework for the Internet of Things. IEEE Access **9**, 24168–24186 (2021)
10. ENISA: Pseudonymisation techniques and best practices (Issue November) (2019). https://doi.org/10.2824/247711
11. EU G. General data protection regulation
12. Said, A.M., Yahyaoui, A., Yaakoubi, F., Abdellatif, T.: Machine learning based rank attack detection for smart hospital infrastructure. In: Jmaiel, M., Mokhtari, M., Abdulrazak, B., Aloulou, H., Kallel, S. (eds.) ICOST 2020. LNCS, vol. 12157, pp. 28–40. Springer, Cham (2020). https://doi.org/10.1007/978-3-030-51517-1_3

13. Miao, X., et al.: Distributed online one-class support vector machine for anomaly detection over networks. IEEE Trans. Cybernet. **49**(4), 1475–1488 (2018)
14. Qiu, J., et al.: A survey of machine learning for big data processing. EURASIP J. Adv. Signal Process. **2016**(1), 1–16 (2016)
15. Thein, K.M.M.: Apache kafka: next generation distributed messaging system. Int. J. Sci. Eng. Technol. Res. **3**(47), 9478–9483 (2014)
16. Šabić, E., et al.: Healthcare and anomaly detection: using machine learning to predict anomalies in heart rate data. AI Soc. **36**(1), 149–158 (2021)
17. Wan, J., A. A. H. Al-awlaqi, M., Li, M.S., O'Grady, M., Gu, X., Wang, J., Cao, N.: Wearable IoT enabled real-time health monitoring system. EURASIP J. Wirel. Commun. Netw. **2018**(1), 1–10 (2018). https://doi.org/10.1186/s13638-018-1308-x
18. Ajitha, U., Aswathi, P.A., Sasidharan, A., Salman, V.A., Anand, V., Arvind, A.: IoT based heart attack detection and alert system. Int. J. Eng. Manage. Res. (IJEMR) **7**(2), 285–288 (2017)
19. Lunardi, R.C., et al.: Distributed access control on IoT ledger-based architecture. In: NOMS 2018–2018 IEEE/IFIP Network Operations and Management Symposium. IEEE (2018)
20. Vora, J., et al.: Ensuring privacy and security in e-health records. In: 2018 International Conference on Computer, Information and Telecommunication Systems (CITS). IEEE (2018)
21. Gong, T., et al.: A medical healthcare system for privacy protection based on IoT. In: 2015 Seventh International Symposium on Parallel Architectures, Algorithms and Programming (PAAP). IEEE (2015)
22. Boussada, R., et al.: Privacy-preserving aware data transmission for IoT-based e-health. Comput. Networks **162**, 106866 (2019)
23. Ben-Hassen, H., Dghais, W., Hamdi, B.: An E-health system for monitoring elderly health based on Internet of Things and Fog computing. Health Inf. Sci. Syst. **7**(1), 1–9 (2019)
24. Yahyaoui, A., et al.: Machine learning based network intrusion detection for data streaming IoT applications. In: 2021 21st ACIS International Winter Conference on Software Engineering, Artificial Intelligence, Networking and Parallel/Distributed Computing (SNPD-Winter). IEEE (2021)
25. Lin, J., Niu, J., Li, H.: PCD: a privacy-preserving predictive clinical decision scheme with E-health big data based on RNN. In: 2017 IEEE Conference on Computer Communications Workshops (INFOCOM WKSHPS). IEEE (2017)
26. Mackowiak, P.A., Wasserman, S.S., Levine, M.M.: A critical appraisal of 98.6 F, the upper limit of the normal body temperature, and other legacies of Carl Reinhold August Wunderlich. JAMA **268**, 1578–1580 (1992)
27. https://www.kaggle.com/datasets/johnsmith88/heart-disease-dataset
28. Scikit-Learn. https://scikit-learn.org/stable/auto_examples/svm/plot_oneclass.html

Tool Paper - SEMA: Symbolic Execution Toolchain for Malware Analysis

Charles-Henry Bertrand Van Ouytsel$^{(\boxtimes)}$, Christophe Crochet$^{(\boxtimes)}$,
Khanh Huu The Dam$^{(\boxtimes)}$, and Axel Legay$^{(\boxtimes)}$

UCLouvain, Pl. de l'Université 1, 1348 Louvain-la-Neuve, Belgium
{charles-henry.bertrand,christophe.crochet,khan.dam,
axel.legay}@uclouvain.be

Abstract. Today, malware threats are more dangerous than ever with thousand of new samples emerging everyday. There exists a wide range of static and dynamic tools to detect malware signatures. Unfortunately, most of those tools are helpless when coming to automatic detection of polymorphic malwares, i.e., malware signature variants belonging to the same family. Recent work propose to handle those difficulties with symbolic execution and machine learning. Contrary to classical analysis, symbolic execution offers a deep exploration of malware's code and, consequently, contribute to building more informative signatures. Those can then be generalized to an entire family via machine learning training. The contribution of this tool paper is the presentation of SEMA - a Symbolic Execution open-source toolchain for Malware Analysis. SEMA is based on a dedicated extension of ANGR, a well-known symbolic analyser that can be used to extract API calls and their corresponding arguments. Especially, we extend ANGR with strategies to create representative signatures based on System Call Dependency graph (SCDG). Those SCDGs can be exploited in two machine learning modules based on graphs and vectors. Last but not least, SEMA offers the first federating learning module for symbolic malware analysis.

Keywords: Malware analysis · Symbolic execution · Federated learning · Malware Classification/Detection · Automation tool · Open source

1 Context

Approximately 450K new malware emerge every day. For companies, the average cost of an attack is 2.4 millions dollars [3]. Detection and classification of malware is an important challenge. There exists a wide range of static and dynamic tools to detect malware signatures [8]. Most of those tools are helpless when coming to automatic detection of polymorphic malwares, i.e., malware signature variants

Charles-Henry Bertrand Van Ouytsel is FRIA grantee of the Belgian Fund for Scientific Research (FNRS-F.R.S.).

that belong to the same family. Unfortunately, studies show that most infection faced by industries are caused by a polymorphic variant of known malware [23].

Let us illustrate the situation with a simple malware whose objective is to display the string "I'm evil". Imagine that, using a honeypot, we captured a first version of the malware that contains the string as an argument of a printf function. Static analysis tools such as Yara [22] could detect such malware by matching the pattern "I'm evil" directly in the binary file. Unfortunately, this detection can easily be tricked by creating a variant. This variant could be obtained by splitting the string as shown in Line 16 and 17 of Code 1. A solution to this problem is to exploit dynamic analysis. Such analysis allows the malware analyst to monitor the execution of a malware at each step (via, e.g., a sandbox). In addition to inspecting the instructions of the file, dynamic analysis makes it possible to explore the content of the memory with tools such as Volatility [2] or Cuckoo sandbox [18]. Let us consider Code 1 again, in which the string I'm evil is not present in the code, but it will be present during the execution. Indeed, it is obtained as the result of the strcat function via the symbolic function func (Lines 14–15) applied to the arguments I'm (Line 16) and evil (Line 17). However, this solution is not a panacea. Indeed, dynamic analysis focuses on one concrete execution in a dedicated environment. The malware could detect that it is in an environment where he is being observed and decide to escape detection by hiding its behavior [4]. Malware Code 1 uses a time trigger, i.e., Sleep(500000) (Line 3) and check (Line 5) if the sleep action has really been completed (uptimeBis-uptime). It also checks for the presence of a debugger (function IsDebuggerPresent) in the isolated environment. If one of those conditions is met, the malware will naively perform harmless behaviours, i.e., showing the hello world! message at Line 6. If none of them is detected, its malign behaviour will be executed.

```
1    ULONGLONG uptime
2        = GetTickCount();
3    Sleep(500000);
4    ULONGLONG uptimeBis =
         GetTickCount();
5    if ((uptimeBis - uptime)<500000
6        || IsDebuggerPresent()){
7    MessageBox(NULL,"Hello world!",
8               "", MB_OK);
9    }else{
10       char message[20] = "";
11   HINSTANCE hlib =
12       LoadLibrary("msvcrt.dll");
13   MYPROC func =
14       (MYPROC) GetProcAddress(hlib,
15                  "strcat");
16   (func) (message, "I'm ");
17   (func) (message, "evil!!");
18   MessageBox(NULL, message, "",
         MB_OK);   }
```

Code 1. Malware code example

```
1    ULONGLONG uptime
2        = GetTickCount();
3    Sleep(500000);
4    ULONGLONG uptimeBis =
         GetTickCount();
5    if ((uptimeBis - uptime)<500000
6        || IsDebuggerPresent()) {
7    MessageBox(NULL,"Hello world!",
8               "", MB_OK);
9    }else {
10       char* fl[2] = {"cat","str"};
11   char buf[10],message[20];
12   strcpy(buf, fl[1]);
13   strcat(buf, fl[0]);
14   HINSTANCE hlib = LoadLibrary("
         msvcrt.dll");
15   MYPROC func =
16       (MYPROC) GetProcAddress(hlib,
17                  buf);
18   (func) (message, "I'm ");
19   (func) (message, "evil!!");
20   MessageBox(NULL, message, "",
         MB_OK);   }
```

Code 2. Variant of the code in Code 1

A way to detect such behavior is to explore all the execution paths of the file under analysis. This approach is used in tools such as STAMAD [15]. STA-MAD translates the program into a push-down system from which the program's behaviour can be extracted into a data dependency graph over APIs. Such graph, whose structure is directly obtained by the disassembly procedure, is built in a static manner by inspecting the disassembly code. Consequently, the approach can be tricked by obfuscation such as the one presented in Code 2 that hide the strcat call via string combinations (Lines 10–13). To tackle those challenges, we offer SEMA, a Symbolic Execution open-source toolchain for Malware Analysis.

2   The SEMA Toolset in a Nutshell

STAMAD [15] explores all behaviors of the system statically via disassembling. This may lead to obfuscation problems such as those listed above. A solution to get around those issues is to apply Symbolic Execution [10,11]. There, the program is symbolically executed with symbolic input variables in place of concrete values. The main advantage being that all calls that are executed will be present in the symbolic trace. Consequently, symbolic analysis can be seen as a multi-trace analysis extension of dynamic malware analysis. Symbolic traces are merged to build a *System Call Dependency Graph* (SCDG). SCDGs are graphical representations of API interactions [12,13,16,19]. Note that, as the number of symbolic traces may grow exponentially, it is rare to obtain a complete SCDG in a reasonable amount of time. This is problematic as detection/classification shall be as fast as possible. Consequently, SEMA implements heuristics from [7] to explore "interesting" parts of the program and obtain a compact SCDG.

Once the SCDG is built, SEMA uses machine learning algorithms for classification and detection. In its current version, SEMA implements three machine learning techniques. The first one is based on graph mining and exploits the well-known *gspan* [25] algorithm. This procedure, which is based on graph isomorphism, is able to extract a common sub-graph from a set of SCDGs of malware that belong to the same family. This sub-graph represents the signature of the family and can then be used in the detection process. The second approach is based on graph kernel, i.e., a function measuring the similarity between pairs of graphs. Such functions, which allows us to detect similarities that are beyond isomorphism [9,24], can be exploited in Support Vector Machine (SVM) [7] algorithms. The last technique uses an autoencoder to compute vectors representing each SCDG and then applies deep neural network algorithms as described in [14].

Last but not least, in the spirit of what has been done for Android in [17], SEMA offers the first federating learning module for symbolic malware analysis. There, each client trains its own classifier with its own malware and only shares the parameters of the trainer via homomorphic encryption [20]. This addition aligns with SEMA's goal of allowing as many open source contributions as possible (new strategies, new learning algorithms) while maintaining the confidentiality of the malware sets used by the clients.

3   The Architecture of SEMA

SEMA is an open source tool [5] to analyse, detect and classify malware. It is implemented in Python (version 3.8) with already more 10,000 lines of code. It is designed to be highly modular to facilitate public contributions to its different core blocks. The architecture of SEMA consists in three main components: SEMA-SCDGs, SEMA-Classifier, and SEMA-Federated Learning.

SEMA-SCDGs is implemented as an extension of the Angr symbolic execution framework [21]. This extension is dedicated to the efficient computation of SCDGs for malware analysis. SEMA-SCDGs is able to handle ELF and PE files at the exception of .NET files or malware exhibiting control flow manipulation/virtualization. It implements all the heuristics (infinite loop, state-space search strategies, graph compaction, ...) proposed in [7]. An interface allows to create its own exploration methods or plugins to improve malware exploration depending on specific needs. Most of the windows API functions have their signatures stored in JSON files corresponding to different windows library. Thanks to those information, SEMA-SCDGs can keep the stack consistent during symbolic execution and offer a default behaviour when meeting those functions : extracting the arguments from the stack and returning a symbolic value from the API function. Some frequent API calls (more than 80) have been implemented as Simprocedures which consists of a summary of their effect on the control flow of the executable. Finally, SCDGs are outputed as JSON files containing the calls and arguments found during exploration.

SEMA-Classifier implements the malware detection/classification component. It takes multiple JSON files containing SCDGs as an input and allows to train classifiers and save them. As said in Sect. 2, models are based either on graph mining with *gSpan* [25], on graph kernel and support vector machine, or on deep learning. Similarly to SEMA-SCDGs, SEMA-Classifier is highly modular and allows to easily add new classifiers. This module can also load previously trained models and use them on unknown binaries to classify them.

The last component, SEMA-Federated Learning, offers a federated learning version of SEMA. There, n devices communicate with each other via a server in order to train an accurate classifier for malware detection. Each client trains its model with its own data set. In the current version of SEMA, we restrict ourselves to the deep neural approach where each trained model can be characterized by a set of parameters. Such parameters are shared with a server that uses a secured aggregator to obtain a better training from individual ones without having access to individual data. The latter is done thanks to homomorphic encryption. This new model is again dispatched to the client to improve its training [6].

4   SEMA in Action

SEMA is accessible via the command lines that are described in the GIT repository [5]. Let us illustrate some of these commands. Assume that we want to exploit the module SEMA-SCDGs to create the SCDG corresponding to a given binary named `Example.exe` located in `databases/`. This can be done with the following command:

```
python3 ToolchainSCDG/ToolChainSCDG.py --verbose databases/Example.exe
```

The options for this command are described in [5]. As an example, the `-method` CBFS option will prioritize an exploration with breadth-first search. The option `-symb_loop NUM` is used to limit the number of loop iterations to NUM).

We can then use `SEMA-Classifier` to train the classifier on SCDGs that are already computed and saved, e.g., in `output/save-SCDG/` directory)

```
python3 ToolchainClassifier/ToolChainClassifier.py --train output/save-SCDG/
```

By default, the classification model used is a Support Vector Machine. A switch to Gspan classification is available via the `-classifier gspan` option. These two modules can be combined to analyse and classify binaries, which is done with the following command:

```
python3 ToolChainClassifier.py FOLDER/FILE
```

Finally, thanks to `SEMA-Federated Learning` Module, we deploy a collaborative learning among two (or more) clients as follows:

```
#First, we launch client 1 and client 2.
./run_worker.sh --hostname=client1 and ./run_worker.sh --hostname=client2
#Then, we launch the tool at the master node.
python3 ToolChainFL.py --hostnames client1 client2 BIN_FOLDER SCDG_FOLDER
```

The classifiers obtained by these commands can then be used to classify a new malware using deep learning with the following command:

```
python3 ToolChainFL.py --classification --classifier dl NEW_PROGRAM
```

It should be noted that SEMA has been made compatible with pypy3. A dataset containing malware extracted from [1] is included in the project. A collection of SHA-256 hashes from more than 1800 samples within 15 families is also included. Both have been tested on the entire toolchain. Different combination of parameters has been tested regarding exploration, SCDGs building and classifiers. Those experiments highlights the benefits of graph kernels to make a better usage of SCDGs.

5   Conclusion

This short paper presents SEMA, a new open source toolchain for malware analysis via symbolic execution and (federated) machine learning. The tool is able to detect variants of malware that are out of scope of classical static/dynamic analysis. This clearly shows the usefulness of introducing techniques from formal verification into this discipline. SEMA is fully open source and easily extendable to new strategies for symbolic analysis or for classification. As future work, we plan to study such strategies as well as to consider other aggregator schemes such as multiparty computation. We also plan to extend the federated learning component with other machine learning algorithms.

References

1. MalwareBazaar. https://bazaar.abuse.ch/
2. Volatility. https://github.com/volatilityfoundation/volatility
3. Accenture: Eighth Annual Cost of Cybercrime Study. https://www.accenture.com/us-en/insights/security/eighth-annual-cost-cybercrime-study
4. Afianian, A., Niksefat, S., Sadeghiyan, B., Baptiste, D.: Malware dynamic analysis evasion techniques: a survey. ACM Comput. Surv. (CSUR) **52**(6), 1–28 (2019)
5. Bertrand Van Ouytsel, C.H., Crochet, C., Dam, K.H.T., Legay, A.: SEMA. https://github.com/csvl/SEMA-ToolChain
6. Bertrand Van Ouytsel, C.H., Dam, K.H.T., Legay, A.: Symbolic analysis meets federated learning to enhance malware identifier. In: ARES (2022)
7. Bertrand Van Ouytsel, C.H., Legay, A.: Malware analysis with symbolic execution and graph kernel. arXiv preprint arXiv:2204.05632 (2022)
8. Biondi, F., Given-Wilson, T., Legay, A., Puodzius, C., Quilbeuf, J.: Tutorial: an overview of malware detection and evasion techniques. In: Margaria, T., Steffen, B. (eds.) ISoLA 2018. LNCS, vol. 11244, pp. 565–586. Springer, Cham (2018). https://doi.org/10.1007/978-3-030-03418-4_34
9. Bonfante, G., Kaczmarek, M., Marion, J.Y.: Architecture of a morphological malware detector. J. Comput. Virol. **5**(3), 263–270 (2009)
10. Brumley, D., Hartwig, C., Liang, Z., Newsome, J., Song, D., Yin, H.: Automatically identifying trigger-based behavior in malware. In: Lee, W., Wang, C., Dagon, D. (eds.) Botnet Detection. ADIS, vol. 36, pp. 65–88. Springer, Boston (2008). https://doi.org/10.1007/978-0-387-68768-1_4
11. Cadar, C., Sen, K.: Symbolic execution for software testing: three decades later. Commun. ACM **56**(2), 82–90 (2013)
12. Canali, D., Lanzi, A., Balzarotti, D., Kruegel, C., Christodorescu, M., Kirda, E.: A quantitative study of accuracy in system call-based malware detection. In: ISSTA, pp. 122–132 (2012)
13. Christodorescu, M., Jha, S., Kruegel, C.: Mining specifications of malicious behavior. In: FSE, pp. 5–14 (2007)
14. Dam, K.H.T., Given-Wilson, T., Legay, A.: Unsupervised behavioural mining and clustering for malware family identification. In: SAC 2021, pp. 374–383. ACM (2021)
15. Dam, K.H.T., Touili, T.: STAMAD: a static malware detector. In: ARES (2019)
16. Fredrikson, M., Jha, S., Christodorescu, M., Sailer, R., Yan, X.: Synthesizing near-optimal malware specifications from suspicious behaviors. In: S&P. IEEE (2010)
17. Galvez, R., Moonsamy, V., Díaz, C.: Less is more: a privacy-respecting android malware classifier using federated learning. PET **2021**(4), 96–116 (2021)
18. Jamalpur, S., Navya, Y.S., Raja, P., Tagore, G., Rao, G.R.K.: Dynamic malware analysis using cuckoo sandbox. In: ICICCT, pp. 1056–1060. IEEE (2018)
19. Macedo, H.D., Touili, T.: Mining malware specifications through static reachability analysis. In: Crampton, J., Jajodia, S., Mayes, K. (eds.) ESORICS 2013. LNCS, vol. 8134, pp. 517–535. Springer, Heidelberg (2013). https://doi.org/10.1007/978-3-642-40203-6_29
20. Microsoft SEAL. https://github.com/Microsoft/SEAL
21. Shoshitaishvili, Y., et al.: SoK: (state of) the art of war: offensive techniques in binary analysis. In: S&P (2016)
22. VirusTotal: Yara. http://virustotal.github.io/yara/

23. WebRoot: Next Generation Threaths Exposed. https://webroot-cms-cdn.s3. amazonaws.com/7814/5617/2382/Webroot-2016-Threat-Brief.pdf
24. Xu, X., Liu, C., Feng, Q., Yin, H., Song, L., Song, D.: Neural network-based graph embedding for cross-platform binary code similarity detection. In: CCS, pp. 363–376 (2017)
25. Yan, X., Han, J.: gSpan: graph-based substructure pattern mining. In: 2002 IEEE International Conference on Data Mining, pp. 721–724. IEEE (2002)

Blockchain Survey for Security and Privacy in the e-Health Ecosystem

Maher Boughdiri[1]([email]), Takoua Abdellatif[1,2], and Tesnim Abdellatif[3]

[1] SERCOM Laboratory, University of Carthage, 1054 Carthage, Tunisia
`maher.boughdiri@ept.ucar.tn`
[2] ENISo, University of Sousse, 4002 Sousse, Tunisia
[3] Informal Systems, Paris, France

Abstract. This survey paper focuses on the use of blockchain technology to ensure security and privacy properties in e-health applications. For that, background information on blockchain technology was conducted, followed by a classification of e-health applications based on data life-cycle components related to security and privacy concerns. Then, we discuss the security and privacy requirements of an e-health system and how blockchain can address these requirements, accompanied by a detailed examination of the data security and privacy solutions offered by five blockchain platforms. Lastly, we provide some guidelines and recommendations for using blockchain to secure e-health applications and preserve patient privacy. This work provides technical and intuitive insights into concepts, requirements, development, and deployment technologies for healthcare professionals and system designers interested in adopting blockchain to maintain the security and privacy of healthcare systems.

Keywords: e-health · Blockchain · Security · Privacy · Blockchain platforms

1 Introduction

Healthcare digitalization or e-health as it is commonly known, has recently been a topic of interest for researchers and scientists. Its goal is to find a cost-effective solution to improve therapy and patient care, as well as to assist users in making better-informed decisions about their health [1]. It involves many industries, such as hospitals, diagnostic labs, pharmacies, doctors, and insurance companies, to synthesize a complete image analysis of the patient. However, integrating medical data scattered across a variety of stakeholders, protecting sensitive information against unauthorized breaches, and providing patients control over their data access are more challenging [2]. Furthermore, the widespread adoption of the internet of things (IoT) in e-health to improve communication between patients and health professionals for treatment effectiveness and patient monitoring raises security and privacy concerns [3].

Blockchain is a distributed technology [4] that has recently emerged as a key tool in the e-health sector. It has the potential to address e-health data management issues, system interoperability, secure access and share of medical records,

S. Kallel et al. (Eds.): CRiSIS 2022, LNCS 13857, pp. 69–84, 2023.
https://doi.org/10.1007/978-3-031-31108-6_6

and patient privacy. Blockchain-based e-health systems can achieve an enormous level of access control and protection against unauthorized users for medical data. It also provides a patient-centric and transparent data sharing process to boost trust among healthcare stakeholders while preserving the privacy of patients, as well as, distributed data management to get beyond the single point of failure of centralized systems. In addition, it achieves medical data integrity and authenticity through a data provenance mechanism based on cryptographic hash functions. [5]. This technology has evolved in a number of e-health industries to improve medical data security and privacy, including electronic health records, pharmaceuticals supply chain management, clinical trials, and more [6]. Alongside, to meet the growing demand for blockchain solutions, several blockchain platforms have improved their data privacy and security solutions. Others were released with built-in security and privacy mechanisms.

This survey aims to provide a guideline to healthcare system designers and developers who want to employ blockchain technology to address security and privacy concerns. For that, the following steps are established: a classification of e-health applications; an analysis of the security and privacy requirements of these applications; and a discussion about the benefits of blockchain adoption to fulfill the requirements. Thanks to a proposed Framework, the system designer can determine which platforms are appropriate for her/his healthcare application. Indeed, the Framework allows for providing necessary guidelines and recommendations for using blockchain to secure e-health applications.

Earlier survey work [6–9,11,13,19] generally addresses two topics at the same time: either e-health and security or blockchain and e-health or blockchain and security. In this survey, we focus on the intersection of the three topics: e-health applications, security and privacy requirements, and blockchain platforms. Furthermore, we classify e-health applications based on the data life cycle related to security and privacy issues rather than the e-health fields. For that, we distinguish data collection, data sharing, data storage, and data processing components. This classification allows us to cover a wide range of applications and anticipate future e-health application needs. We provide a Framework based on the following criteria: data life cycle components in e-health applications, data security and privacy requirements, and existent blockchain platforms. This assists developers and healthcare professionals in determining the best solution for deploying blockchain to protect their applications and in selecting a suitable platform given the security and privacy requirements of an e-health application.

The remainder of this paper is structured as follows: Sect. 3 reviews the state of the art on the use of blockchain technology for e-health systems. Section 4 presents background information on blockchain technology and classification of different e-health applications. Section 5 details the security and privacy requirements of e-health applications. Section 6 examines blockchain platforms' data privacy and security solutions. Finally, before concluding the article with possible future directions, we give some guidelines to secure e-health applications with blockchain technology.

2   Research Strategy

Since it is a survey paper, our main purpose is to integrate and update the findings of the past studies regarding the same topic. We made sure to gather relevant studies from various scientific databases between 2018 and 2022 to carry out the review, such as Google Scholar, IEEE Xplore, IEEE Access journal, PubMed, Elsevier Science Direct, Web of Science, Springer, and MDPI journals. Only blockchain research applied to eHealth, blockchain for security and privacy, and blockchain platforms were chosen as selection criteria. Papers not related to our study were excluded.

To answer the question: what kind of blockchain is appropriate for e-health security and privacy? We begin by identifying components affiliated with e-health applications following the data life cycle. Therefore, we distinguish data collection, data storage, data sharing, and data processing components. Then, we list the security and privacy requirements for the different components. On the other hand, we study the different blockchain technologies and solutions by examining five platforms' levels of data security and privacy. A Framework is then proposed to attribute appropriate blockchain technologies and solutions to each component requirement. A system designer has to specify the data life-cycle components he or she needs, the security requirements of his or her application, and then use the Framework to identify the appropriate technology to use.

3   State of the Art

Several surveys on the adoption of blockchain technology in various healthcare applications have already been published. In this section, works are discussed considering three criteria: e-health application classification, security and privacy requirement identification, and blockchain technologies categorization based on each platform's security and privacy solutions.

In [7], authors provide a systematic review of the adoption of blockchain technology in e-health applications. This study answers four main questions: What is the advanced profile for implementing blockchain in the healthcare industry? What are the most common applications of blockchain in healthcare? What are the current issues that prior blockchain-based healthcare studies have identified? and What are the potential healthcare avenues that would benefit from blockchain implementation? Additionally, Hölbl et al. [8] and Agbo et al. [9] published systematic reviews that analyzed the applications of blockchain for different healthcare fields and highlighted the challenges, most used platforms, and possible research directions. Other surveys have focused on the adoption of blockchain in a specific healthcare application, such as Electronic Health Record (EHR) [11], supply chain management [13], Clinical Trials [14], and more. However, compared to our work, these works categorize various e-health applications according to the e-health domain, which is limited to classifying the numerous applications in the e-health industry as well as future applications and identifying their security and privacy needs. Adding to that, none of these works examines the key features of blockchain in maintaining privacy and security in the health field, as well as the security and privacy levels of blockchain platforms.

In [5] and [16], security and privacy requirements of healthcare data are considered. They address the potential of blockchain technology to fulfill these requirements. Authors of [15] focused on the security and privacy requirements for blockchain-based electronic medical data sharing. They provided a comprehensive analysis of its security and privacy risks and needs, as well as techniques and strategies for implementing these security and privacy aspects. Further, some other research analyzes the capability of blockchain for specific requirements such as access control [17] and identity management [18], or specified use case like cloud-based e-health applications [19] and the Internet of Medical Things (IoMT) [20]. These works do not include a consideration of e-health applications classification and component related to their security and privacy identification as well as the suitable blockchain platform for implementation.

Some blockchain platforms for healthcare are compared in [22] and [23], however little emphasis is placed on each platform's privacy and security levels. Thus, e-health system developers can not decide which platform is appropriate for securing their applications and protecting patient privacy.

Compared to the state-of-the-art, our main work contributions are as follows:

(1) We provide a Framework for classifying e-health applications based on data life-cycle components rather than application fields. This allows us to address a much larger range of applications than the existing ones.

(2) This survey addresses three fields at the same time: e-health application classification; security and privacy requirement identification; and blockchain technologies categorization because it focuses on a specific topic, which is blockchain usage in securing e-health systems. The other surveys have a larger scope and address two of the discussed fields at the same time.

4   Background

4.1   Blockchain Technology Overview

Blockchain is an immutable and distributed ledger technology for peer-to-peer networks that allows data to be stored and shared securely and transparently across several network nodes [24]. Due to the use of consensus mechanisms and cryptographic techniques, blockchain platforms provide several benefits such as accountability, traceability, transparency, and security of the data stored in the network, commonly called ledger. It provides a fully decentralized root of trust that avoids the use of central authorities, allowing confidence to be built between previously untrustworthy or unknown stakeholders and consumers. On the blockchain, a smart contract is a self-executing, self-verifying, and tamper-proof computer program. If the program's rules are met, smart contracts enforce the agreement between various system entities without the involvement of a third party. Smart contracts that incorporate blockchain technology can perform tasks in real-time at a low cost and with increased security.

The Blockchain architecture is dependent on the access privileges granted to the network entities to read and write on the ledger and reach consensus agreements. Three main blockchain architectures can be distinguished [26]:

- **Public blockchain (permissionless)** is an open network that anyone can join without revealing any personal information, read, write, and participate in the consensus mechanism. It is a fully decentralized network that connects unidentified parties.
- **Private blockchain (permissioned)** is a network where the participating nodes must be granted access to the network, via an invitation or permission, to perform operations over the distributed ledger or participate in consensus. Thus, the governing organization determines the level of security, permissions, authorizations, and accessibility.
- **Consortium blockchain (Federated)** is a combination of public and private blockchains. The governance is shared by different stakeholders. Its fundamental goal is to increase cooperative effects in order to tackle a certain industry's persistent issues. Consortium blockchain can be used by organizations with common goals to improve data security, accountability, and transparency.

4.2 e-Health Applications

Healthcare data is a collection of all the information relevant to organizations and individuals involved in the e-health industry. As follows, we identify application components relevant to an e-health application's security and privacy based on the data life-cycle. This allows us to classify various existing and future e-health applications.

- **Data collection**: the acquisition of medical data related to patients and healthcare providers faces numerous security and privacy challenges. This process requires data authenticity, integrity, and availability to improve healthcare quality and reduce medical errors. One example of data collection-related security and privacy problems is the **Internet of Medical Things (IoMT)**. IoMT's remote patient monitoring service consists of a set of medical IoT devices equipped with a variety of intelligent sensors that can sense their environment and collect biomedical signals from patients, allowing healthcare professionals to obtain a complete real-time image of the patient's health conditions and make an appropriate decision. However, the integration and the connectivity of medical things in the IoMT environment introduce various vulnerabilities and privacy concerns. IoMT devices are vulnerable to numerous wireless and network attacks due to their dependency on wireless connections. An attacker can compromise an IoT device and alter its data or breach a patient's critical information [27].
- **Data storage**: medical data gathered from various patients or healthcare organizations should be kept safe and should preserve patients' privacy. This is more challenging, especially when distributed storage is needed due to

granular access control, consistency, immutability, and auditability requirements. **Electronic health records (EHR)** are the most prevalent system for patient medical data storage. It contains a patient's personal information, physiological health metrics, medical history, laboratory test results, and pharmaceutical prescription data. EHRs are created by healthcare providers based on the diagnoses of healthcare professionals and laboratories [11]. Security and privacy issues in this e-health application are owing to the distributed data storage component. Maintaining a distributed, auditable, and consistent EHR among several healthcare providers to synthesize a complete analysis of the patient, as well as, providing patient-centric health records (patients own their medical data access) to address patients' self-sovereignty are more demanding. Further, as these medical records are so large, a high storage capacity is required. On-chain and off-chain collaboration storage model has been developed to efficiently solve this problem [12]. Indeed, off-chain data can be any structured or unstructured data that is too large to be effectively stored on the Blockchain, or that must be modified or destroyed, and only a pointer to this data is retained on the ledger (On-chain) for auditability and transparency needs. Off-chain transactions also provide greater confidentiality and anonymity to participants since information is not publicly broadcast to all blockchain network peers.

- **Data sharing**: integrating and exchanging patients' medical data scattered across different healthcare providers is a critical need for e-health service development. However, the confidentiality, integrity, and unlinkability of data as well as user authentication and fine-grained access control should be provided for security and privacy considerations. Maintaining data traceability for accountability purposes enables more suitable and efficient use of healthcare information by legitimate users, and prevents any potential misuse that may jeopardize patient privacy. In the **Pharmaceutical Supply Chain**, verifying the provenance of medical products and their authenticity is a major challenge for the healthcare sector because of the complexities of product and transaction flows. Indeed, counterfeit drugs are a huge public health issue that has a significant influence on human lives and treatment outcomes. It affects all pharmaceutical stakeholders as its actors falsify information, such as improper labeling, as well as, incorrect and erroneous ingredients. Hence, authenticity and traceability, when sharing medical goods' information, in the pharmaceutical industry are extremely crucial [13].

- **Data processing** refers to the analysis and the exploitation of collected and stored data. This process should provide data security and privacy preservation. **Disease Diagnostic** is an example of a use case where security and privacy problems are associated with data processing components. Since medical data is inextricably linked to the diagnostic' accuracy, its authenticity, integrity, and consistency are critical. Furthermore, one of the key issues in this components is when highly de-identified patient data is required. Healthcare professionals rely on the analysis of vast volumes of anonymous data to offer a picture of how a disease is dispersed as accurately as possible without knowing any patient's personal information [9].

5 Security and Privacy Requirements for e-Health Applications

Centralizing data management is one of the key reasons for security and privacy concerns in the healthcare industry. Data interoperability among diverse healthcare stakeholders, system security, and, most importantly, the confidentiality and privacy of patient medical information are some of these issues. The single point of control created by the centralized handling of medical data by affiliated companies creates security concerns and exposes the system to threats and vulnerabilities. Since healthcare data includes personal and sensitive information about patients and healthcare providers, a successful cyberattack on the control point can compromise the data integrity and confidentiality of all the related systems, as well as, illegitimately steal and breach some private data for financial gains. Similarly, ambiguity in the ownership of patient data leads to privacy concerns and to the issue of illegal access to stored data and its manipulation without the patient's permission [2].

The key features of blockchain as a secure, immutable, transparent, and decentralized technology have the potential to address these security and privacy requirements in the healthcare system. Therefore, blockchain networks are used to securely store and share patient data across many healthcare providers. As well as, assisting in gaining insight, improving medical record analysis, and properly identifying major and even dangerous medical errors. Also, the performance, security, and transparency of medical data sharing and storing in the healthcare system can all be improved, which can help alleviate concerns about data tampering in healthcare.

Medical data of different healthcare industries are extremely privacy-sensitive. Therefore, healthcare stakeholders should place a greater emphasis on the security and privacy of these sensitive data. It should be fully safeguarded, with the essential cyberattack protection, data encryption, user authentication and fine-grained access control, as well as security operations and certifications that match the most recent standards.

The following, is a list of security and privacy requirements for a healthcare applications and how blockchain can meet these criteria [15]:

- **(R1) Integrity of data**: refers to the accuracy of medical information in a transaction. It should not be tampered during the process of broadcasting, mining, and storing on the blockchain ledger. This property can be achieved by the inherent hash chained storage mechanism of the blockchain.
- **(R2) Authenticity of data**: refers to the truthfulness of medical data, users of a healthcare blockchain must verify that medical data in a transaction is genuine, that it was supplied by the rightful owner, and that it had not been faked. This property can be ensured by a digital signature signed by the owner of the medical data who generates and submits the transaction to blockchain network, allowing users to validate the transaction's legitimacy by verifying the signature with sender's public key.

– **(R3) Confidentiality of data**: refers to the property that sensitive data kept in the blockchain ledger is not divulged to unauthorized people or organizations. Since the blockchain health data is fully encrypted, unauthorized parties can not access it. Also, the ability to create private transactions supported by some blockchain technology offers a high level of confidentiality to medical data.

– **(R4) Traceability and auditability**: refers to the feature of keeping a log of every access and update of data, as well as capturing user activity in the healthcare system in chronological order. Hence, any nodes of the network can deny the provided data. Since every transaction is cryptographically associated with a user and its hash is maintained on the distributed ledger in chronological order(timestamped), we held a fully traceable history log.

– **(R5) Availability of data**: healthcare data must be provided when needed without delay for timely diagnosis and treatment. The blockchain's hash chain structure prevents malevolent users from deleting or altering transactions. Adding to that, the blockchain's distributed network topology and consensus mechanism with Byzantine fault make some attacks like DDoS attack more challenging.

– **(R6) Authentication of users**: refers to the trustworthiness of the requesting entity. Only the authentic party has access to or can edit the health data. This feature can be ensured using public key cryptography techniques as well as using wallet for identity management.

– **(R7) Anonymity of users**: refers to the concealment of a patient's identity from the public and unauthorized entities. It ensures that the data is maintained in such a way that patient identification remains anonymous. It can be ensured through public key infrastructure, identity mixing services, anonymous signature and non-interactive zero-knowledge proof method.

– **(R8) Unlinkability of transactions**: unlike the anonymity property stated above (not disclosing real identity), users demand that transactions relating to their medical data cannot be linked. Because once all of a person's transactions are connected, it is simple to infer other information about the user, such as the chronic disease, by combining transaction statistics with some background knowledge about the user. Anonymity of users can ensure the unlinkability of their transactions.

– **(R9) Granular access control**: refers to the feature that only authorized users have access to the medical data. Patients may require minimum disclosure of their medical data and related information when they are shared with others in a healthcare blockchain system. The use of public-key cryptography and smart contract can ensure this requirement.

– **(R10) Patient control** : members of the blockchain network are unable to share medical data without the patient's authorization. In fact, patients should be able to choose who has access to which parts of their medical information. Using smart contracts and data encryption, patients can maintain control over their own data and identities (self-sovereign identity) [21].

– **(R11) Consistency of data**: refers to the requirement that medical data in each transaction kept in the node ledger are consistent with other nodes. The blockchain consensus mechanism ensures this feature by requiring nodes to confirm new blocks and maintain consistency by time-stamping and attaching the freshly generated block to the ledger.

6   Blockchain Platforms and Their Security Solutions

Blockchain has been described as a disruptive technology with the potential to significantly impact a wide range of sectors. In this section, we focus on the platforms providing the best-suited security and privacy built-ins for healthcare applications. A snapshot of five platforms' best practices and data privacy solutions is captured by analyzing how effectively these technologies address the (**Ri**) requirements described in Sect. 5.

6.1   Hyperledger Fabric

Hyperledger Fabric is a private blockchain technology maintained and created by the Linux Foundation and IBM, with a significant focus on privacy and security levels [28]. Fabric's security is built on Transport Layer Security (TLS) protocol and certificate processing to ensure data integrity (**R1**) and authenticity (**R2**). The functional element of this security is dependent on the correct set up of the Hyperledger certificate authority (CA) and the Access Control List (ACL) with proper key management. In addition to smart contract (chaincode) capabilities to meet (**R10**) requirement, Fabric uses some added levels for privacy and security enforcement:

- Fabric uses a Membership Service Provider (MSP) to authenticate, authorize, and manage identities on a permissioned blockchain network. This identity management layer enables the development of security policies that specify which entities are permitted to do which operations, hence addressing the (**R6**) criteria.
- Fabric's Channels enable a set of entities to build a private ledger that separates their interactions from those of other entities. It is a sub-network of the real Hyperledger network that has its own set of regulations for access. Thus, preserving the confidentiality (**R3**) of information exclusively within the nodes that are in the channel. In addition, Fabric supports creating private data collections (private transactions), which allows a subset of organizations on the network to endorse, commit, or query private data without having to construct a separate channel. This meets the (**R9**) needs by offering transaction privacy at a more fine-grained level than channels.
- Fabric allows anonymous client authentication using: Identity Mixer or with Zero-Knowledge Asset Transfer (ZKAT). Strong privacy is promoted where not only the anonymity (**R7**) of transaction participants is preserved but also the complete unlinkability (**R8**) of the exchanged assets.
- Fabric consensus algorithm built on Crash Fault Tolerant (CFT) consensus algorithms ensures network availability (**R5**). It also addresses (**R4**) and (**R11**) by maintaining time-stamped transaction on the ledger.

6.2 Hyperledger Besu

PegaSys designed and maintains Hyperledger Besu [30], an open-source Ethereum client that includes a private data manager called "Orion" and an Ethereum node. Privacy in the Besu platform refers to the ability to keep transactions private among involved entities. Thus, other parties are unable to view the transaction content, sender, or list of participants ((**R3**) criteria). Besu private transactions are restricted or unrestricted. Only the nodes participating in the transaction receive and store the payload of restricted private transactions. However, the payload of an unrestricted private transaction is sent to all nodes in the network, but only the nodes involved in the transaction can read it ((**R9**) need). This functionality is implemented thanks to the "Orion" Private Transaction Manager. Orion maintains transactions that are only shared amongst relevant peers, and a hash of the transaction is stored on an Ethereum blockchain network of choice, allowing peers to check transaction ordering (**R4**) and integrity (**R1**) from a shared and trustworthy source. It's also responsible for generating and maintaining private/public key pairs to authenticate users (**R6**) as well as managing all nodes in the network. Further, Besu enables smart contract deployment to require the (**R10**) need, as well as, a consensus mechanism based on Byzantine Fault Tolerant (BFT) for the availability (**R5**) and consistency of data (**R11**) [29].

6.3 Quorum

Quorum is an Ethereum-based distributed ledger system maintained by ConsenSys enterprise that allows the building of permissioned blockchain networks with transaction privacy support [31]. The Tessera Privacy Manager provides the core aspects of Quorum privacy. The payload of private transactions is encrypted, resulting in only the nodes indicated in the transaction having access to the payload information ((**R3**) need). It is responsible for managing the quorum network nodes, peers' key information for authentication (**R6**), providing the cryptography operations ((**R1**) criteria), and maintaining a local off-chain database to store encrypted payload data. The centralized platform security of Quorum is based on end-to-end encryption and TLS protocol, ensuring that all aspects of the platform are secure at all times. Quorum uses EthSigner to sign transactions, fulfilling the (**R2**)requirement. It deploys GoQuorum smart contract to meet (**R9**) and (**R10**) requirements. Further, it uses the "Quorum-Chain" consensus algorithm which is based on majority voting to validate and create a time-stamped block on the ledger ((**R4**) and (**R11**)). For better fault tolerance, Quorum employs the Istanbul BFT consensus mechanism (**R5**).

6.4 Corda R3

Corda R3 is an open-source distributed ledger technology maintained by the R3 organizations [23]. It can be applied to establish networks in which several peers

reach a distributed agreement on a transaction order that is only visible to transaction participant ((**R3**) need). It is flexible and scalable and ensures a high level
of privacy and security. Corda requires that each node verify its identity before
being allowed to join the network ((**R6**) need). A notary is a node responsible
for authenticating identities and disseminating certificates, adding to verify the
uniqueness ((**R1**) and (**R2**) needs) and timestamping (**R4**) of the transactions
without requiring worldwide broadcasting. Corda ensures that data stored by
actors is consistent (**R11**) as operations to change that data are performed.
Corda's confidential identities preserve the privacy of the user's identity, but not
the asset's details. There is an ongoing investigation of zero-knowledge proofs
(ZKPs) and/or trusted execution environments (TEEs) that allow verification
of a transaction without revealing the content [32]. Corda employs Byzantine
Fault Tolerant State Machine Replication (BFT-SMaRt) to address the (**R5**)
requirement.

6.5   Cosmos

Cosmos [33] is a constantly growing ecosystem managed by the Interchain Foundation (ICF). It's a network of independent and interoperable blockchains that
can securely exchange data with one another. Cosmos' mission is to address some
of the challenges faced by other blockchains, such as scalability, usability, and
governance, by providing appropriate tools for developers to easily build separate blockchains for a range of use cases. Establishing an Internet of blockchains
network allows blockchains to maintain sovereignty, execute transactions quickly,
and communicate with other blockchains in the Cosmos ecosystem. This vision
is achieved through a set of open-source tools like the Tendermint consensus
algorithm, Cosmos SDK, and Inter-Blockchain Communication protocol (IBC)
designed to let people build custom, secure(addressing (**R1**), (**R2**) and (**R3**)),
scalable, and interoperable blockchain applications rapidly. The Cosmos SDK
allows developers to implement modules that satisfy their application's business
logic, such as the Auth and Authz modules for authentication (**R6**) and authorization (**R9**) needs. Adding to that, It deploys Tendermint BFT consensus to
guarantee data availability as long as less than a third of validators are not malicious (**R5**). The hub and zones of the Cosmos network communicate with each
other via the IBC protocol, maintaining consistency (**R11**) and keeping track
of each asset held by a zone ((**R4**) need).

   To achieve privacy in Cosmos blockchain systems, several projects have
emerged aiming to implement new protocols and layers, such as Oasis Labs
Network, Nym protocol, and Secret Network [34]:

– **Oasis Network** is a privacy-focused smart contract platform built on the
  Cosmos SDK. This project prioritizes applications that require data privacy
  and user confidentiality. It accomplishes this by isolating its consensus layer
  from its contract execution layer and offering a built-in interface for privacy-
  preserving computation between the two. The consensus layer serves as a hub
  that secures the network and achieves consensus on transaction legitimacy

using a Proof-of-Stake (PoS) mechanism. The execution layer is made up of a number of parallel runtimes ("ParaTimes") for different types of computations that all plug into the consensus layer.

- **Nym protocol** is a full-stack privacy protocol that enables developers to create blockchain apps that provide consumers with strong guarantees against metadata leaking at both the network and authentication and payment levels. It enables privacy-enhancing data transport and decentralized identity by using anonymous authentication credentials based on the Coconut signature technique. Nym credentials can include all of the data required for a specific service (including zero-knowledge proofs of private data), and they are confirmed in a decentralized and public manner without tying a user to the service they want to use.

- **Secret Network** is a strong blockchain platform built on the Cosmos SDK that addresses the blockchain's lack of user privacy. It promotes smart contract generation and makes data privacy a standard feature. As a result, developers will be able to construct decentralized apps that protect user data while maintaining privacy. The protocol enables "programmable privacy" which is defined as an application's capacity to create arbitrarily complex data privacy measures.

7   A Security Framework for Blockchain-Based e-Health Applications

In this section, we will discuss when blockchain is required in e-health applications. When should it be applied? providing guidelines for selecting the appropriate blockchain platform given a healthcare application's security needs.

7.1   When Blockchain Can be Used in e-Health Applications ?

The security and privacy issues of an e-health system depend on the e-health use case and the involved entities. For that, the decision tree provided in Fig. 1 can be used as a general guide to adopting blockchain for the protection of an e-health application. It can assist in determining the best moment to use blockchain technology in a healthcare application to address security and privacy concerns.

Consider a clinical trial application in which a group of healthcare providers wants to test novel medications on human subjects. During the trial, data were collected from the subjects at predetermined intervals, including vital signs, changes in symptoms, side effects, or complications caused by the study medicine, and then shared among the involved investigators. Clinical trial data are highly sensitive and their access control is restricted so traceability, auditability, and immutability are highly required. Furthermore, patients participating in this experiment demand control over their identities and their medical data (Self Sovereign Identity), as well as, the ability to discuss what they wish anonymously. Following the decision tree, we manipulate digital medical data that is shared and

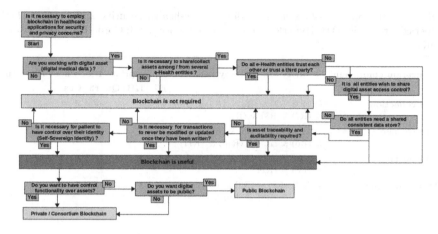

Fig. 1. Blockchain decision tree for e-health applications security and privacy

collected among different stakeholders. They don't share trust and access control. Also, immutability, auditability, and traceability of data are needed even if it is shared. Adding to that, subjects must have control over their identities and their medical information. Thus, we may infer that blockchain technology is effective in this context for securing and protecting patient privacy. Because medical information should not be made public in this scenario, private or consortium blockchains are most suited.

7.2 Which Blockchain Solution to Use?

The implementation of blockchain technology can help e-health applications meet their security and privacy requirements. It can authenticate and authorize users, and grant data granular access control and self-ownership of patients' data. It also offers data auditing and time-stamping, which could aid patients in identifying any unauthorized modification of medical data over time. Blockchain's data unlinkability and patient anonymity characteristics help to boost medical research and development in the healthcare sector without compromising patient personnel information. Thus, developers should have a thorough examination of specific applications' security and privacy needs before selecting blockchain platforms, techniques, and mechanisms for deployment. Using the provided Framework, they can select the suitable platform after identifying components related to the security and privacy of their applications. Table 1 defines the appropriate blockchain platform, when necessary, to meet the security and privacy of each specified healthcare application's component.

As example, let us consider a remote patient monitoring where security and privacy concerns are related to data collection component. This component requires (R1), (R2), (R3), (R5), (R6), (R7), (R8), and (R10) needs. We can adopt any of the five blockchain platforms to meet these requirements. However, for an Insurance claims application where security and privacy concerns are

Table 1. Appropriate blockchain platform for e-health security and privacy (**HF**: Hyperledger Fabric, **HB**: Hyperledger Besu, **Qu**: Quorum, **r3**: Corda R3, **Cos**: Cosmos SDK)

Application component	Security and Privacy needs	Appropriate Blockchain Platform				
		HF	HB	Qu	r3	Cos
Data collection	(R1) & (R2) & (R3) & (R5) & (R6) & (R7) &(R8) & (R10)	✓	✓	✓	✓	✓
Data storage	(R1) & (R2) & (R3) & (R4) & (R5) & (R6) & (R9) & (R10) & (R11)	✓	✓	✓	✓	✓
Data Sharing	(R1) & (R2) & (R3) & (R4) & (R5) & (R8) & (R11)	✓	✗	✗	✓	✗
Data processing	(R1) & (R2) & (R3) &(R4)& (R6) & (R7) & (R8) & (R9) & (R10)	✓	✗	✗	✗	✗

related to data processing and where unlinkability of transactions is required, only the Hyperledger Fabric blockchain technology can be adopted.

A question is raised when the system designer is faced with a new application where all the data life-cycle components have to be provided and then multiple blockchain technologies are selected following the Framework we propose. In this particular case, blockchain interoperability and connectivity are required. This refers to the ability of different blockchain networks to interconnect with each other without restrictions and to co-exist in a single system, especially given the variety of mechanisms, protocols, and platforms used by each network. In this particular case, **Cosmos** blockchain can be adopted to interconnect these various networks for a secure transfer of medical data among different providers implementing blockchain technology. The Cosmos Hub interchain's security mechanism and privacy layers offer strong data security and patient privacy at inter-blockchain systems.

8   Conclusions and Future Work

In this paper, we demonstrated the great potential of blockchain technology in addressing the security and privacy requirements in the e-health ecosystem. At first, in the background section, we presented an overview of blockchain technology, its key features, essential mechanisms and concepts. We then provided a Framework based on data life-cycle components to classify e-health applications. Then, we discussed the security and privacy requirements for an e-health application and how blockchain can meet these needs. By examining the security and privacy of data solutions offered by various blockchain platforms: Hyperledger Fabric, Hyperledger Besu, Quorum, Corda R3 and Cosmos, we provided guidelines to choose the appropriate solution for e-health use cases depending on their requirements and to the needed data life-cycle components (collection, storage, sharing, processing).

As a future work, we aim to explore this work in the implementation of a consortium blockchain in healthcare logistics, enabling several hospitals to collaborate while managing emergency cases, especially when it comes to maintaining the confidentiality and privacy of medical data during the act of medical regulation. The presented Framework will be very useful to ask the right questions regarding the application components to provide, their requirements in terms of security and privacy and then the blockchain technology to choose.

References

1. Hussien, H.M., Yasin, S.M., Udzir, S.N.I., Zaidan, A.A., Zaidan, B.B.: A systematic review for enabling of develop a blockchain technology in healthcare application: taxonomy, substantially analysis, motivations, challenges, recommendations and future direction. J. Med. Syst. **43**(10), 1–35 (2019). https://doi.org/10.1007/s10916-019-1445-8

2. Hathaliya, J.J., Tanwar, S.: An exhaustive survey on security and privacy issues in Healthcare. Comput. Commun. 4, 311–335 (2020)

3. Amaraweera, S.P., Halgamuge, M.N.: Internet of Things in the healthcare sector: overview of security and privacy issues. In: Mahmood, Z. (ed.) Security, Privacy and Trust in the IoT Environment, pp. 153–179. Springer, Cham (2019). https://doi.org/10.1007/978-3-030-18075-1_8

4. Chukwu, E., Garg, L.: A systematic review of blockchain in healthcare: frameworks, prototypes, and implementations. IEEE Access **8**, 21196–21214 (2020)

5. Shi, S., He, D., Li, L., Kumar, K., Choo, R.: Applications of blockchain in ensuring the security and privacy of electronic health record systems: a survey. Comput. Secur. **97**, 101966 (2020)

6. Haleem, A., Javaid, M., Singh, R.P., Suman, R., Rab, S.: Blockchain technology applications in healthcare: an overview. Int. J. Intell. Networks **2**, 130–139 (2021)

7. Saeed, H., et al.: Blockchain technology in healthcare: a systematic review. PLoS ONE **17**(4), e0266462 (2022)

8. Hölbl, M., Kompara, M., Kamišalić, A., Zlatolas, L.N.: A systematic review of the use of blockchain in healthcare. Symmetry **10**(10), 470 (2018)

9. Hussien, H.M., Yasin, S.M., Udzir, S.N.I., Zaidan, A.A., Zaidan, B.B.: A systematic review for enabling of develop a blockchain technology in healthcare application: taxonomy, substantially analysis, motivations, challenges, recommendations and future direction. J. Med. Syst. **43**(10), 1–35 (2019). https://doi.org/10.1007/s10916-019-1445-8

10. Hepp, T., Sharinghousen, M., Ehret, P., et al.: On-chain vs. off-chain storage for supply-and blockchain integration. IT Inf. Technol. **60**(5–6), 283–291 (2018)

11. Mayer, H., da Costa, C.A., da Rosa Righi, R.D.R.: Electronic health records in a Blockchain: a systematic review. Health Inform. J. **26**(2), 1273–1288 (2020)

12. Sun, Y., Zhang, R., Wang, X., Gao, K., Liu, L.: A decentralizing attribute-based signature for healthcare blockchain. In: 2018 27th International Conference on Computer Communication and Networks (ICCCN) (2018)

13. Reda, M., Kanga, D.B., Fatima, T., Azouazi, M.: Blockchain in health supply chain management: state of art challenges and opportunities. In: The International Workshop on Artificial Intelligence and Smart City Applications (IWAISCA), Procedia Computer Science 17 (2020)

14. Omar, I.A., Jayaraman, R., Salah, K., Yaqoob, I., Ellahham, S.: Applications of blockchain technology in clinical trials: review and open challenges. Arabian J. Sci. Eng. **46**(4), 3001–3015 (2021)

15. Zhang, R., Xue, R., Liu, L.: Security and Privacy for Healthcare Blockchains. IEEE Trans. Serv. Comput. **15**, 3668–3686 (2021)
16. Tariq, N., Qamar, A., Asim, M., Khan, F.A.: Blockchain and smart healthcare security: a survey. Procedia Comput. Sci. **175**, 615–620 (2020)
17. Sookhak, M., Jabbarpour, S.S., Yu, F.R.: Blockchain and smart contract for access control in healthcare: a survey, issues and challenges, and open issues. J. Network Comput. Appl. **178**, 102950 (2021)
18. Liu, Y., He, D., Obaidat, M.S., Kumar, N., Khan, M.K., Choo, K.-K.R.: Blockchain-based identity management systems: a review. J. Network Comput. Appl. **166**, 102731 (2020)
19. Sahi, A., Lai, D., Li, Y.: A review of the state of the art in privacy and security in the eHealth cloud. IEEE Access **9**, 104127–104141 (2021)
20. Dilawar, N., Rizwan, M., Ahmad, F., Akram, S.: Blockchain: securing internet of medical things (IoMT). Int. J. Adv. Comput. Sci. Appl. (IJACSA) **10**(1) (2019)
21. Houtan, B., Hafid, A.S., Makrakis, D.: A survey on blockchain-based self-sovereign patient identity in healthcare. IEEE Access **8**, 90478–90494 (2020)
22. Saraf, C., Sabadra, S.: Blockchain platforms: a compendium. In: IEEE International Conference on Innovative Research and Development (ICIRD), Thailand (2018)
23. Polge, J., Robert, J., Le Traon, Y.: Permissioned blockchain Frameworks in the industry: a comparison. ICT Express (2020)
24. Khatoon, A.: A blockchain-based smart contract system for healthcare management. Electronics **9**(1), 94 (2020)
25. Rajasekaran, A.S., Azees, M., Al-Turjman, F.: A comprehensive survey on blockchain technology. Sustain. Energy Technol. Assess. **52**, 102039 (2022)
26. Ray, P.P., Dash, D., Salah, K., Kumar, N.: Blockchain for IoT-based healthcare: background, consensus, platforms, and use cases. IEEE Syst. J. **15**(1), 85–94 (2021)
27. Elhoseny, M., et al.: Security and privacy issues in medical internet of things: overview, countermeasures, challenges and future directions. Sustainability **13**(21), 11645 (2021)
28. Brotsis, S., Kolokotronis, N., Limniotis, K., Bendiab, G., Shiaeles, S.: On the security and privacy of hyperledger fabric: challenges and open issues. In: 2020 IEEE World Congress on Services (SERVICES), pp. 197–204. IEEE (2020)
29. Manuel, J., Plaza, P., Renwick, R., Ehrke-Rabel, T., Hergueta, R.F.: Blockchain security focus whitepaper (I). In: European Union's Horizon 2020 Research and Innovation Programme. SOTER, pp. 52–55 (2020)
30. Palma, S.D., Pareschi, R., Zappone, F.: What is your Distributed (Hyper)Ledger? In: 2021 IEEE/ACM 4th WETSEB, pp. 27–33 (2021)
31. Mazzoni, M., Corradi, A., Di Nicola, V.: Performance evaluation of permissioned blockchains for financial applications: The ConsenSys Quorum case study. Blockchain: Research and Applications, 100026 (2021)
32. Koens, T., King, S., van den Bos, M., van Wijk, C., Koren, A.: Solutions for the corda security and privacy trade-off: having your cake and eating it. ING Enterprise (2020)
33. Cosmos, Kwon and Buchman: Cosmos whitepaper: a network of distributed ledgers. https://v1.cosmos.network/resources/. Accessed 29 May 2022
34. Medium. https://medium.com/zero-knowledge-validator/privacy-in-cosmos-event-review-143f4058b5d6. Accessed 29 May 2022

Towards a Dynamic Testing Approach for Checking the Correctness of Ethereum Smart Contracts

Mohamed Amin Hammami, Mariam Lahami[✉], and Afef Jmal Maâlej

ReDCAD Laboratory, National School of Engineers of Sfax, University of Sfax,
BP 1173, 3038 Sfax, Tunisia
{mariam.lahami,afef.jmal}@redcad.org

Abstract. One of the most essential concepts related to the development of Blockchain oriented software is smart contracts. Once deployed on the blockchain, these pieces of code cannot be altered due to the immutability feature of the blockchain technology. Therefore, it is necessary to verify and validate smart contracts before their deployment. This paper presents a model-based testing approach for validating and checking the correctness of Ethereum smart contracts. The adopted process comprises essentially four steps: (1) modelling the smart contract and its blockchain environment as UPPAAL Timed Automata, (2) generating abstract test cases by UPPAAL CO√ER tool, (3) executing in a dynamic manner the generated test cases, and finally (4) analyzing the obtained test results and generating test reports. To illustrate our proposal, we apply it on Ethereum Blockchain and especially on the electronic voting case study.

Keywords: Blockchain · Smart contracts · Ethereum · Dynamic Testing · Model-based testing · UPPAAL Timed automata · Verification · Validation

1 Introduction

Blockchain technology is emerging the last decade and has garnered a lot of attention in several domains [21], such as finance, supply chain management [26], intelligent transportation [18] and health [4, 10]. Indeed, Blockchain is a distributed ledger made up of a chain of linked blocks in which transactions are stored. The interest in such a technology has increased due to its main characteristics such as decentralization, transparency, immutability and security. For instance, the immutability is achieved by sharing the same copies of the ledger in a decentralized way across different peer-to-peer nodes.

Another reason for this new trend is related to the concept of *Smart contracts* which are pieces of code that are defined, executed and recorded on the Blockchain. They enable the implementation of business logic within the distributed ledger. By the way, developing Blockchain oriented Software (BoS) can be easily achieved.

However, several defects and vulnerabilities can be introduced in smart contracts and can lead to serious problems and attacks such as asset losses. Consequently, checking their correctness and guaranteeing their high quality remains a crucial requirement to be considered.

As one of the key methods to get confidence in these Blockchain oriented Software, software testing captured researchers interest. It has been often applied to check

ⓒ The Author(s), under exclusive license to Springer Nature Switzerland AG 2023
S. Kallel et al. (Eds.): CRiSIS 2022, LNCS 13857, pp. 85–100, 2023.
https://doi.org/10.1007/978-3-031-31108-6_7

functional and non-functional requirements. Its ultimate goal is to detect the presence of faults in the System Under Test (SUT). In this respect, the literature comprises a myriad of techniques and methods (i.e., static testing [25,32], dynamic testing [5,7,19,23,24], etc.) for efficiently testing BoS. As our main focus in this paper is dynamic testing, we have identified several studies that have considered dynamic testing of BoS, especially at the smart contract level such as [5,7,19,23,24]. The majority have dealt with structural testing approaches and required the source code of the smart contract to generate tests and execute them. Model-based testing technique, in which test cases are derived from formal test models, is rarely discussed.

To overcome this limitation, we provide a model-based testing approach for BoS, called *MBT4BoS*, that checks the correctness of smart contracts deployed on Ethereum Blockchain. Our proposal ensures firstly the modelling of smart contracts and the blockchain environment using UPPAAL Timed Automata formalism while considering essentially Ethereum gas mechanism. Secondly, the well-established tool UPPAAL CO√ER is reused to generate effectively new abstract test cases. Thirdly, a Web-based interface is proposed to easily execute tests, analyze test results and generate test reports. The implemented tool for test execution and reporting is named *BC Test Runner*. As a proof of concept, the proposed approach is illustrated through the electronic voting application.

The rest of this paper is organized as follows. Section 2 provides background materials for understanding the research problem. Subsequently, Sect. 3 draws comparison with related work in the context of dynamic testing of BoS. The model-based testing approach for BoS is outlined in Sect. 4. Afterwards, its application to the electronic voting case study is highlighted in Sect. 5. Finally, we conclude, in Sect. 6, with a summary of paper contributions, and we identify potential areas of future research.

2   Background Materials

In this section, we give a brief discussion on topics related to Blockchain (BC), Smart Contracts (SCs), and software testing concepts. All these key concepts are important to fully understand our contribution in the following sections.

2.1   Blockchain

Nakamoto et al. [28] introduce for the first time the concept of *Blockchain* as the technology underlying Bitcoin. This emerging technology is defined as a distributed ledger maintained over a peer-to-peer network. It is used in several platforms such as Ethereum [1] and Hyperledger [2].

As depicted in Fig. 1, Blockchain is composed of a linked list of blocks. Each block contains mainly a given number of transactions that have occurred within the network. The transaction can be seen as data exchange or token transfers. Each block is made up of two parts: the header and the body. The header of a given block contains several fields, particularly a timestamp of when the block was produced and the identifier of the previous block. The latter is obtained by executing a cryptographic hash function (e.g., SHA256, KECCAK256, etc.). By this way, blocks are connected to each other like a linked list [6]. In the body of the block, transaction details are stored such as price, asset, ownership, etc.

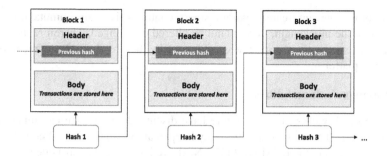

Fig. 1. Blockchain structure.

2.2 Smart Contracts

Smart Contracts (SCs) are one of the most interesting features that have been introduced by several platforms such as Ethereum and Hyperledger with the aim of attaching business logic code to transactions. A SC is seen as an autonomous programming code that is deployed on the blockchain and is executed when some events occur. In the case of Ethereum, smart contracts are implemented in a Turing complete language called Solidity[1]. Solidity language is very similar to JavaScript. It supports features like libraries, inheritance and user-defined types. Using the solidity compiler *solc*, they are compiled to the Ethereum Virtual Machine (EVM) bytecode.

A concrete example of smart contract is illustrated in Listing 1.1. The first line specifies the compiler version, then the keyword contract declares the contract with its name similarly to any object oriented language. In line 3, a state variable is also declared as unsigned integer (uint). Next, several functions are defined either to modify the state variable or to read its content.

```
1   pragma solidity ^0.5.3;
2   contract SimpleStorage{
3       uint storedData;
4       function set(uint x)public{
5           storedData=x;
6       }
7       function get() public view returns (uint){
8           return storedData;
9       }
10      function increment(uint n)public{
11          storedData=storedData+n;
12          return;
13      }
14      function decrement(uint n)public{
15          storedData=storedData-n;
16          return ;
17  }}
```

Listing 1.1. Code snippet of the SimpleStorage smart contract.

---

[1] https://solidity.readthedocs.io/.

The most relevant feature within smart contracts is their immutability. Once deployed on the blockchain, they cannot be altered or changed. Therefore, it is highly required to ensure their correctness and security before their deployment on the blockchain platform.

2.3 Common Vulnerabilities

Several research works in the literature have discussed smart contract vulnerabilities such as [12, 30]. These vulnerabilities may happen at the smart contract code level, the blockchain level and the EVM level [27]. Next, we introduce the most cited vulnerabilities in the literature:

- **Reentrancy.** It is a solidity-level vulnerability. It occurs when a given smart contract calls an entrusted function in another contract. The malicious callee can take control of the data flow and makes its attack. This kind of vulnerabilities was the cause of the DAO attack.
- **Gasless send.** It is a solidity-level vulnerability. When using the function send to transfer ether to a contract, it may end up with an out-of-gas exception.
- **Timestamp dependency.** It is a blockchain level vulnerability. In fact, any operation on the blockchain has its timestamp (e.g., smart contract creation, block creation, etc.). A malicious miner can manipulate the timestamp of the generated block for malicious purposes.

It is highly demanded to detect such vulnerabilities while developing blockchain oriented software. Thus, adopting verification techniques such as software testing is mandatory to ensure the quality and trustworthiness of BoS.

2.4 Blockchain Testing Techniques

One of the most important activities for Blockchain Oriented Software Engineering (BOSE) is the testing activity. Indeed, it is defined as the process of validating and ensuring the quality of a System Under Test (SUT) [13]. It is usually performed with the purpose of assessing the conformance of a system to its specifications.

Software testing can be static or dynamic. Static testing does not involve software execution, but analyses the source code structure, syntax and data-flow, and is also called *Static analysis*. Contrary to static testing, dynamic testing considers testing the dynamic behavior of a SUT while it is running. Test cases are conceived by specifying test inputs and expected outputs. The purpose of dynamic testing is to check whether the actual outputs correspond to the expected ones.

In the case of testing blockchain oriented software, we identify in the literature several kinds of testing techniques that are performed with the aim of increasing confidence and trustworthiness of BoS. For instance, we cite *Smart contract testing* (i.e., applying unit testing on smart contract code), *Performance testing* (i.e., verifying performance and latency within blockchain network), *Node testing* (i.e., testing the block size, chain size and data transfer) and *Security testing* (i.e., identifying whether there is any piece in the Blockchain application that is vulnerable to malicious attacks).

Regarding Model-based testing (MBT), it is a software testing technique in which different test cases are derived from a test model that describes the functional aspects of the SUT. The advantage of choosing this type of test in our work is to improve the detection of errors in case of testing BoS and to reduce the cost and time of the test phase [33].

3 Related Work

Although testing blockchain oriented software should cover several layers: application layer (e.g., DApps), smart contract layer, blockchain layer (e.g., blocks, transactions), consensus layer and network layer, testing efforts are concentrated essentially on testing smart contracts and ensuring their functional correctness. In this direction, we have identified two research lines: white-box testing and black-box testing approaches [22].

The first research line, *white-box testing*, is based on the investigation of internal logic and structure of the smart contract code. Up to our knowledge, the majority of studied papers focus on mutation testing [5,7,15,17,23,34] and show that this testing technique has a good impact on smart contract quality. Indeed, mutation testing is considered as a fault-based software testing technique generally used to evaluate the adequacy of test cases and their fault detection capabilities.

In this direction, a well established approach is proposed in [23] providing a mutation testing tool for Ethereum smart contracts called, MuSC. This proposal takes as input a smart contract under test and transforms its source files to Abstract Syntax Tree (AST) version. Next, it generates various mutants that implement traditional mutation operators and new ones according to the characteristics of solidity language. The obtained mutants are then transformed back to solidity source files with injected faults for compilation, execution and testing purposes. It also provides user-friendly interface to create test nets and to display test reports. The latter include execution results for each mutant (i.e., pass or fail) and the total mutation score.

Similarly, authors in [17] developed a RegularMutator tool for mutation analysis. Its major goal is to improve the test suites in order to find defects as well as to increase the effectiveness and the fault detection capabilities of test suites. Taken as input a Truffle project, RegularMutator generates mutants for each source file in the project. Once mutant files are generated, it substitutes the original files with the mutant ones, executes project test suites, and then, the test output is analysed. The main problem within this approach is its high computational cost of executing a set of tests when generating numerous mutants.

Yet another potential research topic to explore is discussed here which consists in testing Decentralized Applications (DApp). A DApp is a Web application made up of two parts: the front-end and the back-end. The following two studies [14,36] touch several research areas including smart contract analysis and automated Web application testing. They overcome the lack of effective methods and tools for testing DApps since the existing ones either focus on testing front-end code or back-end programs but they ignore the interaction between them. These approaches focus on DAPP testing including Web testing of graphical user interfaces and also smart contract testing whereas our proposal deals with model based testing of smart contracts without access to source code.

The second research line, *Black-box testing*, includes several testing approaches that apply testing activities without having any knowledge of the internal structure of BoS. The most used ones in the studied context are fuzz testing and model-based testing.

Regarding fuzz testing perspective, we introduce the Fuse project [9], a fuzz testing service for smart contracts and Dapp testing. Fuse assists developers for test diagnosis via test scenario visualization. The first prototype developed in the context of Fuse project is ContractFuzzer [19] that detects seven security vulnerabilities of Ethereum smart contracts. The proposed approach generates fuzzing inputs from the ABI specification of the smart contract. It also defines test oracles for detecting the supported real world vulnerabilities within smart contracts. ContractFuzzer was performed on 6991 real-world Ethereum SCs showed that it has identified 459 SCs vulnerabilities, including the DAO and Parity Wallet attacks.

A similar approach to ContractFuzzer is sFuzz, an adaptive fuzzing engine for EVM smart contracts [29]. sFuzz is made up of three components: *runner* that manages test case execution, *liboracles* that supports eight oracles inspired by the previous researches [19,25] and *libfuzzer* which implements the test suite generation algorithm. The latter is based on a feedback-guided fuzzing technique which transforms the test generation problem into an optimization problem and uses feedbacks as an objective function in solving the optimization problem. This proposal is based on adaptive strategy since it is possible to change the objective function adaptively based on the feedback to evolve the test suite with the aim of improving its branch coverage. Due to its effectiveness and its reliability, sFuzz has already gained interest from multiple companies and research organizations. However, fuzz-based approaches may suffer from false positive detection as a reported vulnerability may be a false positive[2].

Regarding the model-based testing perspective, authors in [31] propose a model driven approach that generates smart contract code from UML diagrams (i.e., Use Cases and Activity diagrams). They also point out the necessity of applying testing technique in the early stage of Software Development Life Cycle (SDLC), especially in the context of blockchain oriented software. However, this approach is still immature since no test tool implementation for the discussed ideas were introduced. Similarly, the work in [20] proposes a complete software testing life cycle to test BoS projects. The proposal is composed of four phases including system overview, test design, test planning and test execution. Test generation issue was not discussed and solutions to reduce test cost and effort are not given.

Up to our best knowledge, ModCon tool [24] is very closer to our MBT approach. In fact, it uses an explicit abstract model of the target smart contract in order to generate test cases automatically. This tool shows its effectiveness specifically for enterprise SC applications written in Solidity from permissioned/consortium blockchains. It allows SC developers to input their test model for the SC under test. Compared to our solution, ModCon did not model blockchain environment and focused only on modelling and testing functional aspects of single smart contracts.

4 Proposed Approach

In this section, we describe the main steps of our model-based testing approach MBT4BoS. It is divided into four steps as shown in Fig. 2: (1) modelling the smart contract and its blockchain environment as UPPAAL Timed Automata, (2) generating

---

[2] Some test cases fail but there is no bug and the program is working correctly.

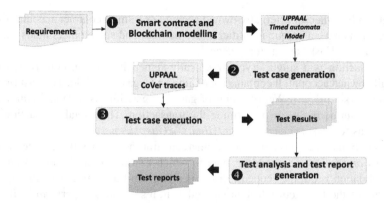

Fig. 2. Architecture of the model-based testing approach: MBT4BoS.

abstract test cases by UPPAAL CO√ER tool, (3) dynamically executing the generated test cases, and finally (4) analyzing the obtained test results and generating test reports. In the following subsections, these modules are deeply discussed.

4.1 Modelling the Smart Contract and Its Blockchain Environment

In this step, our aim consists of designing an abstract test model from which test cases are automatically generated. The purpose of this test model is to specify the expected behaviours of the system under test with reference to its requirements. To do so, we adopt a popular and widespread formalism for specifying critical systems, called Timed Automata (TA). In fact, we model a given smart contract and its blockchain environment as a network of timed automata.

From smart contract modeling perspective, a timed automata is defined by the tuple

$$(S, s_0, \mathcal{A}ct, C, Inv, \mathcal{V}, \mathcal{T}), \text{ where:}$$

– S is a finite set of states.
– $s_0 \in S$ is the initial state and $i_0 \in I$ represents the initial input action that corresponds to the constructor of the smart contract.
– $\mathcal{A}ct$ is a finite set of Input and output actions. The Input actions correspond to smart contract function calls.
– C is a finite set of clocks that are used to model temporal constraints.
– $\mathcal{V}$ is the set of state variables. Every variable $x \in \mathcal{V}$ is a global variable and can be accessed at every state $s \in S$.
– $\mathcal{T}$ is a finite set of transitions, where $e = \langle l, g, r, a, l' \rangle \in \mathcal{T}$ corresponds to the transition from l to l', g is the guard associated to e, r is the set of clock to be reset and a is a label of e. We note $l \xrightarrow{g,r,a} l'$.

From the blockchain modelling perspective, we consider only accounts, transactions and gas mechanism in Ethereum blockchain. Consensus algorithms and mining are out the scope of this paper. As introduced in the Ethereum Yellow paper [35], an Ethereum account can be either an externally owned account or a smart contract account. Both of these accounts have a unique identifier called *address* and some others fields such as a balance[3], a codeHash[4] and a storageRoot[5].

A transaction is a single cryptographically-signed instruction constructed by an externally owned account. It contains a gasLimit and a gasPrice field. The gasPrice indicates the market price in Wei of a unit of gas. The gasLimit is the maximum amount of gas that can be burnt for performing the transaction. Thus, total transaction fee is calculated as follows: $txFee = Gas unit(limits) * Gas price per unit$.

At this point, we consider that an ethereum transaction has three states *created, confirmed and failed*. The pending state in which transaction in the pool waiting for minor validation is out the scope of this paper. A given transaction is confirmed when the sender of the transaction has enough ether in his account to perform it. It can be failed if the sender does not provide the gas needed to complete it.

4.2   Test Case Generation

Test generation within a model-based testing process is the generation of tests from the previously designed model. This generation is based on behaviours from the test model and on test selection criteria chosen by the validation engineer. In our case, the used test generation technique is based on model checking. The main idea is to formulate the test generation problem as a reachability problem that can be solved with the model checker tool UPPAAL [8]. However, instead of using model annotations and reachability properties to express coverage criteria, the observer language is used. The use of the observer language simplifies the expression of coverage criteria.

Therefore, we reuse the finding of Hessel et al. [16] by exploiting its extension of UPPAAL namely UPPAAL CO√ER[6]. This tool takes as inputs a model, an observer and a configuration file. The model is specified as a network of UPPAAL timed automata (.xml) that comprises a SUT part and an environment part. The observer (.obs) expresses the coverage criterion that guides the model exploration during test case generation. In our context, we use an observer that handle *edge coverage* criteria[7]. The configuration file (.cfg) describes mainly the interactions between the system part and the environment part in terms of input/output signals. As output, it produces a test suite containing a set of timed traces (.xml).

Our test generation module is built upon this well-elaborated tool. We use UPPAAL CO√ER and its generic and formal specification language for coverage criteria to generate abstract test cases for checking the correctness of smart contracts. The concretization of tests is done manually.

---

[3] The number of Wei owned by this address.

[4] The hash of the EVM code of this account.

[5] The hash of the root node of a Merkle Patricia tree encoding the storage contents of the account.

[6] http://user.it.uu.se/ hessel/CoVer/index.php.

[7] A test case should traverse all edges of a given timed automaton.

4.3 Test Case Execution

The generated test cases can be executed manually or automatically. Manual test execution involves a human tester executing the generated test cases by interacting with the system under test, following the test case instructions. Automated test execution involves translating the generated test cases into automatically executable test scripts.

At this level, we have developed a test tool *BC Test Runner* which allows to automate the execution of generated tests by stimulating smart contracts deployed on a local blockchain, called *Ganache* and also the generation of test reports. As highlighted in Fig. 3, this test tool consists of a Web-based front-end and a server-side backend. The front-end accepts two inputs from testers: a set of test cases generated from the given test model by UPPAAL CO√ER and a Json file obtained after the compilation of the smart contract. This file contains all the specifications of the smart contract. The backend comprises several modules: such as *Test Executor*, *Test result analyzer* and *Report generator*. The communication with the smart contract is done through the Web3.js library.

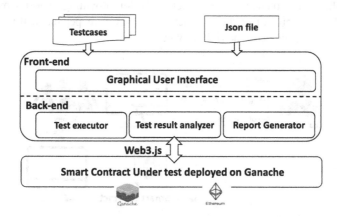

Fig. 3. Architecture of the test tool BC Test Runner

The *Test Executor* module is responsible for stimulating the smart contract with test input data and retrieving the results. To do so, it reads from the Json file the address of the contract and its ABI (Application Binary Interface) in order to invoke its functions. The ABI is the binary interface that describes the smart contract and its functions, i.e. function names, parameters, return types, etc. From the second entry which is a text file that contains the test cases (i.e., input values and expected results separated by (;)), it sends test inputs to the deployed smart contract, then collects the obtained results and compares them to the expected ones. Then, *Pass* or *Fail* verdicts are then generated for each test case.

4.4 Test Result Analysis and Test Report Generation

This step consists of analyzing the test execution results which are stored in log files during the test execution and also generating test reports. Regarding test result analysis,

BC Test Runner includes the module *Test results analyser* which performs the analysis of results by calculating the percentage of Pass verdicts and the percentage of Fail verdicts. Then, test reports are generated by the module *Report Generator* as trace text files.

5   Illustration

At present, we introduce the case study that we used to illustrate our MBT approach. Moreover, the elaborated test models for the studied smart contract and the implemented test tool are presented.

5.1   Case Study Description

Decentralized electronic voting systems, relying on Blockchain technology, are emerging as new solutions to handle security concerns of traditional electronic voting systems. With blockchain technology, the E-voting system can guarantee transparency and confidentiality. The idea is to create one contract per ballot, providing a short name for each proposal. Then, the creator of the contract, known as chair person, will register each address individually and give the right to vote.

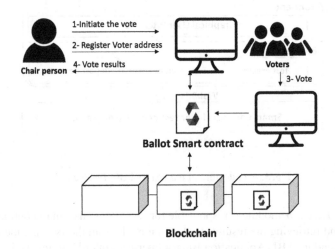

Fig. 4. A simplified electronic voting system deployed on blockchain.

As depicted in Fig. 4, the chair person initiates the vote by deploying the *Ballot* contract while providing a short name for each proposal. Then, he registers voters individually. We assume here that the registration period is equal to ten days. When the registration phase is closed and the vote phase is opened, voters can vote by choosing the proposal identifier. At the end of the voting period which is equal to one day, the system will return the proposal with the largest number of votes. It is worth to note that we have adopted the *Ballot* smart contract which is introduced in solidity's documentation with minors modifications [3].

```
 1  contract ballot {
 2      struct Voter {
 3          uint weight; // weight is accumulated by delegation
 4          bool voted; // if true, that person already voted
 5          address delegate; // person delegated to
 6          uint vote; // index of the voted proposal
 7      }
 8      struct Proposal {
 9      string name; // short name (up to 32 bytes)
10          uint voteCount; // number of accumulated votes
11      }
12      address public chairperson;
13      function register(address voter) public {
14          require(
15              msg.sender == chairperson,
16              "Only chairperson can give right to vote."
17          );
18          require(
19              !voters[voter].voted,
20              "The voter already voted."
21          );
22          require(voters[voter].weight == 0);
23          voters[voter].weight = 1;
24      }
```

Listing 1.2. Code snippet of the Vote smart contract.

5.2   Modelling the E-voting System

In the following, we present the timed automaton specification of the Ballot smart contract which will be then used as a reference in our approach.

The Ballot Smart Contract Automaton

As shown in Fig. 5, at the initial state named *initial* which is marked by double circle, the clock *(c)* is initialized to zero. The first transition corresponds to the reception of a request to invoke the register function of the smart contract $(Tx\_Contractcall\_register[e][ch]?)$. Reaching the state $(Accepting\_registration)$, the model evolves to the state *initial*, either through the transition that corresponds to the failed registration $(registration\_failed[e][ch]!)$ if the return value of the function *register* is *false*, or through the transition that corresponds to the confirmed registration $(registration\_confirmed[e][ch]!)$ if the return value of the function *register* is *true*. In this case, the procedure $(Registration\_Confirmed(e))$ stores the address of the voter (e) on the Ballot smart contract.

Returning to the initial state, the model evolves either to $(Accepting\_registration)$ state and it does the same scenario if the clock delay is less than or equal to 10 days $(c <= 10)$, or to $(Registration\_closed)$ state if the clock delay is greater than 10 days $(c > 10)$. In this case, the clock is set to zero. Reaching $(Registration\_closed)$ state, the transition to be enabled corresponds to the reception of a request to invoke the voting function $(Tx\_Contractcall\_vote[e][P\_Num]?)$.

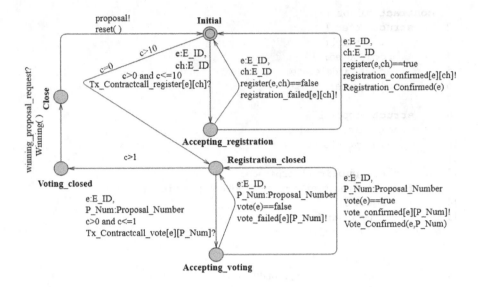

Fig. 5. Ballot smart contract automaton.

When reaching (*Accepting_voting*) state, the model may change its state to the previous one, either through the transition that corresponds to the failed vote (*vote_failed*[*e*][*P_Num*]!) if the return value of the vote function is *false*, or through the transition (*vote_confirmed*[*e*][*P_Num*]!) that corresponds to the confirmed vote if the return value of the function *vote* is *true*. In this case, the (*Vote_Confirmed*(*e*, *P_Num*)) procedure records the voter's vote on the blockchain.

When returning to the state (*Registration_closed*), the model can evolve either to the state (*Accepting_voting*) and it follows the same scenario if the clock delay is less than or equal to one day ($c <= 1$), or to the state (*Voting_closed*) if the clock delay is greater than one day($c > 1$). Reaching the state (*Voting_closed*), the transition to be enabled corresponds to the reception of a request of the winning proposal (*winning_proposal_request*?). In this case, the procedure *(winning())* returns the proposal having obtained the greatest number of votes. When the state *(close)* is reached, the transition to be fired corresponds to the emission of the winning proposition *proposal!*. At the end, the model returns to the initial state.

Transaction Automaton

This automaton has three states. As illustrated in Fig. 6, starting from the initial state *T0*, the model evolves, either towards the state *T1*, or towards the state *T2*, according to the request which it receives.

For instance, the transition *Register_request*[*e*][*ch*]? is enabled and the state *T1* is reached. As a result, the model may evolve to the previous state *T0*, through the transition that corresponds to the erroneous transaction (*Tx_errored!*) if the value of *gasUsed* is higher than the value of *gaslimit* or the account balance of the chairperson is lower than the transaction fee. Otherwise, the transition which corresponds to the invocation of the register function of the smart contract (*Tx_Contractcall_register*[*e*][*ch*]!) is

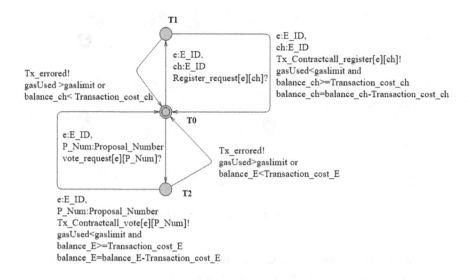

Fig. 6. Transaction Automaton.

enabled if the value of *gasUsed* is less than the value of *gaslimit* and the account balance of the chairperson is greater than or equal to the transaction fee. In this case, the transaction cost is removed from the chairperson's balance.

5.3 Test Case Generation

From the elaborated formal models, UPPAAL CO√ER is used to generate abstract test cases. For space limitation, only two test sequences are illustrated as follows:

- **Valid Register**: Register_request[id][chairperson]! Register_request[e][ch]? .0,gasUsed,balance_ch.Tx_Contractcall_register[e][ch]!.1,gasUsed,balance_ch .Tx_Contractcall_register[e][ch]?registration_confirmed[e][ch]! registration_confirmed[id][chairperson]?;
- **Failed Register**: Register_request[id][chairperson]! Register_request[e][ch]? .10,gasUsed,balance_ch. Tx_errored! .11,gasUsed,balance_ch Tx_errored?;

5.4 Test Tool Implementation

In this section, we present our test tool *BC Test Runner*, which is written in JavaScript and HTML. It is connected with the local blockchain (Ganache) through *Web3.js* library. This tool allows us to invoke smart contracts deployed on the local blockchain using their specifications (address, ABI). It provides an interface that consists of three sub-interfaces as illustrated in Fig. 7.

The sub-interface (1) allows the tester to select the smart contract specification file (.json) and test cases (.txt) then to start the test process through the button *Start Test* or to generate test reports through the button *Generate Report*. The sub-interface (2)

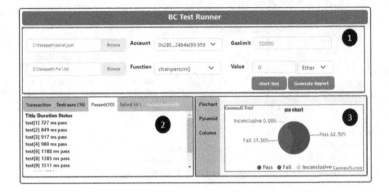

Fig. 7. The user interface of BC Test Runner.

displays the number of test cases executed, their verdicts and their test duration. The sub-interface (3) highlights test results as a pie chart.

6   Conclusion

In this paper, we provided a model-based testing approach for BoS, called MBT4BoS, that tests smart contracts deployed on Ethereum Blockchain. Our approach ensured the modelling both of smart contracts and the blockchain environment while considering essentially Ethereum gas mechanism. To do so, UPPAAL Timed Automata were used to elaborate test models. Then, new abstract test cases were adequately generated by using an extension of UPPAAL called UPPAAL CO√ER. We also proposed a Web-based interface to execute tests, analyze test results and generate test reports. In order to show the efficiency of MBT4BoS, we illustrated our solution using the Vote case study.

At the end of this work, we can distinguish several perspectives. First, we consider the automatic generation of test cases by proposing a test generation algorithm and integrating it into our solution MBT4BoS and into our test tool *BC Test Runner*. In addition, we can improve the current version of our test tool to integrate it into other modules, which will allow more accurate determination of anomalies and better analysis of test results. Another area to explore is combining model checking and testing to enhance the efficiency of BoS formal verification [11].

References

1. Blockchain platform: Ethereum. https://ethereum.org/en/. Accessed Mar 2022
2. Blockchain platform: Hyperledger. https://www.hyperledger.org/. Accessed Mar 2022
3. Solidity   examples.   https://docs.soliditylang.org/en/v0.5.11/solidity-by-example.html. Accessed Mar 2022
4. Abbas, A., Alroobaea, R., Krichen, M., Rubaiee, S., Vimal, S., Almansour, F.M.: Blockchain-assisted secured data management framework for health information analysis based on internet of medical things, pp. 1–14. Personal and Ubiquitous Computing (2021)

5. Akca, S., Rajan, A., Peng, C.: Solanalyser: a framework for analysing and testing smart contracts. In: Proceeding of the 26th Asia-Pacific Software Engineering Conference (APSEC), pp. 482–489 (2019)
6. Ali, M.S., Vecchio, M., Pincheira, M., Dolui, K., Antonelli, F., Rehmani, M.H.: Applications of blockchains in the internet of things: a comprehensive survey. IEEE Commun. Surv. Tutor. **21**(2), 1676–1717 (2018)
7. Andesta, E., Faghih, F., Fooladgar, M.: Testing smart contracts gets smarter. In: Proceeding of the 10th International Conference on Computer and Knowledge Engineering (ICCKE 2020), pp. 405–412 (2020)
8. Behrmann, G., David, A., Larsen, K.G.: A tutorial on uppaal. In: Proceeding of the International School on Formal Methods for the Design of Computer, Communication, and Software Systems, SFM-RT 2004. Revised Lectures, vol. 3185, pp. 200–237 (2004)
9. Chan, W., Jiang, B.: Fuse: an architecture for smart contract fuzz testing service. In: Proceeding of The 25th Asia-Pacific Software Engineering Conference (APSEC), pp. 707–708 (2018)
10. Ben Fekih, R., Lahami, M.: Application of blockchain technology in healthcare: a comprehensive study. In: Jmaiel, M., Mokhtari, M., Abdulrazak, B., Aloulou, H., Kallel, S. (eds.) ICOST 2020. LNCS, vol. 12157, pp. 268–276. Springer, Cham (2020). https://doi.org/10.1007/978-3-030-51517-1_23
11. Fekih, R.B., Lahami, M., Jmaiel, M., Ali, A.B., Genestier, P.: Towards model checking approach for smart contract validation in the EIP-1559 ethereum. In: Proceeding of the 46th IEEE Annual Computers, Software, and Applications Conference, COMPSAC 2022, Los Alamitos, CA, USA, pp. 83–88. IEEE (2022)
12. Feng, X., Wang, Q., Zhu, X., Wen, S.: Bug searching in smart contract. CoRR abs/1905.00799 (2019)
13. Freedman, R.: Testability of software components. IEEE Trans. Software Eng. **17**(6), 553–564 (1991)
14. Gao, J., et al.: Towards automated testing of blockchain-based decentralized applications. In: Proceeding of IEEE/ACM 27th International Conference on Program Comprehension (ICPC), pp. 294–299 (2019)
15. Hartel, P., Schumi, R.: Mutation testing of smart contracts at scale. In: Ahrendt, W., Wehrheim, H. (eds.) TAP 2020. LNCS, vol. 12165, pp. 23–42. Springer, Cham (2020). https://doi.org/10.1007/978-3-030-50995-8_2
16. Hessel, A., Larsen, K.G., Mikucionis, M., Nielsen, B., Pettersson, P., Skou, A.: Testing real-time systems using uppaal. In: Hierons, R.M., Bowen, J.P., Harman, M. (eds.) Formal Methods and Testing, pp. 77–117 (2008)
17. Ivanova, Y., Khritankov, A.: Regularmutator: a mutation testing tool for solidity smart contracts. Procedia Comput. Sci. **178**, 75–83 (2020)
18. Jabbar, R., et al.: Blockchain technology for intelligent transportation systems: a systematic literature review. IEEE Access **10**, 20995–21031 (2022)
19. Jiang, B., Liu, Y., Chan, W.K.: Contractfuzzer: fuzzing smart contracts for vulnerability detection. In: Proceedings of the 33rd ACM/IEEE International Conference on Automated Software Engineering, pp. 259–269 (2018)
20. Kakadiya, A.: Block-chain oriented software testing approach. Int. Res. J. Eng. Technol. (IRJET) (2017)
21. Krichen, M., Ammi, M., Mihoub, A., Almutiq, M.: Blockchain for modern applications: a survey. Sensors **22**(14), 5274 (2022)
22. Lahami, M., Maâlej, A.J., Krichen, M., Hammami, M.A.: A comprehensive review of testing blockchain oriented software. In: Proceedings of the 17th International Conference on Evaluation of Novel Approaches to Software Engineering, ENASE 2022, Online Streaming, April 25–26, 2022, pp. 355–362. SCITEPRESS (2022)

23. Li, Z., Wu, H., Xu, J., Wang, X., Zhang, L., Chen, Z.: MUSC: a tool for mutation testing of ethereum smart contract. In: Proceeding of the 34th IEEE/ACM International Conference on Automated Software Engineering (ASE 2019), pp. 1198–1201 (2019)
24. Liu, Y., Li, Y., Lin, S.W., Yan, Q.: MODCON: a model-based testing platform for smart contracts. In: Proceedings of the 28th ACM Joint Meeting on European Software Engineering Conference and Symposium on the Foundations of Software Engineering, pp. 1601–1605 (2020)
25. Luu, L., Chu, D.H., Olickel, H., Saxena, P., Hobor, A.: Making smart contracts smarter. In: Proceedings of the ACM SIGSAC Conference on Computer and Communications Security, pp. 254–269 (2016)
26. Mars, R., Youssouf, J., Cheikhrouhou, S., Turki, M.: Towards a blockchain-based approach to fight drugs counterfeit. In: Proceedings of the Tunisian-Algerian Joint Conference on Applied Computing (TACC 2021), Tabarka, Tunisia, pp. 197–208 (2021)
27. Mense, A., Flatscher, M.: Security vulnerabilities in ethereum smart contracts. In: Proceedings of the 20th International Conference on Information Integration and Web-Based Applications & Services, pp. 375–380 (2018)
28. Nakamoto, S., et al.: Bitcoin: a peer-to-peer electronic cash system (2008)
29. Nguyen, T.D., Pham, L.H., Sun, J., Lin, Y., Minh, Q.T.: Sfuzz: an efficient adaptive fuzzer for solidity smart contracts. In: Proceedings of the ACM/IEEE 42nd International Conference on Software Engineering, pp. 778–788 (2020)
30. Praitheeshan, P., Pan, L., Yu, J., Liu, J.K., Doss, R.: Security analysis methods on ethereum smart contract vulnerabilities: A survey. CoRR abs/1908.08605 (2019)
31. Sánchez-Gómez, N., Morales-Trujillo, L., Torres-Valderrama, J.: Towards an approach for applying early testing to smart contracts. In: Proceedings of the 15th International Conference on Web Information Systems and Technologies - APMDWE, pp. 445–453 (2019)
32. Tsankov, P., Dan, A., Drachsler-Cohen, D., Gervais, A., Bünzli, F., Vechev, M.: Securify: practical security analysis of smart contracts. In: Proceeding of the ACM SIGSAC Conference on Computer and Communications Security, pp. 67–82 (2018)
33. Utting, M., Legeard, B.: Practical Model-Based Testing: A Tools Approach. Morgan Kaufmann Publishers Inc. (2006)
34. Wang, X., Wu, H., Sun, W., Zhao, Y.: Towards generating cost-effective test-suite for ethereum smart contract. In: Proceeding of the IEEE 26th International Conference on Software Analysis, Evolution and Reengineering (SANER), pp. 549–553 (2019)
35. Wood, G., et al.: Ethereum: A secure decentralised generalised transaction ledger. Ethereum project yellow paper **151**(2014), 1–32 (2014)
36. Wu, Z., et al.: Kaya: a testing framework for blockchain-based decentralized applications. In: Proceeding of the IEEE International Conference on Software Maintenance and Evolution (ICSME 2020), pp. 826–829 (2020)

Blockchain Olive Oil Supply Chain

Tarek Frikha[1] (ID), Jalel Ktari[1(✉)] (ID), and Habib Hamam[2,3,4,5] (ID)

[1] CES Lab, ENIS, University of Sfax, Sfax, Tunisia
{tarek.frikha,jalel.ktari}@enis.tn
[2] Faculty of Engineering, Univ de Moncton, Moncton, NB E1A3E9, Canada
habib.hamam@umoncton.ca
[3] International Institute of Technology and Management, Commune d'Akanda,
BP: 1989 Libreville, Gabon
[4] Spectrum of Knowledge Production and Skills Development, 3027 Sfax, Tunisia
[5] School of Electrical Engineering, Department of Electrical and Electronic Engineering
Science, University of Johannesburg, Johannesburg 2006, South Africa

Abstract. In Tunisia, one of the major problems in the olive oil industry is marketing. Several factors have an impact such as quality, originality, lobbying, subvention, and Extra Virgin Olive Oil certification. The major issue is still traceability of the production process to ensure that food provenance is always guaranteed. Such fine-grained traceability can be achieved by applying Blockchain technologies. Blockchain can be used as a solution that should bring visibility to the oil supply chain. It is proposed to guarantee the veracity of the product's information at the different stages. We use the Ethereum Blockchain to program the smart contract. This smart contract allows us to configure our system to follow the manufacturing process of olive oil from the farmer through the oil factory to the customer. In this paper we present a general-purpose approach for the oil supply chain management, proposing a system that can be configured for productions. The primary purpose is to provide a methodology to facilitate and make more efficient the development of such applications. It is based on general smart contracts and apps interacting with the same smart contracts. We use IoT to configure sensors. These sensors are the data source for the supply chain process.

Keywords: Olive oil · Ethereum Blockchain · Traceability · Raspbian OS · IoT

1 Introduction

Tunisia is the world's third-largest exporter of olive oil. For decades, Tunisian olive oil has been shipped in bulk to other olive oil-producing countries like Italy and Spain where it was mixed with local oils and marketed under Italian or Spanish brand names. Today, Tunisia continues to be a large exporter of its olive oil, the majority of which still leaves the country in bulk containers. However, Tunisia's 'liquid gold' is also increasingly being exported in bottles under Tunisian brand names.

The main factors that influence the quality of olive oil are agricultural practices, environmental conditions, olive processing, and storage and distribution. Furthermore, olive

S. Kallel et al. (Eds.): CRiSIS 2022, LNCS 13857, pp. 101–113, 2023.
https://doi.org/10.1007/978-3-031-31108-6_8

crushing influences the organoleptic and nutritional qualities. However, it is commonly observed that information concerning these factors is not transparently shared among partners. Thus, customers are often confronted with many labels on oil bottles and with no means of verification.

As such there is an interest for preserving or certifying the quality of Extra Virgin Olive Oil. As top quality commands high prices, oil is vulnerable to fraud and adulteration throughout its transformation process. Customers are increasingly sensitive about the oil quality and the use of safe practice. Ensuring the authentication of olive oil quality is critical for customers Fig. 1.

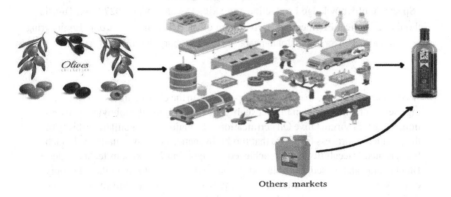

Fig. 1. A fraud in transformation process

Blockchain technology is increasingly supported for various applications such as e-health [1, 2], industry 4.0 [3, 4], voting [5], agriculture, including tracing and establishing the provenance of products. The data transparency and inclusivity of blockchain technology may significantly reduce the related food safety risks underlying deliberate fraud, poor management, and lack of regulation.

In this paper, we will focus on the implementation of a system to track the flow of olive oil from the farmer to the producer without having to go through intermediaries or fodder sources as shown in Fig. 1. Our system is based on the permissioned Ethereum blockchain in order to have the desired traceability. This document is structured around 4 parts. We start with a state of the art, then we go through the approach implemented. We then move on to the results obtained before closing with a conclusion and somes perspectives.

2 Related Work

In many countries, food legislation is particularly strict and the implementations of traceability systems are mandatory but are unable to insure consumers against fraud. For this reason innovative methods for traceability systems based on product identification are needed. Deterring food fraud requires interdisciplinary research combining food science, food law, supply chain management, and other fields such as informatics, mathematics and statistics. In this context, a distributed ledger technology such as Blockchain provides a full and immutable audit trail of transactions data for all stages of the food supply chain allowing for transparency and verifiable and immutable records in the form of digital certificates. Immutability of the data enables the technology to be considered for regulated industries such as agri-food.

As reported by Galvez et al. [6] in his research paper most blockchain systems for traceability management have been developed since 2015. Numerous research papers, Ezzeddini et al. [7], Costa et al. [8], Ktari et al. [9], Antonucci et al. [10] just to cite a few, have shown that using blockchain can advantageously help to achieve traceability by irreversibly and immutably storing data. Although many studies are promising that the application of blockchain technologies to the agri-food supply chain can ensure the food traceability and some companies have launched pilot or proof of concept projects to manage their supply chains with blockchain technology, certain limits remain to be considered and addressed. Blockchain can link all aspects of the food supply chain with a traceable and immutable data system (Fig. 2).

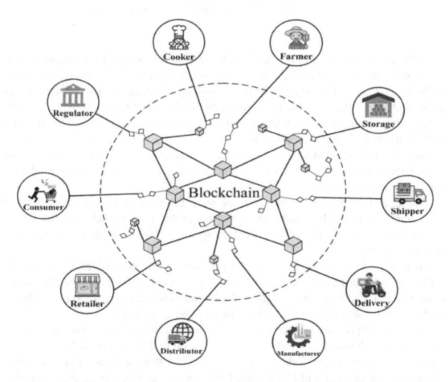

Fig. 2. Blockchain participants in the food supply chain [11]

Nowadays, numerous companies are developing blockchain technology globally, including Coinbase, Chronicled, Facebook, Circle, Binance, SALT Lending, Ripple,

Steem, etc. Most of them are in the field of finance. Other companies working to incorporate blockchain technology into the agricultural-food industry include IBM, Ripe.io, Transparent Path, Greenfence, OpenSC, Carrefour, Nestle, Hungry Coin, FoodlogIQ, and the like. These companies are summarized in Table 1 [11–13].

Table 1. Examples of collaboration models using blockchain technology in agri-food area.

Blockchain Company	Food Company Partners	Food Products	Country
IBM	Walmart, Carrefour, Nestle, Unilever, Farmer Connect, Tyson,	Mousseline, scallop, pork, lettuce, mango slices, chicken,	USA, china, France
SAP	Target, Kelloggs, Tate & Lyle, Johnsonville, Natura	yellowfin tuna,	USA
FoodlogIQ	Tyson Foods, Subway, UK's Food Standards Agency	Tomato, coffee,	USA
BloomBloc	Malaysian Palm Oil Council (MPOC)	Palm oil	Malysia
OpenSC	Nestlé	Milk and palm oil	Switzerland

On the other hand, researchers study blockchain-based food supply chain traceability.

Yu and Huang [14] put forth the traceability solution for broiler chickens by combining the blockchain technology and RFID technology. With the solution, smart devices can be used to scan the traceable QR code on the chicken claw ring to retrieve the corresponding data and information, where the chicken claw ring is designed into an "inverted tooth" shape to prevent its secondary use.

Tian et al. [15, 16] developed an agricultural food supply chain traceability system, covering the whole process of data acquisition and information management of all links of the entire supply chain.

Yang et al. [17] used Hyperledger as the traceability chain to store information in the local database, which is useful in solving the problem of blockchain deficiency in massive data storage. However, it is disadvantageous in high cost, slow data transition rate, low security, etc.

Xie et al. [18] utilized the IoT technology to carry out ETH-based tracing of agricultural products, ensuring that data will not be maliciously tampered or damaged. However, on the data storage layer, data storage is blockchain-based; thus the network overheads will become increasingly greater with the increase of data volume.

Hao et al. [19] researched the traceability storage solution based on the blockchain technology, which stores the crop growth information in IPFS and provides analysis of crop growth data by virtue of the auxiliary database. Although the solution overcomes the data storage constraint of blockchain, the focus of the system is on the acquisition of crop growth information, and thus the solution is not favorable to the information tracing subsequent to crop processing.

Caro et al. propose an integrated solution of a blockchain platform named Agri-BlockIoT in the agriculture supply chain [20]. AgriBlockIoT is a fully distributed system which uses the blockchain technology in combination with IoT devices in order to collect and distribute traceability data. The proposed solution was tested with two different blockchain platforms, namely Ethereum and Hyperledger Sawtooth. Trial results showed that Ethereum performed considerably better compared to Hyperledger Sawtooth, in terms of latency, CPU and network usage. AgriBlockIoT enables the integration of IoT and blockchain technologies, creating transparent, fault-tolerant, immutable and auditable records which can be used for an agri-food traceability system.

Furthermore, Lin et al. propose another system based on blockchain and IoT technologies for the agriculture supply chain [21]. Specifically, the authors try to combine the technologies of blockchain, IoT, low-power wide-area network (LPWAN) and existing enterprise resource planning (ERP). The proposed platform, which aims to solve food safety and trust issues of the traditional agri-food supply chain, involves all parties within a typical agriculture supply chain ecosystem. [22].

Mondal et al., describes a blockchain–IoT based system which utilizes the proof of object (PoO) concept as an alternative to the blockchain's proof of work (PoW) [23–25] and proof of stake (PoS). PoO is a validation method where the owner of the object is obliged to prove the possession. As long as the other stakeholders validate this claim, a consensus is reached and a new block is added in the blockchain. The authors follow an analytical approach and present trial results for the proposed model regarding the implementation of the consensus algorithm, the security issues and the sensor technology involved [26].

Based on the different approaches used in the state of the art and given the Tunisian technological, retail and infrastructural constraints, we propose in this paper an approach that can help not only to improve the olive oil quality but also to optimize the selling price.

Cutting out the middleman is the best way to avoid fraud and minimize possible commissions. The result is a very high-quality oil with low prices. We will try to describe the most suitable process.

3 Proposed Approach

The aim of the proposed work is to allow the implementation of a supply chain system allowing the follow-up of the routing of the olive oil from the producer to the customer through the oil factory. The proposed system as indicated allows to bypass the intermediaries in order to minimize the cost of the production and to secure the system. Anyone who is not part of our blockchain is automatically excluded.

This system therefore allows us to maintain the quality of our production. Our reliable system is performed by the implementation of smart contracts to store critical data that are immutable and ensure the monitoring and securing of olive production. That is why there is a need of:

- Implementation of a web application for data entry.
- Transfer, processing and storage of information in the Blockchain

- Blockchain implementation on Raspberry PI
- Secure data tracking

    As for the farmer

- Access the system by completing the registration process.
- To put on sale its products, i.e. the olives. The necessary details about the product.

    Concerning the producer

- Access the system by completing the registration process.
- To buy the raw materials offered for sale by the farmer.
- He can also put the oil up for sale.

    As for the customer

- The client can access the system.
- He can check the production line through which the product was passed.

Figure 3 represents the different actors and the steps that will be followed in the implementation of our system.

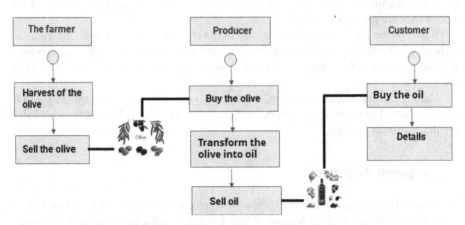

Fig. 3. Implemented proposed system

The system proposed in our paper is presented in Fig. 4. The different people who interfere in our system are presented in this figure.

Thus we have the farmer, the industrial (manufacturing, processing and packaging, quality inspection, transport and logistics) and the customer.

Each member of our system will propose a Blockchain node. This node will be implemented on a Raspberry PI3. The smart contract will run to record each transaction performed. The result of the implementation of our system will be illustrated in the results part.

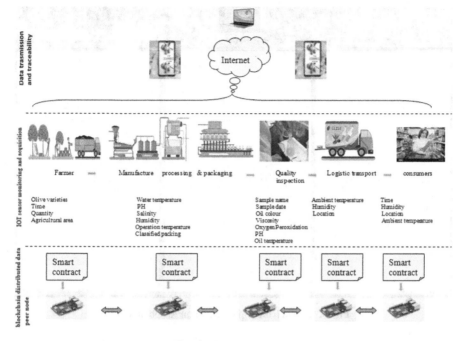

Fig. 4. Global approach

4 Obtained Results

With the objective of setting up an efficient system allowing to trace the routing of the production of olive trees from the farmer to the customer without having to go through intermediaries, we will highlight the system that has been set up. We will first present the Blockchain part implemented on a Raspberry PI 3 platform. Then, we will describe the mobile application that allows tracking and controlling the different transactions.

4.1 Implemented Blockchain on Raspberry Pi

Several embedded platforms can be used such as FPGAs [27, 28], GPUs [29], etc. We chose to use a Raspberry Pi platform for the implementation of our application. This choice is due to several reasons:

In terms of low power consumption [30–33], the raspberry PI has the characteristics of a PC with a minimalist configuration. It offers a multiprocessor architecture with a GPU that allows access to a good computational capacity. It offers different peripherals to be able to connect and use several peripherals. Since the data does not require significant computational capabilities, we will use the Raspberry Pi as receptacle for our blockchain. We will therefore use Ethereum as the Blockchain implemented on Raspberry. The result of our work is described in Fig. 5. We see the Blockchain, and the different transactions performed. In this figure we use a virtual machine in which we installed the Raspbian OS. The data were recorded using smart contracts.

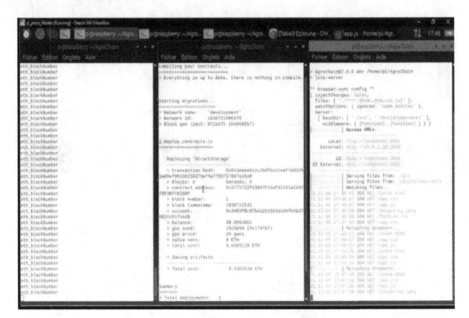

Fig. 5. Blockchain implemented on Raspbian OS

However, the implementation of our blockchain goes through several steps that require the use of several tools. We will use Ganache to test our custom Ethereum blockchain. The truffle tool will be the provider of our smart contract and finally metamask will be our crypto wallet. Figure 6 describes the different tools used that we have already described.

After the smart contract, the ganache result was represented in Fig. 6. We can notice that all transaction are hashed to secure it. Figure 7 illustrates it.

After describing the Blockchain implementation part, we will highlight the mobile part used to consult as well as pass our transactions via Blockchain.

4.2 Web Application

In the application part, we are going to propose our system which has been realized using Flatter. We see in the Fig. 8 our Web application that has been realized. The goal is to also to use a mobile application that can be used both on Android and IoS. In this figure we can find the agriculture registration part.

Fig. 6. Blockchain implementation used tools

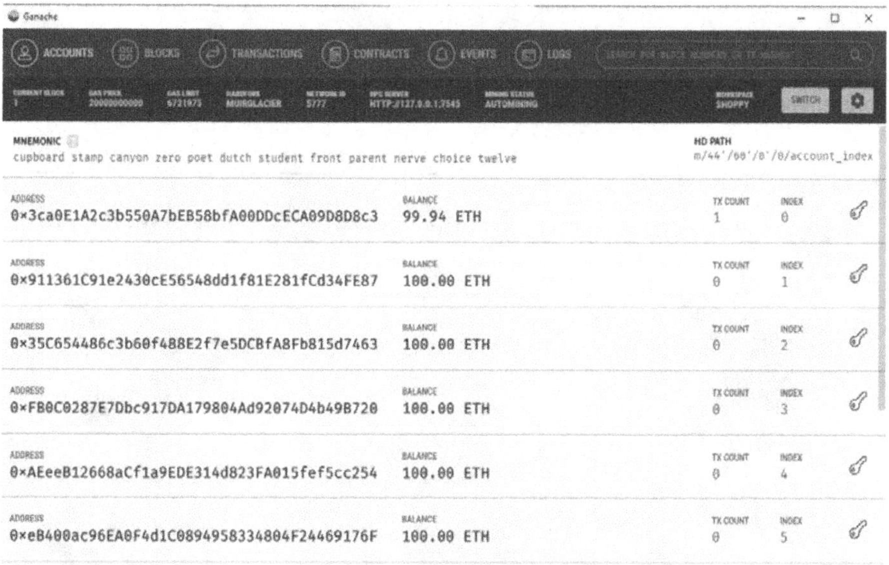

Fig. 7. Ganache result example

Fig. 8. Monitoring & securing production: agriculture interface

After selling olive to the manufacturer to extract olive oil, the transaction was saved on the Blockchain. In Fig. 9, we find the confirmation of the executed transaction. It represents the oil manufacturer interface.

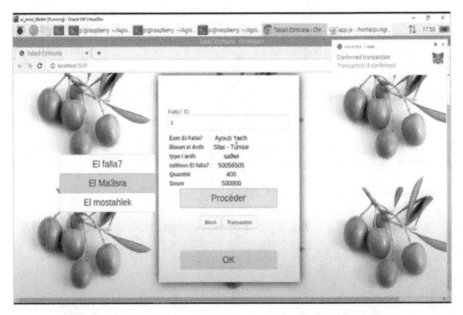

Fig. 9. Monitoring & securing production: oil manufacturer interface

The third application actor was the customer. He can access to the system to check the identity of the olive producer as well as the oil manufacturer before buying his oil. Figure 10 illustrates it.

Fig. 10. Monitoring & securing production: customer interface

It is important to notice that each actor in our system has access to a crypto-wallet Meta mask in order to perform the necessary transactions in our system. Each transaction done by the system needs ethereum gas to be validated. This crypto-money is displayed via meta mask.

5 Conclusion

In this paper, we have presented a system to highlight the security of information related to the production of olive oil using the Blockchain.

The steps showing the importance of our system have been set up and described taking into account the Tunisian context related to olive oil.

Several perspectives can be added to this work. Indeed, in order to have a system using intelligent agriculture, we can add several sensors to minimize human intervention.

We can use artificial intelligence to automate the state of the olives but also the type and quality of the olive oil obtained.

References

1. Ktari, J., Frikha, T., Ben Amor, N., Louraidh, L., Elmannai, H., Hamdi, M.: IoMT-based platform for E-health monitoring based on the blockchain. Electron. J. **11**, 2314 (2022). https://doi.org/10.3390/electronics11152314

2. Frikha, T., Abdennour, N., Chaabane, F., Ghorbel, O., Ayedi, R., Shahin, O.R., Cheikhrouhou, O.: Source localization of EEG brainwaves activities via mother wavelets families for SWT decomposition. J. Healthcare Eng. (2021)

3. Ktari, J., Frikha, T., Hamdi, M., Elmannai, H., Hamam, H.: Lightweight AI framework for industry 4.0 case study: water meter recognition. Big Data Cogn. Comput. **6**, 72 (2022). https://doi.org/10.3390/bdcc6030072

4. Ktari, J., Frikha, T., Yousfi, M.A., Belghith, M.K., Sanei, N.: Embedded Keccak implementation on FPGA. In 2022 IEEE International Conference on Design & Test of Integrated Micro & Nano-Systems (DTS), pp.01–05. https://doi.org/10.1109/DTS55284.2022.9809847

5. Chaabane, F., Ktari, J., Frikha, T., Hamam, H.: Low power blockchained E-vote platform for university environment. Future Internet **14**(9), 269 (2022). https://doi.org/10.3390/fi14090269

6. Galvez, F., Mejuto, J.C., Simal-Gandara, J.: Future challenges on the use of blockchain for food traceability analysis, pp. 222–232, oct 2018. TrAC Trends in Analytical Chemistry

7. Ezzeddini, L., Ktari, J., Zouaoui, I., Talha, A., Jarray, N., Frikha, T.: Blockchain for the electronic voting system: case study: student representative vote in Tunisian institute. In: 2022 15th International Conference on Security of Information and Networks (SIN), pp. 01–07. IEEE (2022)

8. Costa, C., Antonucci, F., Pallottino, F., Aguzzi, J., Sarria, D., Menesatti, P.: A review on agri-food supply chain traceability by means of rfid technology. Food Bioprocess Technol. **6**(2), 353–366 (2013)

9. Ktari, J., Frikha, T., Chaabane, F., Hamdi, M., Hamam, H.: Agricultural lightweight embedded blockchain system: a case study in olive oil. Electronics **11**(20), 3394 (2022). https://doi.org/10.3390/electronics11203394

10. Antonucci, F., Figorilli, S., Costa, C., Pallottino, F., Raso, L., Menesatti, P.: A review on blockchain applications in the agri-food sector. J. Sci. Food Agric. **99**(14), 6129–6138 (2019)

11. Xu, J., Guo, S., Xie, D., Yan, Y.: Blockchain: a new safeguard for agri-foods. Artif. Intell. Agriculture **4**, 153–161 (2020)

12. Singh, M.: Can Blockchain Technology Support Agricultural Sustainability? January 2022 https://doi.org/10.22541/au.164192086.60828523/v1

13. Kamble, S., Gunasekaran, A., Sharma, R.: Modeling the blockchain enabled traceability in agriculture supply chain. Int. J. Inf. Manag. **52**, 101967 (2020)

14. Xie, J., et al.: A survey of blockchain technology applied to smart cities: research issues and challenges. IEEE Commun. Surv. Tutorials **21**(3), 2794–2830 (2019)

15. Tian, F.: An agri-food supply chain traceability system for China based on RFID & blockchain technology. In: Proceedings of the 2016 13th International Conference on Service Systems and Service Management, pp. 1–6, Kunming, China, June 2016

16. Tian, F.: A supply chain traceability system for food safety based on HACCP blockchain & Internet of things. In: Proceedings of the 2017 International Conference on Service Systems and Service Management, pp. 1–6, Dalian, China, Jun 2017

17. Yang, X., Li, M., Yu, H., Wang, M., Xu, D., Sun, C.: A trusted blockchain-based traceability system for fruit and vegetable agricultural products. IEEE Access **9**, 36282–36293 (2021)

18. Xie, C., Sun, Y., Luo, H.: Secured data storage scheme based on block chain for agricultural products tracking. In: Proceedings of the 2017 3rd International Conference on Big Data Computing and Communications, pp. 45–50, Chengdu, China (2017)

19. Hao, J.T., Sun, Y., Luo, H.: A safe and efficient storage scheme based on blockchain and IPFS for agricultural products tracking. J. Comput. **29**(6), 158–167 (2018)

20. Caro, M.P., Ali, M.S., Vecchio, M., Giaffreda, R.: Blockchain-based traceability in Agri-Food supply chain management: a practical implementation. In 2018 IoT Vertical and Topical Summit on Agriculture-Tuscany (IOT Tuscany), pp. 1–4. IEEE (2018)

21. Lin, J., Shen, Z., Zhang, A., Chai, Y.: Blockchain and IoT based food traceability for smart agriculture. In: Proceedings of the 3rd International Conference on Crowd Science and Engineering-ICCSE'18, Singapore, 28–31 July 2018; Volume 3, p. 3 (2018)
22. Demestichas, K., Peppes, N., Alexakis, T.: Blockchain in agriculture traceability systems: a review. Appl. Sci. **10**(12), 4113 (2020). https://doi.org/10.3390/app10124113
23. Frikha, T., Chaari, A., Chaabane, F., Cheikhrouhou, O., Zaguia, A.: Healthcare and fitness data management using the IoT-based blockchain platform. J. Healthc. Eng. **2021**, 9978863 (2021)
24. Frikha, T., Chaabane, F., Aouinti, N., Cheikhrouhou, O., Ben Amor, N., Kerrouche, A.: Implementation of blockchain consensus algorithm on embedded architecture. Secur. Commun. Netw. **2021**, 9918697 (2021)
25. Allouche, M., Frikha, T., Mitrea, M., Memmi, G., Chaabane, F.: Lightweight blockchain processing. case study: scanned document tracking on Tezos Blockchain. Appl. Sci. **11**, 7169 (2021). https://doi.org/10.3390/app11157169
26. Mondal, S., Wijewardena, K., Karuppuswami, S., Kriti, F., Kumar, D., Chahal, P.: Blockchain inspired RFID-based information architecture for food supply chain. IEEE Internet Things J. **6**, 5803–5813 (2019)
27. Frikha, T., Ben Amor, N., Diguet, J.-P., Abid, M.: A novel Xilinx-based architecture for 3D-graphics. Multimed. Tools Appl. **78**(11), 14947–14970 (2019)
28. Frikha, T., Ben Amor, N., Lahbib, K., Diguet, J.-P., Abid, M.: A data adaptation approach for a hw/sw mixed architecture (case study: 3d application) WSEAS Transactions on circuit and systems
29. Dhouioui, M., Frikha, T.: Design and implementation of a radar and camera-based obstacle classification system using machine-learning techniques. J. Real-Time Image Proc. **18**(6), 2403–2415 (2021). https://doi.org/10.1007/s11554-021-01117-8
30. Ktari, J., Abid, M.: A low power design methodology based on high level models. In: International Conference on Embedded Systems & Applications, USA 2008, pp. 10–15. https://dblp.org/rec/conf/csreaESA/KtariA08.html
31. Ktari, J., Abid, M.: A low power design space exploration methodology based on high level models and confidence interval. J. Low Power Electron. (2009). https://doi.org/10.1166/jolpe.2009.1003
32. Ktari, J., Abid, M.: System level power and energy modeling for signal processing applications. In: 2007 2nd IEEE, International Design and Test Workshop, Egypt, pp. 218–221 (2007). https://doi.org/10.1109/IDT.2007.4437463
33. Ktari, J., Abid, M., Julien, N., Laurent, J.: Power consumption and performance's library on DSPs: case study MPEG2. J. Comput. Sci. **3**, 168–173 (2007)

Impact of EIP-1559 on Transactions in the Ethereum Blockchain and Its Rollups

Salah Gontara(✉) 📷, Amine Boufaied, and Ouajdi Korbaa 📷

MARS Research Laboratory, Université de Sousse Tunisia, LR17ES054011 Hammam Sousse, Tunisia
gontara.salah@gmail.com, ouajdi.korbaa@Centraliens-Lille.org

Abstract. EIP-1559 is an Ethereum Improvement Proposal that aims to modify the transaction fee system on Ethereum and has also been adapted by some of its layer 2 Rollups. It would reduce fees paid by its users and help make its cryptocurrency a deflationary currency by burning a certain amount of it during operations. However, this modification does not only bring advantages. In this paper, we conduct a practical study to show how it affects the transactions on the Ethereum Blockchain as well as its layer 2 scaling solutions (Rollups) Polygon and Arbitrum in term of gas fees and waiting times.

Keywords: Blockchain · EIP-1559 · Ethereum · Polygon · Arbitrum · waiting time · gas fees

1 Introduction

To perform a transaction on any public Blockchain, a gas fee is required to be paid to the miners or the validators as an incentive for them to maintain the blockchain and be part of a healthy consensus [1]. This is valid in Proof-of-Work blockchains like Ethereum and Proof-of-Stake blockchains like Polygon and Arbitrum.

Ethereum is a decentralized and open source blockchain system that has its own cryptocurrency: Ether (ETH). Ethereum also acts as a platform for a multitude of other cryptocurrencies namely ERC-20 tokens but also for the deployment and execution of decentralized programs called smart contracts [2].

To execute these smart contracts or simply transfer Ether, gas fees are required to be paid for these operations and have lately been amounting to very high costs due to the large demand and the lack of scalability of the Ethereum network. To curb these costs, a number of Ethereum Improvement Proposals (EIPs) have been implemented [3].

However, some EIPs like EIP-1559 have been controversial as they divide the users' opinion about their efficiency. We show in this paper why this is the case, especially since it's implemented on layer-2 of the Ethereum as well [4].

Several works [4–6] have highlighted the consequences of EIP-1559 on the Ethereum blockchain, however, its impact on the Ethereum Rollups like Polygon and Arbitrum hasn't been studied. Our study will prove how this improvement proposal have different consequences on Rollups when compared to the Ethereum blockchain.

© The Author(s), under exclusive license to Springer Nature Switzerland AG 2023
S. Kallel et al. (Eds.): CRiSIS 2022, LNCS 13857, pp. 114–126, 2023.
https://doi.org/10.1007/978-3-031-31108-6_9

The remainder of this paper is organized as follows. We offer a brief description of Ethereum L1 and L2 as well as EIP-1559 in Sect. 2. Section 3 describes our proposed testing approach. We present and explain the testing results in Sect. 4. Finally, a conclusion is provided in Sect. 5.

2   Background

2.1   Layers 1 and 2 in Ethereum

Ethereum 1.0 (L1)
Ethereum is a decentralized exchange network allowing users to create smart contracts. These smart contracts are based on a computer protocol to verify or enforce a mutual contract. They are deployed and publicly viewable in a blockchain. It is based on Proof-Of-Work [1]. EIP-1559 went live on Ethereum on august 2021 as part of the London Fork. It is considered a layer 1 (L1) network since it's the main blockchain network other Rollups are implemented on. Ethereum is planning to become Proof-of-Stake with ETH 2.0 [7].

Polygon (L2)
Polygon was born from an observation: Ethereum is the first smart contract platform in the world, but it is reaching its limits. Users and developers suffer from high latency and gas costs. The current Ethereum architecture does not allow to customize its technology stack. Developers are fleeing to secondary blockchains like it, compatible with EVM [8]. Figure 1 shows a simple representation of the scaling mechanism implemented between Ethereum and Polygon as a layer 2 (L2) Scaling solution based on Proof-of-Stake where transactions are validated instead of mined. EIP-1559 went live on Polygon on January 2022.

Arbitrum (L2)
Arbitrum takes data storage and computation and moves it off the Ethereum mainchain. By processing transactions in a separate environment, via the ArbOS, Arbitrum can clear transactions more quickly and it's not affected by network congestion on Ethereum. The primary difference between Arbitrum and Polygon is the security mechanism. Arbitrum is secured by the Ethereum base layer and does not have its own token. Polygon is secured by its own Proof-of-Stake consensus mechanism, where stakers lock up the MATIC token to get a reward for validating transactions [8]. Arbitrum uses an EIP-1559-like mechanism since its launch for the developers as a Dev mainnet in May 2021. It is inspired to be tailored to its needs but is still very similar in many aspects.

2.2   Eip-1559

Presenting EIPs
Ethereum Improvement Proposals (EIPs) are feature and process proposal documents

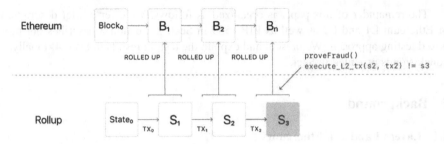

Fig. 1. Ethereum scaling mechanism

that propose potential changes to the Ethereum blockchain. Any member of the Ethereum community can submit them to the Ethereum platform.

Usually, developers or groups of developers submit an EIP based on changes they believe will improve the Ethereum protocol and network. Proposals are evaluated and discussed by Ethereum's core developers, who manage its repository on the GitHub platform. EIPs go through several stages of evaluation. If they are eventually accepted, they are usually bundled together to form updates called forks [3].

There are several categories of Ethereum improvement proposals:

- The Standard Track EIPs relate to changes that will affect most or all Ethereum implementations. These include network protocol improvements and changes in transaction regulations.
- Networking EIPs are proposed changes to network protocol specifications.
- Meta EIPs relate to requests and operations applied to areas other than the network protocol.
- The EIP Interface offers enhancements to standards and user specifications.
- Ethereum Request for Comments (ERC) EIPs relate to application standards and conventions.
- Informational EIPs are linked to guidelines for the actual design of Ethereum.
- Core EIPs are proposals that require a consensus fork.

The reason for adopting this model of organization is due to the requirement for a high level of organization in the decentralized development communities to manage and decide on the next improvements that will be incorporated into the project. In this way, any developer can present an improvement proposal that will be discussed in the community, and depending on its impact, it may or may not be included in the Ethereum protocol [3].

Transaction Fee Mechanism in EIP-1559

This EIP aims to change the way commissions are managed within the network. For this, the EIP-1559 creates a commission burning mechanism that prevents Ethereum from having higher inflation and, at the same time, expands or shrinks the capacity of Ethereum blocks to include more transactions to reduce network congestion.

Legacy transaction mechanism (TFM), prior to EIP-1559 is considered a first-price auction where users submit their own bid for their transaction. Their bids are then set to outbid their competitors to gain their transactions mined first. Outbidding leads to overpaid transactions, which is a problem in Ethereum due to high Ether price but isn't relatively an issue on Rollups since token prices are very low in the layer 2 scaling solutions [3]. The gas fee is paid with Ether in Ethereum, Matic in Polygon and Arb in Arbitrum. It's defined with the following equation:

$$\text{GasFee} = GasUsed \times GasPrice \tag{1}$$

EIP-1559 introduces four major changes to the transaction fee mechanism (TFM) on Ethereum. A list of notations related to EIP-1559 is presented in Table 1.

Regarding block size, EIP-1559 makes the fixed-sized blocks variable. The block gas limit is doubled from 15 million to 30 million, while the block gas target is still set at 15 million. As we will introduce below, a novel gas price mechanism ensures that block gas used remains around block gas target on average [4].

EIP-1559 has a base fee parameter depending on the network consensus. Base fee is the minimum gas price that every transaction must pay to be included in a block. Base fee adjusts in a dynamic Markov process according to the block gas used in the previous block. If the block gas is greater than the target, the base fee for the next block increases, and vice versa. The base fee of the next block is determined solely by its present state. The dynamics of the base fee is represented as follows [4, 5]:

$$BaseFee_{h+1} = BaseFee_h \left(1 + \frac{1}{8} \frac{GasUsed_h - GasTarget}{GasTarget} \right) \tag{2}$$

EIP-1559 also affects consensus security as it changes the distribution of block size.

For their new TFMs, Polygon implements EIP-1559 as it is but Arbitrum adapts it from Ethereum (L1) to calculate its own gas fees, as shown in the following equation:

$$GasFee = L2\_GasUsed + \left(\frac{L1\_CalldataPrice * L1\_CalldataSize}{L2\_GasPrice} \right)$$

Table 1. Notations related to EIP-1559 and Arbitrum's new TFM

Notation	Description
BaseFee	The minimum GasUsed multiplier required for a transaction to be included in a block. The result of BaseFee times GasUsed is the part of the transaction fee that is burned
MaxPriorityFee	The maximum GasUsed multiplier that a user is willing to pay to the miner

(continued)

Table 1. (*continued*)

Notation	Description
MaxFee	The maximum GasUsed multiplier that a user is willing to pay for a transaction
GasPrice	Only legacy transactions use it, which represents the GasUsed multiplier that a user is willing to pay for a transaction
GasUsed	The total amount of gas used by a transaction
GasTarget	The target of gas that blocks are expected to use on average, which is set by the protocol
GasFee	The actual transaction fee that a user pays
L2_GasUsed	Same as GasUsed but for Arbitrum (L2)
L2_GasPrice	Same as GasPrice but for Arbitrum (L2)
L1_CalldataPrice	Current price of the Calldata in Ethereum (L1)
L1_CalldataSize	Size in raw data of the transaction

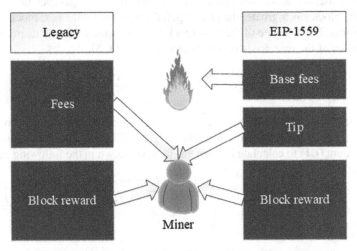

Fig. 2. Simple representation of legacy TFM and EIP-1559

3   Testing Approach

3.1   Smart Contract

To test EIP-1559's TFM, we write a smart contract that includes functions to handle event emission, variable storage and address table modification. These functions are known to have high opcode gas fees [9].

The smart contract is deployed on Ethereum, Polygon and Arbitrum testnets from the address 0x6F0A14Fb2631f5530E5F3CBc0f7aC99091A8882E with both legacy and new TFMs and has its addresses presented in Table 2.

Table 2. Smart Contract Deployment Information

Network	Transaction Type	Address
Ethereum Rinkeby	Legacy	0xFdEDD8E629105a08Bb06F38981a9Bc392CA636Ba
Ethereum Rinkeby	EIP-1559	0xFcC80689817FCaC06AA346b660105C439647BEdA
Polygon Mumbai	Legacy	0xD5CA0277bfD3d9D9883d7f79fbe17395E2e83820
Polygon Mumbai	EIP-1559	0x68219Ca5964416b028DcA439D9A6886af2C8FCae
Arbitrum Rinkeby	Legacy	0x68219Ca5964416b028DcA439D9A6886af2C8FCae
Arbitrum Rinkeby	EIP-1559	0xD5CA0277bfD3d9D9883d7f79fbe17395E2e83820

These deployments and their transactions' logs can be easily viewed on the listed blockchain explorers:

- Etherscan (Rinkeby): rinkeby.etherscan.io
- Polygonscan (Mumbai): mumbai.polygonscan.com
- Arbiscan (Rinkeby): testnet.arbiscan.io

The following is the code for the Smart Contract used in our testing, written, and compiled with Solidity 0.8.12:

```
// SPDX-License-Identifier: MIT
pragma solidity >= 0.8.4 < 0.9.0;
contract EIP1559_Testing {
    address admin;
    mapping(address => uint) index;
    address[] allowedAddresses;
    constructor() {
        admin = msg.sender;
    }
    event EventREQ(
        uint req_value_0,
        string req_value_1,
        string req_value_2,
        string req_value_3,
        string req_value_4
    );
    function sendEvent(uint _req_value_0, string calldata
_req_value_1, string calldata _req_value_2, string
calldata _req_value_3, string calldata _req_value_4) ex-
ternal payable {
        if (!isAllowed(msg.sender)) {

            revert('wrong address');
        }
        emit EventREQ(_req_value_0, _req_value_1,
_req_value_2, _req_value_3, _req_value_4);
    }
    function addAllowed(address _allowedAddress) external
{
        if (msg.sender != admin) {
            revert('wrong owner, cant add');
        }
        if (!isAllowed(_allowedAddress)) {
            index[_allowedAddress] = allowedAddress-
es.length;
            allowedAddresses.push(_allowedAddress);
        }
    }
    function isAllowed(address _uA) public view re-
turns(bool) {
        if (index[_uA] > 0) {
            return true;
        }
        return false;
    }
    function transferFunds(address payable recipient,
uint256 amount) external {
        if (msg.sender != admin) {
            revert('wrong owner');
        }
        recipient.transfer(amount * 1E9);
    }

}
```

The structures of our Smart Contract are explained in Table 3.

Table 3. Smart Contract Structures

Structure Name	Type	Description
admin	address	admin address allowed to add other addresses and transfer funds
index	mapping	mapping referencing each allowed address
allowedAddresses	address table	table of allowed addresses
EventREQ	event	testing event with max number of variables
req_value_0	uint	testing integer variable in EventREQ
req_value_[1..4]	string	testing string variables in EventREQ
sendEvent	payable function	emit variables to EventREQ
addAllowed	function	add allowed addresses to some functions
transferFunds	function	transfer Smart contract funds to address

The functions "sendEvent" and "addAllowed" are chosen for the tests as their opcodes have dynamic gas prices needing to be calculated with a TFM each time they're called.

3.2 Interaction with the Smart Contract

To perform the tests while interacting the smart contract, we use the Web3.js framework, in its version 1.7.0 [10].

The following code is an excerpt of our Web3 scripts with the legacy version of the TFM, used in this case to call the function that adds an address to the allowed addresses table of the Smart Contract:

```
const init = async () => {
    try {
        let web3_wallet = new Web3(walletProvider);
        const addresses = await
web3_wallet.eth.getAccounts();
        const contract = new
web3_wallet.eth.Contract(contractABI.abi,
'0xFdEDD8E629105a08Bb06F38981a9Bc392CA636Ba');
        let startTime = Date.now()
        contract.methods
.addAllowed('0xFcC80689817FCaC06AA346b660105C439647BEdA')
.send({
                from: addresses[0] ,
                gasPrice: 2500000000
            })
            .on('receipt', function (receipt) {
                let elapsedTime = Date.now() - startTime
                console.log(elapsedTime);
                console.log(receipt);
            })
    } catch (error) {
        console.error(error);
    }
}
```

To use the previous script with EIP-1559, we simply omit the gasPrice parameter thus the legacy bidding mechanism, enabling the implementation of the EIP-1559 TFM.

The gasPrice used with the legacy TFM is exactly as provided by EIP-1559 to set a similar bidding environment, with the same transaction speeds.

We get the transaction time by calculating the difference between the transaction initiation time by the ABI function and the receipt reception time (valid transaction).

4 Experimentation

4.1 Testing Results

We start by measuring the times of the smart contract deployments. When we first deploy the smart contract, we get longer deployment times with EIP-1559 compared to the legacy TFM. Results are shown in Table 4.

Table 4. Smart Contract deployment times

Network	Transaction Type	Deployment Time
Ethereum Rinkeby	Legacy	8 s
Ethereum Rinkeby	EIP-1559	13 s
Polygon Mumbai	Legacy	8 s
Polygon Mumbai	EIP-1559	12 s
Arbitrum Rinkeby	Legacy	> 1 s
Arbitrum Rinkeby	EIP-1559	2 s

The deployments, done with the Truffle framework [11], show significantly different times between the two TFMs, with the most critical delays due to the EIP-1559 TFM on Ethereum and Polygon.

We analyze next the gas fees used to deploy these smart contracts. Since their numbers do not vary at all over a short amount of time, only one instance is enough to show the difference between EIP-1559 and the legacy transaction fees. The gas fees are represented in Wei, a subunit of Ether (1Eth $= 10^{18}$Wei) and subsequently of Matic and Arb.

The implementation of the EIP-1559 on Polygon is completely identical to the one on Ethereum, so it's only natural to acquire the exact same transaction fees, where legacy fees are slightly cheaper, as shown in Fig. 3.

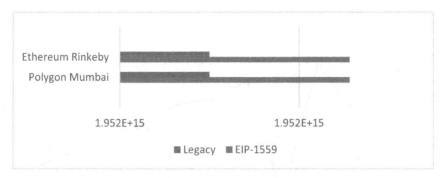

Fig. 3. Resulting transaction fees on Ethereum and Polygon in Wei

However, the transaction mechanism is different on Arbitrum, where the EIP-1559 is implemented differently than on Ethereum and Polygon. And since the transaction fees are on a different scale for Arbitrum, we choose to represent them in a separate graph, as shown in Fig. 4.

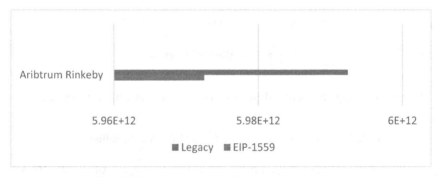

Fig. 4. Obtained transaction fees on Arbitrum in Wei

The optimization of EIP-1559 on Arbitrum allows for cheaper transactions.

Next, we call the functions "addAllowed" and "sendEvent", described in Table 3, 10 times each, simultaneously, using the same endpoints provider, Alchemy.

The times are generated in milliseconds and receipts are all validated on the Blockchain; they can easily be viewed with any blockchain explorer.

The results are displayed in Fig. 5 and 6 respectively, showing the transaction times for Legacy Ethereum, EIP-1559 Ethereum, Legacy Polygon, EIP-1559 Polygon, Legacy Arbitrum and EIP-1559 Arbitrum.

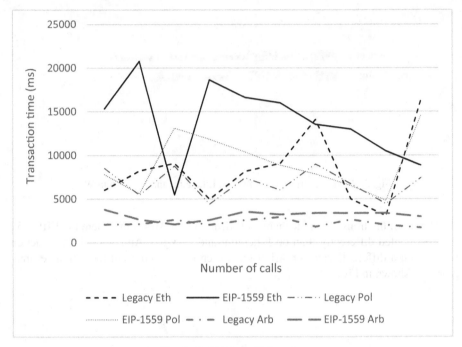

Fig. 5. "addAllowed" function

We get the average times in milliseconds from these transactions in Table 5:

Table 5. Average transaction time for "addAllowed" in milliseconds

Legacy Eth	EIP-1559 Eth	Legacy Pol	EIP-1559 Pol	Legacy Arb	EIP-1559 Arb
8387.9	13866.7	6808.3	9127.3	2259	3100.1

Transaction times are fluctuating due to the time variation before the block creation when the transaction is initiated then mined or validated, but it's still visible how the legacy transaction times are way faster than the EIP-1559 transaction times. We also notice how transactions in Ethereum are slower compared to Polygon, itself slower than Arbitrum. This is coherent with the fact that PoW blockchains (Ethereum) are theoretically slower than PoS blockchains (Arbitrum and Polygon).

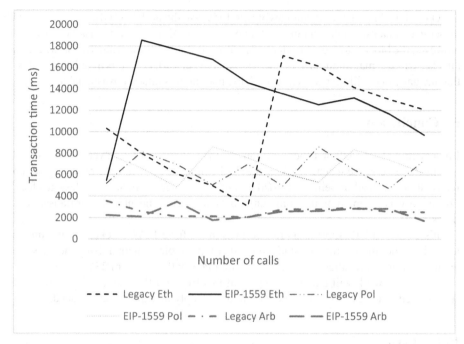

Fig. 6. "sendEvent" function

We get the average times in milliseconds from these transactions in Table 6:

Table 6. Average transaction time for "sendEvent" in milliseconds

Legacy Eth	EIP-1559 Eth	Legacy Pol	EIP-1559 Pol	Legacy Arb	EIP-1559 Arb
10499.8	13368	6450.8	6909.9	2608.2	2433.2

The trend in transaction times is confirmed in the event manipulation function "sendEvent" as Legacy transaction times are shorter than EIP-1559 transaction times and Arbitrum stays faster than Polygon which itself is faster than Ethereum.

4.2 Discussion

We now know that the transaction fees are slightly cheaper in the legacy TFM compared to EIP-1559.

In addition, on layer 2 scaling solutions like Polygon, EIP-1559's implementation is unnecessary as gas fees are already extremely cheap, it only made transactions slower defeating the purpose of a fast PoS blockchain.

Arbitrum's implementation of EIP-1559 doesn't have a significant impact on its transactions since it's modified to suit its needs as a PoS blockchain, keeping transactions times basically unchanged.

One other claim of the advantages of EIP-1559 is to thwart BDoS (Blockchain Denial of Service) attacks, but this claim is still unprovable as it's not advised to attack testnets. However, the block variance introduced in this proposal can present such a risk where an attacker will use maximum-size blocks to spam the network [12]. It is noted nonetheless that the gas price will increase exponentially, making this attack unsustainable.

5 Conclusion

Implementing EIP-1559 on Ethereum, causing the London Fork, was very controversial as it made miners lose incentive, since they're being "tipped" while the base transaction fee is burned instead of being rewarded to them. However, users now pay less gas fees. Overall, it was accepted by the community despite the significantly slower transactions times.

It's clear that EIP-1559 in its raw form is made for a PoW blockchain and unless adequately modified, will only hinder any other type of blockchain, raising the question about its future with Ethereum as it's becoming PoS with Ethereum 2.0.

Our future work will target the impact of this EIP on Ethereum 2.0 to see if it can still be used as is or if it needs to be modified or simply discarded and replaced.

References

1. Zheng, Z., Xie, S., Dai, H., Chen, X., Wang, H.: An overview of blockchain technology: architecture, consensus, and future trends. In: IEEE International Congress on Big Data (BigData Congress), Honolulu, HI, USA (2017)
2. Wood, G.: Ethereum: a secure decentralised generalised transaction ledger. Ethereum project yellow paper, pp. 1–32 (2014)
3. Bez, M., Fornari, G., Vardanega, T.: The scalability challenge of ethereum: an initial quantitative analysis. In: IEEE International Conference on Service-Oriented System Engineering (SOSE), San Francisco, CA, USA (2019)
4. Liu, Y., Yuxuan, L., Kartik, N., Fan, Z., Luyao, Z., Yinhong, Z.: Empirical analysis of EIP-1559: transaction fees, waiting time, and consensus security. arXiv:2201.05574v2 (2022)
5. Moore, I.C., Sidhu, J.: Stochastic properties of EIP-1559 basefees arXiv:2105.03521 (2021)
6. Reijsbergen, D., Sridhar, S., Monnot, B., Leonardos, S., Skoulakis, S., Piliouras, G.: Transaction fees on a honeymoon: ethereum's EIP-1559 one month later. In: IEEE International Conference on Blockchain (2021)
7. Sedlmeir, J., Buhl, H.U., Fridgen, G., Keller, R.: Recent developments in blockchain technology and their impact on energy. CoRR, vol. abs/2102.07886 (2021)
8. Sguanci, C., Spatafora, R., Vergani, A.M.: Layer 2 blockchain scaling: a survey. arXiv preprint arXiv:2107.10881 (2021)
9. Dannen, C.: Introducing Ethereum and solidity. Apress, Berkeley (2017)
10. Lee, W.-M.: Using the web3.js APIs. Apress, Berkeley, CA (2019)
11. Mohanty, D.: Frameworks: Truffle and Embark, Apress. CA, Berkeley (2018)
12. Buterin, V.: Why I think EIP 1559 block variance is nothing to worry about. Ethereum.org (2021). https://notes.ethereum.org/@vbuterin/eip_1559_spikes

Towards a Secure Cross-Blockchain Smart Contract Architecture

Rawya Mars[1](✉)[iD], Saoussen Cheikhrouhou[1,2][iD], Slim Kallel[1,2][iD], Mohamed Sellami[3][iD], and Ahmed Hadj Kacem[1,2][iD]

[1] ReDCAD, ENIS, University of Sfax, Sfax, Tunisia
{rawya.mars,saoussen.cheikhrouhou,slim.kallel,ahmed.kacem}@redcad.tn
[2] Digital Research Center of Sfax, Sfax, Tunisia
[3] SAMOVAR, Télécom SudParis, Institut Polytechnique de Paris, 91120 Palaiseau, France
mohamed.sellami@telecom-sudparis.eu

Abstract. With the speed rise of heterogeneous Blockchain (BC) platforms, interoperability became a critical area of research barrer for a variety of use cases, ranging from supply chain to healthcare. Consequently, a number of BC interoperability solutions were proposed to overcome these issues. One of these is Bifröst, a notary-based BC interoperability Application Programming Interface (API) which enables users or existing applications to interact seamlessly with multiple BCs. An early prototype of Bifröst was built, which proved its feasibility, nonetheless, it failed to allow interactions with Smart Contracts (SCs) across BCs. In this context, we present in this paper an extension of Bifröst architecture enabling secure cross-BC SCs using the Trusted Execution Environment (TEE). The proposed architecture is also fault tolerant by means of a logging module that facilitates the recovery of partially completed transactions in case of a crash.

Keywords: Blockchain (BC) · Interoperability · Smart Contract (SC) · Security · Fault tolerance

1 Introduction

Due to need of different BC capabilities, new independently and heterogeneous technologies, such as Corda [2], Quorum [1], and Hyperledger Fabric [4], were proposed. While these emerging BCs have the ability to satisfy the changing needs of users, they are unable to interact together.

In this regard, BC interoperability has become a highly active research area, although, until today, the tangible progress has been quite slow. In recent years, there have been proposed solutions [5–10,12,13] in order to support BC interoperability through the adoption of centralized intermediaries like notary schemes, decentralized sidechains with non-trivial scalability, and hash-lock schemes dedicated only to the cryptocurrency exchange. Nevertheless, such solutions, BC interoperability remains an unresolved challenge, primarily because (i) the invocation

S. Kallel et al. (Eds.): CRiSIS 2022, LNCS 13857, pp. 127–132, 2023.
https://doi.org/10.1007/978-3-031-31108-6_10

of cross-BC SCs, (ii) fault tolerance in the face of potential crashes, and (iii) security guarantees, such as access control, integrity, identification and authentication, in such approaches have not been properly studied and addressed.

In line with these works, we refer to Bifröst [12], a notary-based BC interoperability API. It permits users to interact with multiple BCs by abstracting the supporting BC's underlying implementation. Yet, there remain certain facets that can still be further improved, which motivates this work. In particular, the invocation of inter-BC SCs, security, and fault tolerance against potential crashes are not addressed. To address these issues, this paper presents an extension of Bifröst architecture.

The rest of this paper is structured as follows. In Sect. 2, we briefly introduce the concept behind BC interoperability. In Sect. 3, a summary of related work is provided. Section 4 gives a brief overview of the fundamentals of Bifröst. In Sect. 5, we detail the proposed architecture. Section 6 outlines the discussion and challenges. Finally, Sect. 7 concludes with suggestions for future directions.

2   Background and Related Work

Interoperability refers to allow two BCs a way to communicate with one another, with the capability of sharing, accessing, and exchanging information across BCs without the need for any intermediate, such as a centralized authority. Buterin [3] identifies three major approaches towards BC interoperability, such as notary schemes, sidechains, Hash-locking. In this paper, the hash locking is inadequate to achieve the portability of an asset in the form of SCs. Also, the principal difference between sidechains and notary schemes consists in their trust model. For the first, sidechains should not enable failure or allow "51% attacks" to occur in sidechains, while most notaries should behave honestly.

Liu et al. [9] present HyperService, a platform for developing decentralized applications across public heterogeneous BCs, for SCs invocation. Specifically, the authors provide a unified model and a high-level language for describing and programming decentralized applications along with a cryptographic protocol, to invoke the SCs across BCs. The results of the evaluation indicated that HyperService is efficient with respect to latency and scalability. Nevertheless, this approach lacks privacy and is vulnerable to front-running attacks since the data is exposed in the intermediate BC.

Fynn et al. [5] adopt a novel approach for interoperating across BCs, called Move operation, to migrate accounts and arbitrary computation across Ethereum virtual machine based chains. However, it requires that these two BCs should support the same execution environments (e.g., virtual machines).

Li et al. [8] presented a privacy-preserving interoperability BC framework called IvyCross, which addresses SCs across BCs. It proposes the use of two TEE-powered hosts in order to achieve a low-cost interoperability along with an extended optimistic concurrency control protocol to ensure correctness of cross-BC executions. However, this approach can fall under attack by an adversary, leading to a so-called single point of failure.

Nissl et al. [10] presented an approach to invoke SCs from other BCs. This approach relies on intermediaries to transfer information between source and target BCs and validators to approve and confirm the information transmitted by the intermediaries in order to finalize transactions.

In industry, two notable projects supporting BC interoperability are Cosmos [7] and Polkadot [13]. They both have in common the same concepts, such as the consensus engine to build BCs, as well as a mainchain (i.e., the Hub in Cosmos and RelayChain for Polkadot) to link individual BCs. Specifically, Cosmos requires the implementation of it consensus mechanism in all zones for ensuring BC consistency. While the intention is to incorporate existing BCs like Ethereum through specific adapter zones, there are no concrete details yet on how this might be achieved. Also, Polkadot protocol is only provided in the form of prototypes and has not been released yet, it is still in its infancy stages of development.

3   Bifröst Extension Proposal

Bifröst architecture consists of three main components: (i) the API which is the entry point of the interaction by exposing functions to the user, (ii) the adapters to convert the user input into a format conforming to the respective BC's required format, and (iii) databases to store the list of the supported BCs and users credentials [12]. Our main goal behind this extension is to provide a secure, error-handling cross-BC SC invocation. Thus, SC invocation, fault tolerance, and security are the requirements that are considered while extending the Bifröst API.

3.1   Smart Contracts Invocation

Lacking the ability to invoke cross-BC SCs, inter-chain transactions involving SCs are unavailable. Consequently, there is an urgent need for an approach that enables: (i) to compose and execute cross-BC SC transactions, and (ii) to formulate and execute nested transactions consisting of SCs. As such, the Bifröst API should be modified to allow calling SCs on a different BC with variables parameters and return values. In actual cross-BC communication, the proposed approach is based on a set of intermediary nodes, which are used to manage communications, as BCs are not natively allowed to communicate with each other [3]. Thus, the call requests and responses will be translated into dedicated BC transactions and the intermediary nodes will simply execute these transactions in the relevant BCs. Before forwarding the call request to the target BC, the RPCServer should verify whether the request is indeed valid. Likewise, the adapter in turn should verify that the given response is valid (i.e., that the respective transaction is included and confirmed on BC B).

3.2   Fault Tolerance

When performing transactions between BCs, the API must have an appropriate level of resiliency and fault tolerance against potential failures. It is especially important to consider the possibility of crashes to ensure the consistency of transactions between BCs. As such, fault handling and crash recovery are required in order to enhance resiliency, prevent failures, and maintain functioning applications. In particular, by designing a crash recovery solution to deal with API interruptions, it ensures that the source and target BCs are modified in a consistent manner, meaning that transactions from the source BC are persisted in the target BC, hence no double spending can occur. This problem could be solved incorporating a transaction logging module to monitor events and trace the source of the error, as shown in Fig. 1. A transaction log, known also as journal, is a record file which contains transaction details, such as content, type and time, among users of systems. Moreover, logs can be used to record and report on events of interest, e.g., debug, error, etc. A transaction log plays an important part in the recovery of both database servers and cryptocurrency based protocols, such as BC. In case of an eventual failure in system, the transaction logs serve to restore a consistent state of the database.

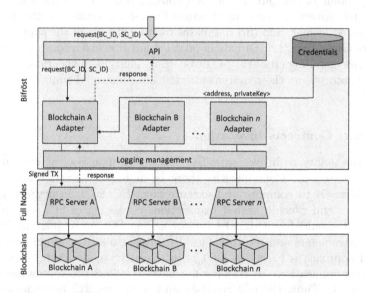

Fig. 1. The architecture of the proposed approach

3.3   Security

As previously stated, Bifröst approach has some limitations as they could be compromised through, for example, providing malicious data, hence decreasing the amount of trust requirements could improve the security of the overall infrastructure. As a result, securing the complete interoperability operations using TEE would eliminate completely the need to trust third parties. The TEE provides an execution environment guaranteeing that all code and data internally stored and executed are protected against potential external, malicious and unauthorized manipulation. The code executed inside a TEE is encrypted and cannot be accessed, not even by the underlying platform, thereby providing privacy. TEE [11] constructs an isolated execution environment enabling hardware protections on both code and data to enforce confidentiality and integrity (Fig. 2).

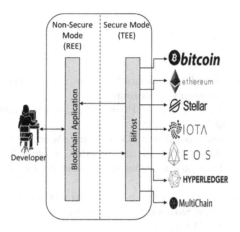

Fig. 2. Securing the interactions of the proposed approach

4   Discussion and Challenges

The proposed approach in this paper is mainly designed to enable interaction between cross-BC SCs with Bifröst. Specifically, this proposal is intended not only to facilitate SC invocations using Bifröst, but also to ensure security and fault tolerance. With the original characteristics of this approach, mainly flexibility, modularity and ease of use, empowering it with TEE enables an interoperability solution with greater security and efficiency. In particular, the remote attestations are prominent, as provable access to the internal state to external parties is a critical feature. Similarly, adding a transaction logging module could help ensure automatic recovery of partially completed transactions. Some challenges, such as data privacy, security, standardisation and decentralisation, are identified.

5   Conclusion and Future Work

In this paper, we aim at developing an extended architecture, for invoking SCs across BCs in secure and fault tolerant manner, of Bifröst, a notary scheme-based BC interoperability API. It allows the transparent interaction of users and applications with multiple BCs. This proposed approach is now in the process of implementation. We leverage the use of TEE to secure SCs invocation across different BCs. Further, we suggest including a logging module to manage the process of logging API events, which allows to check errors and determine what server it came from. Such module maintains logs, thus enabling resuming partially completed transfers, allowing automatic recovery in case of a crash. In future work, we aim to (i) deeply evaluate the efficiency of the proposed extension, such as cost evaluation and security analysis (ii) investigate further recovery and error-handling mechanisms, and (iii) develop a decentralized version of the proposed approach.

References

1. Quorum: A permissioned implementation of ethereum supporting data privacy. https://github.com/ConsenSys/quorum
2. Brown, R.G., Carlyle, J., Grigg, I., Hearn, M.: Corda: an introduction. R3 CEV, August 1(15), 14 (2016)
3. Buterin, V.: Chain interoperability. R3 Research Paper 9 (2016)
4. Cachin, C., et al.: Architecture of the hyperledger blockchain fabric. In: Workshop on Distributed Cryptocurrencies and Consensus Ledgers. vol. 310, pp. 1–4. Chicago, IL (2016)
5. Fynn, E., Bessani, A., Pedone, F.: Smart contracts on the move. In: 2020 50th Annual IEEE/IFIP International Conference on Dependable Systems and Networks (DSN), pp. 233–244. IEEE (2020)
6. Jin, H., Dai, X., Xiao, J.: Towards a novel architecture for enabling interoperability amongst multiple blockchains. In: 2018 IEEE 38th International Conference on Distributed Computing Systems (ICDCS), pp. 1203–1211. IEEE (2018)
7. Kwon, J., Buchman, E.: Cosmos: A network of distributed ledgers. https://cosmos.network/whitepaper (2016)
8. Li, M., et al.: IvyCross: a privacy-preserving and concurrency control framework for blockchain interoperability. Cryptology ePrint Archive (2021)
9. Liu, Z., et al.: HyperService: interoperability and programmability across heterogeneous blockchains. In: Proceedings of the 2019 ACM SIGSAC Conference on Computer and Communications Security, pp. 549–566 (2019)
10. Nissl, M., Sallinger, E., Schulte, S., Borkowski, M.: Towards cross-blockchain smart contracts. In: 2021 IEEE International Conference on Decentralized Applications and Infrastructures (DAPPS), pp. 85–94. IEEE (2021)
11. Sabt, M., Achemlal, M., Bouabdallah, A.: Trusted execution environment: what it is, and what it is not. In: 2015 IEEE Trustcom/BigDataSE/ISPA. vol. 1, pp. 57–64. IEEE (2015)
12. Scheid, E.J., Hegnauer, T., Rodrigues, B., Stiller, B.: Bifröst: a modular blockchain interoperability API. In: 2019 IEEE 44th Conference on Local Computer Networks (LCN), pp. 332–339. IEEE (2019)
13. Wood, G.: Polkadot: vision for a heterogeneous multi-chain framework. White Paper 21, 2327–4662 (2016)

Security Analysis: From Model to System Analysis

Bastien Drouot[(✉)], Valery Monthe[(✉)], Sylvain Guérin, and Joel Champeau[(✉)]

Lab STICC, ENSTA Bretagne, Brest, France
{bastien.drouot,valery.monthe,sylvain.guerin,
joel.champeau}@ensta-bretagne.fr

Abstract. There is a wide range of security solutions on cyber-physical systems, most aimed at preventing an adversary from gaining access to the system. However, to make a cyber-physical system more resilient and discover possible attack scenarios, it is necessary to analyze systems by taking into account their interactions with their environment. Standard formal analysis approaches are based on a model of the system. From a quantitative and qualitative point of view, the results of these analyzes depends on the model abstraction relative to the system. Usually, property verification is performed with formulas expressed in specific logics such as LTL or CTL. One of the problems is the semantic gap between textual requirements and these formalisms. In a security context, attacker interests are also necessary to take into account in the properties expression, in addition to system requirements.

In this article we propose an approach allowing to analyze a real cyber-physical system while taking into account the interests of an attacker and while reducing the semantic gap between the textual requirements and logic formulas. The proposed methodology relies on the property specification patterns and the specification of an interface related to the state of the deployed embedded software. The motivating example used in this article comes from an industrial partner included in a collaborative project.

Keywords: Cyber-Security · Modeling · Formal Methods · Model-Checking · Property Specification · Case Study

1 Introduction

Security of Cyber Physical Systems is a real challenge especially for communicating ones. To improve the security of these systems at design time, formal methods can be used to provide analysis support at behavioral level. This technique is based on the use of formal models which provide system abstraction to mainly focus on the communicating system behavior [3]. To apply efficiently the formal methods, the analyses lead to verify properties regarding the system models. One of the challenges of the approach is to formalize properties from requirements expressions which are mainly textual with a dedicated text structure in the best case.

In a security context, formal properties are not only derived from requirements but must also integrate the potential interests of attackers. These interests provide objectives to the analysis on the system, and include the behavior of attackers interacting with the system. The security property expression is mainly based on temporal logics to take into account propositions which integrate time. In many cases, the expression of these security properties remains an issue for domain experts without experience on formal methods.

So one of our goal is to bridge the gap between the textual security requirements and the formal properties to help the domain expert to conduct an analysis on their system.

Another main drawback of formal methods is the use of models for the system under study. Models are powerful to take into account a dedicated viewpoint of the system and the abstraction relative to this viewpoint provides an efficient focus for the issue to address. In a previous step, we have demonstrated that the formal methods can be applied successfully on our reference system with a full MBSE approach [11]. This previous experiment also allowed us to analyze our results and identify research opportunities. Indeed for embedded systems, application behavior is often dependent on the deployment of the software component on the embedded target. Therefore, models allow analysis but they are not always sufficient to completely guarantee the behavior of the deployed software, especially to know if the system is resilient to attacks.

To avoid the system model drawback, we suggest a methodology based on the analysis of the embedded software code. However the models remain relevant to model the environment. The methodology we propose here is a heterogeneous approach with models for environment specification and the embedded software itself. The base of our approach is the OBP model checker which provides the capacity to take into account heterogeneous formalisms [2,10].

The rest of the paper is organized as follows. In Sect. 2, we present the works on which we base our approach, including the property specification patterns and OBP model checker. In Sect. 3, we introduce the Car Reservation System (CRS), the case study used throughout this paper to illustrate our approach. After that we describe the shared API between system and environment and used to catch the state of the deployed embedded software in Sect. 4. In Sect. 5 we present our implementation of the property specification patterns taking into account the interests of the attacker in security properties. In Sect. 6 we analyse our results and share the lessons learned on our methodology. And we conclude in Sect. 8.

2   Background

2.1   Previous MBSE Approach

In an initial phase, we applied a full MBSE approach [11] on our motivating example based on UPPAAL formal models to perform a methodology on qualitative risk analysis. The goal of our methodology is to identify the risks which are not elicited during the functional analysis and test phases. Based on this experiment, we have identified several key aspects on our methodology: 1) Environment models provide an efficient way to specify the behavior of external entities constraining system behavior. These models define an execution context for the system related to use case scenarios identified by the system designer. 2) Based on models of the system and the environment, we can define security properties to identify risks on system components or behaviors, i.e. an action sequence. The scenarios violating the security properties are possible attacks on the system. 3) The gain obtained with LTL properties is to be put in perspective relatively to the difficulty to express these properties. In fact, these LTL expressions are far from textual requirements. 4) A full MBSE approach is powerful at specification or design time but models remain an issue to take into account the embedded system code. In practice, deployed software is rarely fully derived (generated) from the analyzed model, and contains a significant amount of manual code.

Lessons learned at the end of these first experiments reveal two major issues : 1) how to bridge the gap between the requirements or attacker interests which are informally described and a formal formalism, and 2) how to take into account the real embedded system software in a formal verification approach for security analysis.

2.2   Property Specification Patterns

The purpose of verification is to make sure that a system meets its requirements. A requirement can be simply defined as an expectation or constraint that a service, product or system must satisfy. The property is obtained by describing this expectation or constraint in a formal language, i.e. in the form of a logical formula to be verified. There are several temporal logics that can be used to specify properties: LTL, CTL, TCTL, TLA, TLA+, etc.

Let's take an example: Consider the following requirement: *"the end of task A leads to the end of task B"*. To express this requirement in temporal logic, we must first define atomic propositions, which are predicates whose evaluation result is a boolean. The corresponding logic formula can be written in the chosen temporal logic, such as:

$$P : task\ A\ is\ ended.\quad S : task\quad B\ is\ ended.;\quad CTL : AG\,(\,P \to AF\,(S\,))\quad (1)$$

We can have even more complex formulas. For example, with the requirement: *"After event Q until the arrival of event R, the end of task A leads to the end of task B."*; we would have the following formulas in the CTL logic.

$$CTL : AG(Q \to !E[!R\,U\,(P\,\&!R\,\&\,(E[!S\,U\,R]\,|\,EG(!S\,\&\,!R)))])\qquad (2)$$

We may notice on this example that formulas in temporal logics can be very complex and quickly become incomprehensible to domain experts.

Property specification patterns allow domain specialists to write formal specifications that can be used for model checking. One of the best-known specification models are Dwyer's patterns [6,8]. Dwyer et al. [7] developed a pattern system for property specification. These patterns allow people who are not experts in temporal logic to read and write formal specifications. They are divided in two major groups: order and occurrence. Each pattern has an associated scope, which represents the context in which the property must hold. With Dwyer's patterns, the formulas of Eqs. 1 and 2 are written respectively:

$$Globaly\ S\ Responds\ to\ P \quad (3) \qquad After\ Q\ Until\ R\ (S\ Responds\ to\ P) \quad (4)$$

We thus obtain in Eqs. 3 and 4 logical expressions that are much easier to understand by domain specialists.

2.3 OBP Model Checker

Heim et al. [10] address the state space explosion problem observed in the verification of industrial asynchronous systems. To meet this challenge, they proposed a new approach based on the specification of the context (the environment of the system) and an observation engine called OBP (Observer Based Prover). They start from the idea that, given a property to verify, one does not need to explore all the possible configurations of the complete system. Among all the possible behaviors of the system, a tiny part is sufficiently representative for the property to be verified. Thus, specifying a relevant environment (a context) makes it possible to restrict the behavior of the system to the only parts where the property deserves to be checked.

The OBP model checker is also used coupled with a language interpreter to provide verification and monitoring on embedded models [2]. This capacity is based on a language interface definition between the interpreter and the model checker and also the verification of formal properties on exhaustive exploration of the embedded models. We intensively use these potentialities in our methodology.

3 Motivating Example

This section introduces the case study used throughout this paper to illustrate our approach. The Car Reservation System (CRS) has been designed for a companies with a large car fleet. The CRS system presented in this article is an abstraction of a study system, coming from a collaborative project between companies and research institutions.

3.1 System Presentation

The global context of the system under study is presented by the Fig. 1. This figure aims to highlight the key component, the embedded system, deployed in its environment that includes malicious persons. This critical part of the system is implemented in an embedded software on a dedicated hardware in the car. This software controls the access to the car and takes into account interactions with the user and the IT server part of the CRS system. The embedded software is the main focus of our attention for a security evaluation due to a risk analysis conduct previously [11]. During this analysis, we applied a top-down MBSE methodology based on system specification study. In this context, we have designed a specification formal model to analyze the behavior of the system with regard to the security properties obtained after the risk analysis.

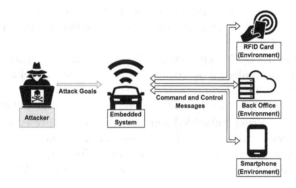

Fig. 1. System Architecture

In this system, each user has an ID stored in a RFID card or in a mobile application. The server or back office is a web server that is used by users to book a vehicle on dedicated day and hours. After a validation, this booking is communicated to the embedded system as a tuple booking ID and user ID. Then, a car session can start. The user can unlock the car, uses it and if necessary temporarily stops using it. The session can resume later or stop if a "stop_booking" request is received. Until the session is not ended, the user can unlock and lock the car again several times to continue the session.

The embedded system interacts with one component at a time, either the server or the ID badge or mobile application. This communication is supported by messages and embedded software process messages in a FIFO mode with a run to completion semantics. A message is dequeued from the FIFO and the effect of this message is executed before any next message consumption.

The server, the mobile and the badge are connected to the embedded system through many technologies and protocols. The system then inherits all the vulnerabilities and weaknesses of these technologies. Our purpose is not target vulnerabilities at this level but malicious persons can exploit them to access or trick the embedded system and potentially change the nominal behavior at application level of the system.

When applying the methodology discussed in the next sections, an interesting goal on our system under study would be, for example, to identify a car unlock situation after session end. The feared events would be that the attacker might want to keep the car locked or unlocked according to the desired outcome.

3.2 General Approach

In our MBSE approach applied previously, we modeled the system under study and the environment entities interacting with the system. This approach is particularly relevant to take into account specific behaviors in the environment notably the attacker one.

One of the issues of this approach is the system model creation. In fact, this model is obviously an abstraction of the system and this model are usually build manually by the system designer.

In this context, in order to increase confidence in embedded software, we aim to consider the real embedded source code. But to preserve flexibility and to formalize several environment hypothesis, we keep the environment models including relevant the entities and attacker model. Figure 2 schematizes our approach grouped into 4 parts, to aim differences with classical MBSE approaches:

1. First part focuses on creating properties to verify. In our cybersecurity context, the formal properties are necessarily based on the attacker interests, in addition to the system requirements. To facilitate the property expression, we use a first level, "Abstract Formalized Properties", to reduce the gap with textual requirements and to be adapted to several temporal logic. In this approach, the attacker succeeds in his attack if a security property is violated (for example by stealing an unlocked vehicle after the end of a reservation). This part is detailed in Sect. 5.
2. The second part focuses on modeling the environment. Against standard approaches based on modeling all the external entities, we take into account the attacker's behavior through a malicious model. This model can define several attacker behaviors like a man in the middle attack, providing a capacity to perform any actions on the system. This environment modeling is detailed in Sect. 4.1.

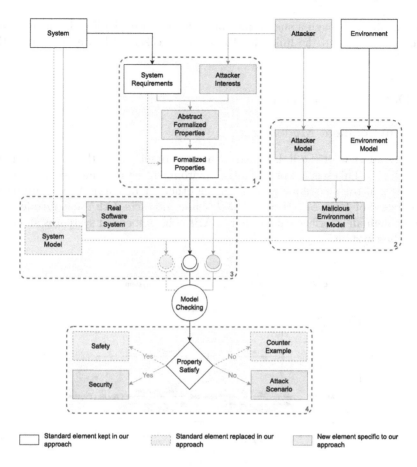

Fig. 2. General Approach

3. The third part focuses on the representation of the system. Unlike the MBSE standard approach (represented in dotted lines in Fig. 2), we suggest an alternative approach having the particularity of directly using the real system code instead of a model. We illustrate our approach in Sect. 4.3 to detail the unavoidable system interface to specify and implement interactions with this system.

4. The last part focuses on property verification. In our approach we define security properties built while taking into account the malicious aspect of the attacker. The objective, for the attacker, Objective of the attacker is here to violate properties to make the system less secure. We give feedback on security property verification in Sect. 6.

So, the main focus of this paper is to define an analysis framework based on several models, in FIACRE language for the environment and a C program for the embedded source code. The interactions between these two parts are defined and controlled through a shared interface, described in the Fig. 3. The contents of this interface and the link with the model checker OBP are detailed in the next section.

4   Detailed Approach

4.1   Environment Modeling

The general view of the link between the environment and the system is illustrated Fig. 3. This schema presents the environment on one side (left part of the schema) and the embedded system on the other (right part). The environment is composed of *User*, *Server* and *Attacker* and interacts with the embedded system through an interface called Shared API. The embedded system is shown as a gray box system.

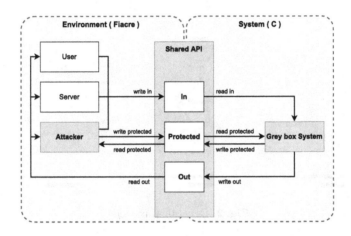

Fig. 3. View on the link between environment and system

This environment written in Fiacre models the behavior of elements interacting with the embedded system. We identify three entity types:

– *User*: These model includes all the interactions that user has with the embedded system, such as: pressing a button, passing an access card, interacting with levers but also losing of GPS or GSM connection. The user interacts and produces only inputs to the system. These inputs are integrated in the "In" part of the shared API.

- *Server*: These models represent interactions with one or more servers communicating with the embedded system. Servers produce only input data for the system, and in some cases a server can take control of some system functionalities bypassing some security rules.
- *Attacker*: In order to represent an attack on the system as accurately as possible, we propose a dedicated model to represent the actions of an attacker. We take as hypothesis that attacker can perform any action on the system and at any time. The goal is to take into account every behavior, even unknown ones. These interactions are translated into accesses that can modify input data in the system ("In" part of the shared API) and also read information from the system ("Out" part of the shared API). As shown in the Fig. 3, we also provide the ability for the attacker to directly modify the internal data of the embedded system (contained here in the "Protected" part of the shared API). This behavior represents a direct and strong attack (rather low level) on the embedded system (memory dump, eavesdropping, sensor manipulation, etc.).

The models of the environment offer several interesting capacities relatively to the security context. First, the power of models provide a quality abstraction to start with a high level of abstraction and after, iteratively adding details into environment models to take into account more complex behaviors. This iterative approach is driven by analyzes that we want to apply on both environment and system, more precisely, according to the properties that come from requirements or attacker interests.

We can also note that modeling the environment provides the possibility, for example, to define several attacker behavior relative to the attacker skills. These skills modify the attacker behavior and specialize its behavior on some scenarios. Several attack contexts can be conceived, evaluated and capitalized through the use of models.

Once the environment has been modeled, we must define how it could behave on the system under study. To act to the system and catch its reaction, we specify a system state API in order to define the interface between environment and system.

4.2 System State and Behavior

The specification of the system state API is based on the definition of variables, encoding the global state of the transition function. This function defines the evolution of the system at each execution step to take into account change of the interface values.

```
 1  // Structure IN
 2  typedef struct{
 3    carRequest        request;
 4    carsharingSource  originOfRequest ;
    ...

16  // Structure OUT
17  typedef struct{
    ...

22  // Structure Protected
23  typedef struct{
24    bool    isApcON;
25    bool    isDoorsLocked;
26    bool    isImmobilizerEnabled;
27    uint8_t currentBooking;
28  } struct_protected;

30  // Shared API
31  typedef struct{
32    struct_in        in;
33    struct_out       out;
34    struct_protected protected;
35  }

37  // System function
38  int fct_run(shared_struct*);
39
```

```
 1  // Structure IN
 2  type fstrut_in is record
 3    request_F        : nat,
 4    originOfRequest_F  : nat,
    ...

15  // Structure OUT
16  type fstrut_out is record
    ...

21  // Structure Protected
22  type fstrut_protected is record
23    isApcON_F                : bool,
24    isDoorsLocked_F          : bool,
25    isImmobilizerEnabled_F   : bool,
26    currentbooking           : nat
27  end record

29  // Shared API
30  type fstrut is record
31    c_in        : fstrut_in,
32    c_out       : fstrut_out,
33    c_protected : fstrut_protected
34  end record

36  // External function
37  extern runSystem (read write fstrut)
       : int is "fct_run"
```

(a) C Source Code   (b) Fiacre Code

Fig. 4. Code of the shared API in C (a) and Fiacre (b)

So, the definition of the system is based on two parts:

– *The interface state definition* : This interface includes all the variables representing the global state of the system program. This interface is shared between the system implementation and the environment models. The interface is implemented on both sides through a C structure including standard C types (Fig. 4a), and a Fiacre representation (Fig. 4b). For example, for each external request the car receives a message implemented as an enumeration name "*carRequest*" in listing 4a line 3, and as a natural in listing 4b line 3. Even internal system variables are included in the interface. Indeed they are necessary to represent the global state of the system and can, in some cases, be modified outside the system. For example, the variable *currentBooking*, line 27 in the listing 4a and line 26 in the listing 4b, encodes the ID of the current reservation. If the value of the *currentBooking* variable is zero, it means that no booking is currently running in the vehicle. An attacker could, during an attack, modify this variable in order to harm the system (vehicle theft, cancel the reservation in progress, etc.) This two representations (listing 4a and listing 4b) implement the share interface between the environment and the embedded system.

– *The system function*: The system is viewed as a function with side effects on the shared API and the environment. This function is like a thread function implementation to execute the behavior of the system, see the declaration of the function line 38 of listing 4a. The environment calls this function as external function, see the declaration line 37 of listing 4b. The function interprets messages from the environment, processes the result relative to the current message through the completion of the resulting action, and finally gives back the result to the environment.

With these two software components, the shared API and the system function, we define an abstract transition system with its transition function which processes the system state. This system state is observable and updated from the environment to provide communication facilities and property evaluation. The properties which come from requirements and attacker interests are evaluated on the system state, based on variable values, and also through several transitions to obtain evaluation of temporal properties.

4.3   The OBP Model Checker

In our framework, the key component to explore all the behavior on the composition of the real system code and environment models, is the OBP model checker. In a standard model checking approach, the system and the environment are modeled like we did in a first step of our methodology [11]. Some approaches emphasize the use of model checking on real software code to help the emergence of errors during sequence of events occurrence [13]. In our approach, we want to highlight two salient points:

– We explore heterogeneous execution states constituted from states of environment models including the attacker, and states of the software system, see the left part of the Fig. 5
– The model checking algorithms are decoupled from the language(s) used, which provides a language independent exploration capability. In our case, we built the Label Transition System (LTS) using exchanges between the model checker and the interpreters via the runtime controller as depicted in the Fig. 5. This controller queries interpreters on the model checker request.

To verify properties on these heterogeneous execution states, we apply a synchronous composition between these states and the interpretation of the properties that is defined as observer automata on the execution states. At each execution step, the automata observer progresses in its behavior if the requested event is observed.

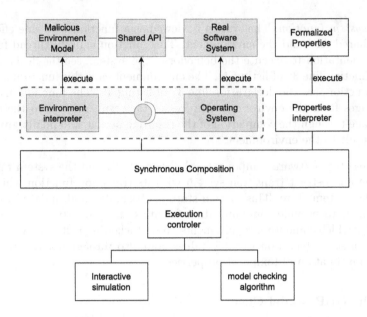

Fig. 5. Architecture of model checking

Based on this approach, properties are evaluated on the heterogeneous LTS composed of the embedded software part and environment model state. So properties take into account the software behavior dived in a malicious environment context. The exhaustive exploration providing by the model checking algorithms gives all the possible scenarios relative to a no limit attacker behavior, defined in the models.

Now the problem remains to define the properties relative to the objectives that we want to obtain during our analyses. Particularly regarding if we are able to translate the attacker interests in relevant property definitions. The goal of the next section is to present our approach relative to property definition and formalisation.

5   Security Property Modelling

In our approach, system requirements and attacker interests are formalized to ensure a formal verification with OBP model checker. The verification is achieved with LTL formulas which are composed with the heterogeneous state from system and environment. One of the problem is the semantic distance between textual requirements and LTL formulas. Many approaches are based on structured text expressions to minimize this distance. One of the main problems is to enforce a strict and constrained format by requirement engineer.

5.1   Raising Abstraction Level of Formal Security Properties

In many cases, the need to formulate the requirements and attacker interests in a purely mathematical expressions creates a pragmatic barrier for requirement engineers to use these techniques. One way to reduce the impact of this barrier would be to bridge the gap between the unstructured textual requirements and mathematical formulas of properties.

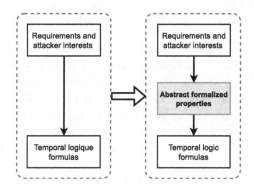

Fig. 6. Abstraction of formal properties from requirements and attacker interests.

Bridging this gap is an objective but the chosen approach must guarantee to obtain formal properties. We have therefore created an intermediate abstraction level using Dywer's patterns (the "Abstract formalized properties" in right part of the Fig. 6). This level facilitates requirement expression because no constrains are applied on the textual requirements. And also ensures the independence from mathematical formalism of formal properties. In our case, the bridge between the textual form of the requirements and Dywer's pattern is achieved manually, to avoid constrains for requirement engineer.

The next section presents in details the security requirements next to attacker interests and their translation into LTL formal logic, through the intermediate step of the Dywer's patterns.

5.2   From Attacker Interests to Formal Security Properties

The risk analysis provides critical elements or potential attacker goals that we must take into account in the security analysis. One of the challenges is therefore to obtain formal properties regarding these attacker interests. As mentioned above, to support this step we use Dywer's patterns to create a link between the conceptual attacker goals and the LTL formulas that are evaluated on the system.

In the following, for each security requirements to be checked we write a sentence closed to the property goal to give the property intention, after we have identified the logic predicates derived from it and we use these predicates to specify the security property using Dwyer's patterns. Finally the LTL properties are derived. The security constraints having been formalized into expressions using Dwyer's patterns, the second step involves translating these expressions into formal properties in a temporal logic. Table 1 summarizes the specifications of the properties expressed using Dwyer's patterns and gives the corresponding Temporal Logic formulas in LTL.

Table 1. mapping between analysed security requirements, properties specification in Dwyer patterns and their corresponding CTL formulas.

R1	::	When ending a session in the Back Office the car should be locked
proposition	::	*P : (BackOffice.booking.isEnding) ∧ (System.car.unlocked)*
Dwyer	::	*Globaly Absence (P)*
CTL property	::	*A [] not (BackOffice.booking.isEnding and System.car.unlocked)*
R2	::	If the user is driving the car, the state of the booking should not be consider as locked in the BackOffice
proposition	::	*P : (System.session.isRunning) ∧ (BackOffice.car.isLocked)*
Dwyer	::	*Globaly Absence (P)*
CTL property	::	*A[] not ((System.start_ session or System.continue_ session) and BackOffice.car_ locked*
R3	::	Once the car is unlocked, at some point in the future, the car should be unbooked and the car can be booked again with correct parameters
proposition	::	*P : !System.car.isLocked ⇒ System.isIdle*
Dwyer	::	*Globaly Universality (P)*
CTL property	::	*A[] (System.car.unlocked ⇒ System.idle)*

Each block of the Table 1 has 4 elements:

1. *Ri*: describes the intention of the business security requirements to be respected and therefore to be verified on the system code;
2. *Proposition (P)*: specifies the requirement Ri in an atomic proposition, i.e. whose value is either true or false. This proposition is formulated using predicates;
3. *Dwyer*: the specification of the property P to check using Dwyer patterns;
4. *CTL property*: the translation of this property P into an CTL formula.

Considering line 1 of Table 1, the need as expressed by the domain expert is as follows: "A session that ends on the backoffice management application requires the vehicle to be locked.". An analysis of this need makes it possible to formulate the security requirement as follows: "*R1: When ending a session in the Back Office the car should be locked*". From this requirement, it is necessary to specify the property to verify and the way to verify it. This requires using a more formal notation, so we use Dwyer's patterns. To do this, a constraint to be checked must be defined. This is expressed in the form of an atomic proposition, that is to say a sentence with a Boolean value (true or false), and is written using predicates.

From R1, we therefore define 2 predicates: *S: System.car.unlocked* (the system detects that the car is locked) and *B: BackOffice.booking.isEnding* (the state of the reservation is at "isEnding" in the Back Office). We would not like to have the situation in which the car is unlocked and the reservation in the Back Office is over. So the situation to avoid during the execution of the system is *S AND B*, hence the proposition *P: S AND B*. Then we choose the right Dwyer pattern that corresponds to this situation: it is the *"Absence"* pattern. This allows us to write *Globaly Absence (P)*. Globaly is the scope and means that the Absence pattern must apply on P during the entire execution of the system. Finally we can deduce the property expressed in the temporal logic CTL. In this formula, *"A"* means for all execution paths and *"[]"* means during the whole execution. So the property *A [] P* with *P= not (BackOffice.booking.isEnding and System.car.unlocked)*, evaluates to true if and only if any reachable state satisfies P.

6   Property Verification Results Analysis

In this paper, we present and test a methodology based on formal property description applied on the real embedded system. In this section, we present the lessons learned after adapting the MBSE formal verification methodology by integrating the real embedded system.

6.1   Model Checking Embedded System Code

While integrating the embedded software code in our methodology, we have identified two main advantages relative to the use of the formal model checking techniques.

- First of all, the use of an agnostic model checker provides the possibility to analyze a composition of heterogeneous languages. In our case we have environment models in FIACRE language and system state of the embedded code. For the communication between these two languages, we must specify a shared API to take into account the system state accessible by the environment. So the entities like sensors or actuators are modeled through environment entities and interact with the system via the shared API. This shared API is also the base for security property proposition evaluations. And again, due the use of this model checker, these properties are based on heterogeneous entities (system and environment) and are applied on the composition of heterogeneous languages. One of the advantages for the security properties is to explore extended behavior for the attacker entity.
- Secondly, the major drawback of the previous MBSE approach is the semantic distance between the embedded code and the system model. In our case, the model was created manually so this distance could be reduced if we had a generation step from model to source code. But in embedded context, the source code necessarily integrates specific platform features like OS, or devices API.

And in a security perspective, many vulnerabilities are coming out while on this platform deployment. So identifying the vulnerabilities at code level is more relevant instead of model level. This experiment implementing approach where the real source code is integrated in the formal verification demonstrates that the debugging phase is improved and the confidence in the developed software is increased. In our case, due to the exhaustive exploration we found that a man in middle attack leads to the system in a case where the door's car remains open after the end of a session. The attacker reaches its goal, the car can be robbed without any obstacle. Our approach based on formal exhaustive exploration provides a one step beyond on debugging phase for embedded software.

Our experiment uses industrial embedded code with all the application functionalities. In order to focus our approach on the application behavior, we have withdrew communication protocols to avoid platform complexity that has no impact on the application behavior. Indeed, all the communications are interpreted as messages received and sent by the application device communication.

6.2 Security Property Verification

Just before focusing on the property verification results, we analyze the semantics of these properties regarding the security perspectives. Indeed, the formulas obtained from the Dwyer's expressions have different meanings relative to the adopted viewpoint. As previously described, the formulas are based on predicates which contain expressions including the system states, in the sense that variable values translating the memory state of the program. A variable can also represent an attractive resource for an attacker like an open door to rob the car, for example.

Table 2. Security Property Modeling.

	System Perspective (+)	Attacker Perspective (-)
Property Successful (+)	Threat causes no risk (+)	Threat causes risk(-)
Property Failed (-)	Threat causes risk(-)	Threat causes no risk (+)

In this context, two viewpoints are considered to analyze property results, like shown in the Table 2. From the designer or system perspective, a successful property means that no risk leads to it. So the system is resilient to the risk expressed by the property. However, if the property verification fails, the system is faulty, or the attack issued was successful in changing the original behavior of the system and thus reached its goal.

Another way to consider the properties is to assume the attacker's perspective. From this point of view, properties ensure that the goals of the attack or risks are reached. So in contrary to the system perspective, a successful verification shows that the system is faulty in the sense that the attack has successfully reached its goals of altering the system's behavior. This means that the system is sensitive to the considered risk, introduced by the attack. In contrast, the failed verification implies that the attack was unsuccessful, and the system is resilient to the attack goal described by the property. Thus, there is no risk caused by this threat. Indeed if the expression of the predicate contains a state of the system favorable to the attacker like for example "the car remains open at the end of a session", the evaluation of this property to true confirms the attacker in these possibilities but does not provide to him an attack scenario. On the other hand, if the negation of this property fails, a counter example is provided by the model checker and represents an attack scenario for the threat.

Therefore, in a context of system security analysis, the expression of properties and their evaluation are elements to put in perspective according to the adopted viewpoints and also according to the objective of the user of verification formalism, designer or attacker. For example, the property R1 *"When ending a session in the Back Office the car should be locked"* of the previous section illustrates this viewpoint perspective in the sense that we adopt the attacker viewpoint and try to find an attack scenario on our system. The proposition *"P : BackOffice.booking.isEnding $\wedge$ System.car.unlocked"* defines the stable state of the system, but the negation of this proposition expresses that we are looking for a system vulnerability and we hope to find a scenario to reach the attacker goal. Note that the Dwyer expression *"Globaly Absence (P)"* is readable and enough expressive to consider the absence of the predicate in all the futures for all the execution paths.

The evaluation of this property provides a counter example by the model checker based on a transition system with 73 870 states and a path with 2 178 transitions, for the first reached counter example. This scenario is reduced to a 4 steps scenario after manual analysis. This scenario is really an attack scenario because in this case, the attacker has the capacity via *a man in middle* attack to send a *"The car is closed"* message to the back office, and so the back office will send a *"End session"* to the car although the car is really open.

With this example we can notice a limitation of our approach which is the interpretation of the model checker results. For now, this analysis is manually accomplished with the know how on the system and the possible threats. But in case of very long scenario, we should provide a dedicated tooling to support the human interpretation.

7   Related Works

Konrad et al. [12] propose a security model that can meet the development needs of secure systems. To maximize understandability, they use well-known notations such as Unified Modeling Language to represent structural and behavioral information. They modified several fields in the design template to convey more security-related information than the original template. Among these fields is the constraint field which was added in the spirit of the Dwyer pattern specification. Lamsweerde [14] offers a constructive approach to modelling, specifying and analyzing application-specific security requirements. His method is based on a goal-oriented framework to generate and resolve obstacles to goal satisfaction. The extended framework tackles malicious obstacles (called anti-objectives) put in place by attackers to threaten security objectives. Threat trees are built systematically by anti-objective refinement until leaf nodes are derived that are either software vulnerabilities observable by the attacker or anti-requirements implementable by that attacker.

Wong et al. [15] propose a model-based approach to express behavioral properties. They describe a PL property specification language for capturing a generalization of Dwyer's property specification models, and translating them into linear temporal logic. Corradini et al. [4] offer a complete chain of web tools that allows modeling, verification and exploitation of the results of BPMN processes. They rely on Dwyer patterns and implement some of these patterns (like the Response pattern) in their tools. Dadeau et al. [5] proposes a property and model-based testing approach using UML/OCL models, driven by temporal property models and a tool to help formalize temporal properties. The models are expressed in the TOCL language, an adaptation of Dwyer's property models to OCL and therefore independent of the underlying temporal logic.

AUtili et al. [1] proposes a comprehensive framework, combining qualitative, real-time and probabilistic property specification models. They rely on Dwyer's patterns to systematically discover new property specification models, which would be absent to cover the three aspects mentioned above. They also offer a natural language interface to map models to chosen temporal logic (LTL, CTL, MTL, TCTL, PLTL, etc.). Gruhn et al. [9] extend Dwyer's pattern system by time-related patterns, to take into account real-time aspects in properties.

Some of the work presented ([14,15]) has deal with the specification of security properties on systems. Others like [1] and [9], have proposed extensions of Dwyer's patterns for real time. The rest ([4,5,15]) provide approaches for using Dwyer patterns on BPMN and UML models.

8   Conclusion

The complexity of cyber-physical systems in general and embedded systems in particular, makes their verification less obvious than other software systems. This verification can be done by using formal methods and specifying properties from security requirements, generally defined in natural language. One of the challenges for the community is to correctly translate the security requirements into formal properties to be verified. This need can be satisfied by giving an extended and expressive formalism to the domain experts to bridge the gap between textual requirements and the formal properties.

To address this issue, we have proposed an approach to raise the abstraction level of the formal description of security properties. The methodology consists in using the Dwyer's patterns to create an intermediate level of abstraction between security requirements and logic formulas to be verified. This formalism is closer to requirement expression and provides a level-independent of temporal logics.

On the other hand, we improve the system debugging by diving the embedded software code in the environment models. The global state is obtained by composing the system state and all environment entity states. The environment includes an attacker entity which provides the possibility to define several attacker behaviors, if needed. The heterogeneity with models and embedded code is supported by the specification of a shared API between the two parts. This shared API exposes the system state description for the model checker and is the input for the synchronous composition with the property observer automaton.

This approach was evaluated on a industrial system for controlling booking and use of vehicles in large car fleet. Security properties have been defined and a vulnerability has been identified at system behavioral level.

In the future, we plan to experiment our approach on other industrial systems and we will study additional tooling to help the interpretation the analysis results.

References

1. Autili, M., Grunske, L., Lumpe, M., Pelliccione, P., Tang, A.: Aligning qualitative, real-time, and probabilistic property specification patterns using a structured English grammar. IEEE Trans. Software Eng. **41**(7), 620–638 (2015)
2. Besnard, V., Teodorov, C., Jouault, F., Brun, M., Dhaussy, P.: Unified verification and monitoring of executable UML specifications. Softw. Syst. Model. **20**(6), 1825–1855 (2021)
3. Chen, H., Dean, D., Wagner, D.A.: Model checking one million lines of c code. In NDSS, vol. 4, pp. 171–185 (2004)
4. Corradini, F., Fornari, F., Polini, A., Re, B., Tiezzi, F., Vandin, A.: A formal approach for the analysis of BPMN collaboration models. J. Syst. Softw. **180**, 111007 (2021)
5. Dadeau, F., Fourneret, E., Bouchelaghem, A.: Temporal property patterns for model-based testing from UML/OCL. Softw. Syst. Model. **18**(2), 865–888 (2019)
6. Dwyer, M.B.: Specification patterns web site. http://patterns.projects.cis.ksu.edu
7. Dwyer, M.B., Avrunin, G.S., Corbett, J.C.: Property specification patterns for finite-state verification. In: Proceedings of the second workshop on Formal methods in software practice, pp. 7–15 (1998)
8. Dwyer, M.B., Avrunin, G.S., Corbett, J.C.: Patterns in property specifications for finite-state verification. In: Proceedings of the 21st International Conference on Software Engineering, pp. 411–420 (1999)
9. Gruhn, V., Laue, R.: Patterns for timed property specifications. Electron. Notes Theoret. Comput. Sci. **153**(2), 117–133 (2006)
10. Heim, S., Dumas, X., Bonnafous, E., Dhaussy, P., Teodorov, C., Leroux, L.: Model checking of scade designed systems. In: 8th European Congress on Embedded Real Time Software and Systems (ERTS 2016) (2016)
11. Hnaini, H., Le Roux, L., Champeau, J., Teodorov, C.: Security property modeling. In: ICISSP, pp. 694–701 (2021)
12. Konrad, S., Cheng, B.H.C., Campbell, L.A., Wassermann, R.: Using security patterns to model and analyze security requirements. Requirements Engineering for High Assurance Systems (RHAS2003), 11 (2003)

13. Musuvathi, M., Park, D.Y.W., Chou, A., Engler, D.R., Dill, D.L.: CMC: a pragmatic approach to model checking real code. ACM SIGOPS Oper. Syst. Rev. **36(SI)**, 75–88 (2002)
14. Van Lamsweerde, A.: Elaborating security requirements by construction of intentional anti-models. In: Proceedings of the 26th International Conference on Software Engineering, pp. 148–157. IEEE (2004)
15. Wong, P.Y.H., Gibbons, J.: Property specifications for workflow modelling. Sci. Comput. Program. **76**(10), 942–967 (2011)

Modeling Train Systems: From High-Level Architecture Graphical Models to Formal Specifications

Racem Bougacha[1,3]($\boxtimes$) iD, Régine Laleau[2] iD, Philippe Bon[3],
Simon Collart-Dutilleul[3], and Rahma Ben Ayed[1]

[1] Institut de Recherche Technologique Railenium, 59300 Famars, France
{racem.bougacha,rahma.ben-ayed}@railenium.eu
[2] Université Paris-Est Créteil LACL, 94010 Créteil, France
laleau@u-pec.fr
[3] COSYS-ESTAS, Univ. Gustave Eiffel, 59650 Villeneuve d'Ascq, France
{racem.bougacha,philippe.bon,simon.collart-dutilleul}@univ-eiffel.fr

Abstract. Model Driven Engineering (MDE) is a software development methodology applied on complex systems, which are composed of many interacting components. This paper proposes a holistic approach based on MDE for modeling and formally verifying the high-level architectures of such systems, in particular railway systems. The approach contains a three-step process. The first one consists in proposing a high-level architecture modeling using SysML. It produces graphical models of system components, represents and documents the system in a simple way to be discussed with stakeholders and allows them to verify if this architecture corresponds to their expected requirements. We have selected diagrams that facilitate SysML high-level architecture design, namely package, block-definition, state-transition and sequence diagrams. The second step consists in transforming SysML models to Event-B formal models. The input meta-models are those of SysML, the output one is the Event-B meta-model. All of them have been adapted to our objectives. The last step is the verification of Event-B formal specifications using provers, model-checkers and animators. Formal specifications are specifically recommended for complex critical systems with high level of integrity to verify their correctness, accuracy and to allow a complete check of the entire system states and properties. We illustrate this approach on a case study of emerging standard of the ATO system running over ERTMS where compliance with the normative documents will ensure the achievement of a number of safety objectives while providing a graphical representation understandable by domain experts.

Keywords: Model-driven engineering · High-level architecture · SysML · Model transformation · Safety · Correct by construction · Event-B method

© The Author(s), under exclusive license to Springer Nature Switzerland AG 2023
S. Kallel et al. (Eds.): CRiSIS 2022, LNCS 13857, pp. 153–168, 2023.
https://doi.org/10.1007/978-3-031-31108-6_12

1   Introduction

Complex systems such as information technology systems, railway systems, air traffic control, and other cyber-physical systems, are composed of a set of subsystems. They generally are heterogeneous in that they integrate various kinds of components as mechanical, electronic, or software components. Therefore their design requires the collaboration of domain experts and the use of a common language to communicate with each other to build and demonstrate the validity of a consistent model. Using a technical norm may avoid a part of this task. Modeling the normative framework in order to generate correct-by-construction components is a way to avoid a difficult task and to ensure that the safety invariant fulfilled by the initial model will remain respected. In the railway domain, the CENELEC 50128 norm[1] clearly recommends the use of formal methods for developing critical software. Using formal methods, safety invariants can be proved and architecture correctness can be traced until the implementation through refinement mechanisms.

The Autonomous Freight Train (AFT) project under the Autonomous Train Program [1] is classified as a critical complex system. Its design depends on solutions that can address interplay between its sub-systems. Here, a first issue is identified, stemming from the fact that complex systems are represented as a layered hierarchy of sub-systems. These sub-systems interact by exchanging information in order to perform the main goal of the global system. Therefore a model of high-level architectures supporting layered hierarchies is needed. Such a high-level architecture must enable the specification of the main functional elements of a system, together with their interfaces and interactions. It constitutes a framework common to all the domain experts involved in the design of the system. In the AFT project, graphical representations of system components have been adopted to specify, view, understand, and document the system in a simple way. Such representations allow all the stakeholders to discuss and agree on the main characteristics of the system to build and allow to check if this high-level architecture corresponds to their expected requirements.

A second issue identified is the non-existence of a holistic approach for designing AFT from a high-level architecture to a formal specification. In fact, graphical models of an architecture are only semi-formal whereas formal methods are specifically recommended for complex systems modeling in order to verify their consistency, as well as safety and security properties. Here, safety is defined as a property of a system which does not in any way endanger neither persons nor environment. It is a central concern in the development process of critical systems particularly railway systems where design errors or system correctness problems cannot, in no way, occur.

In order to achieve these goals, we propose a holistic approach for modeling and formally verifying this type of systems. The approach is based on Model-Driven Engineering (MDE) [31]. Indeed MDE approaches have nowadays been adopted in various domains as they are well adapted to handle the increasing

---

[1] https://standards.globalspec.com/std/2023439/afnor-nf-en-50128.

complexity of complex systems [11]. Our approach is composed of three steps: (i) high-level architecture graphical modeling of the system and its hierarchical layers using the Systems Modeling Language (SysML) [29]. SysML focusses on "big picture" architectural views enriched with state-machine diagrams to define the behavior of each component and sequence diagrams to represent the behavior of the global system and the interactions between the components; (ii) model-to-model transformation to translate graphical models into formal models, in our case Event-B [6] already used in many safety-critical systems [22]. The last step (iii) consists in formally verify the Event-B specifications using the tools associated to Event-B.

Throughout this paper, we use an extract of a case study inspired from ATO over ERTMS system [12].

The paper is structured as follows: Sect. 2 briefly describes Model-Driven Engineering, Query View Transformation, SysML and Event-B. Section 3 discusses the related work. Section 4 presents the proposed approach and details its different steps illustrated on the case study. Finally, Sect. 5 reports our conclusions and presents future work.

2 Background

2.1 Model-Driven Engineering

Model-Driven Engineering is a software engineering specific approach which defines a framework to generate code using successive model transformations and thus to express separately each of the concerns of users, designers, architects, etc. In MDE, the crucial key point is the use of models as primary entities to process them automatically or half automatically. These models are abstract representations of a reality concern and defined with a meta-model [27].

Query View Transformation (QVT) [10] is a language used to transform source models into target models by using a set of rules expressed in an OCL-like language, normalized by OMG (the Object Management Group) [28].

2.2 SysML

The Systems Modeling Language (SysML) [29] is a graphical modeling language supporting the analysis and specification of complex systems that may include hardware, software and humans elements. SysML is based on UML and has been designed to be used in system engineering whereas UML is more appropriated to software engineering. Thus, SysML reuses some UML diagrams and introduces new ones. SysML is composed of nine types of diagrams, each of which is dedicated to represent particular concepts in a system. Over these diagrams, in HLA graphical modeling, we are interested in package, block definition, state machine and sequence diagrams.

2.3 Event-B

Event-B method was introduced by Jean-Raymond Abrial to specify systems rather than just software. An Event-B specification is composed of two elements: *Machine* and *Context*. A *Machine* represents the dynamic part of the model and it specifies the behavioral properties of the system by *variables* and a set of *events* composed of *guards* and *actions*. A *Context* contains the static part of the model. These contexts can be seen by machines. The possible values that the variables hold are restricted using an *invariant* written using a first-order predicate on the state variables. *Proof obligations* are generated to verify that the execution of each event maintains the invariant.

A refinement link, defined between models, allows to enrich or modify a model in order to increase the functionality being modeled, or/and explain how some purposes are achieved. It consists in adding new variables and/or replacing existing variables by new ones. Events can be refined and new ones can be introduced. The refinement of an event has to verify that the guard of the refined event should be stronger than the guard of the abstract one and the effect of the refined action should be stronger than the effect of the abstract one.

Event-B model decomposition is a powerful mechanism to scale the design of large and complex systems. The main idea of the decomposition is to cut a model M into sub-models *M1, ..., Mn*, which can be refined separately and more comfortably than the whole. Many approaches allow to decompose an Event-B model such as generic instantiation [8], shared variable decomposition [5], shared event decomposition [17] and modularization [20].

Event-B method is supported by several industrial tools, such as AtelierB [9], Rodin [7] and ProB [30]. These tools allow to generate proof obligations, automatically and interactively discharge them and to generate executable code. Animation, model-checking and test generation are also possible.

2.4 ATO over ERTMS Case Study Excerpt

Railway Normative Context: A railway system may be controlled using Automatic Train Operation (ATO): this is one of the challenging tasks of the railway industry [21]. In railway, four different grades of automation (GoA) are used. With **GoA1** the driver executes all driving functions manually. With **GoA2** traction and braking are automatic but the driver ensures the environment monitoring and is able to switch towards manual driving if necessary. **GoA3** allows autonomous driving with onboard staff that provides customized functions, e.g. open and closing doors. **GoA4** allows completely autonomous driving without onboard staff. In this paper, we are interested in **GoA2**. This sub-system is activated and deactivated by the driver, which implies the enabling/disabling of the **Railway System**. The driver is also responsible for switching driving mode between manual or automatic. The **GoA2** is composed of two sub-systems : **OnBoard** and **Track**. The **OnBoard** sub-system is responsible for executing the driving mode chosen by the driver and updates the state of the **Track** sub-system with the current driving mode. The European Rail Traffic Management

System (ERTMS) systems is a consequence of the European interoperability directives[2]. Article 16 of the last mentioned directive claims: "the deployment of the European Rail Traffic Management System (ERTMS) on the Union railway network constitutes an important contribution to improving safety levels". People wanting to understand deeper the management and the use of ERTMS as an European standard may consult [19]. In this paper, an excerpt of the case study presented in [12] is treated. In this extract, a railway system is composed of a set of sub-systems and the specification focuses on the **GoA2** functioning in a global framework called ATO over ERTMS. The specification is based on a normative and prenormative documentation. The ATO itself is not specified and the studied system is only the context and interfaces of the ATO. The same phenomenon occurs with relationships with the track system: ERTMS specifies the on-board system and interfaces with the track. As a consequence, the trackside is not specified as it is linked to national specific implementations.

Using Railway Norms for Safety Engineering: Before going into details, it must be recalled that in the railways domain, European safety standards and regulations such as ([3,4]) and Common Safety Method for Risk Assessment [2] establish a system safety process to ensure safe railway operations with a focus on functional safety. One of the three ways of Common Safety Method that must be used for demonstrating that a railway system is safe in Europe, refers to a norm being used as a reference. Considering Clause 6 of the CENELEC 50126 documentation [4], before considering requirements, concepts and system definitions must be documented. System boundaries and interfaces allowing interactions with other systems have to be analysed. Moreover, working context and functioning modes should be taken into account and clearly documented. A railway norm provides most of the above elements and adds some technical solutions in the context of the safety management process. As an example, the functioning modes of ERTMS are presented in Subset 26[3]. The functioning mode is not only described, but a set of scenarios to be run in specific independent laboratories are specified in order to assess that a given system really fulfills the specification: greater degree of safety requires a greater degree of independence for various roles.

Need of a Multi-level Graphical Documentation: Building a SysML model of the used railway norm is an efficient way in safety context. There exists a railway ontology merging main knowledge sources[4]. If your model is built using the railway standard SysML object libraries, it is supposed to be easily understood by a railway expert. Let us remark, that even if is not the focus of the current paper, keeping a SysML model as long as needed to consult system experts seems to be a good strategy, even when a refinement process

---

[2] https://www.eumonitor.eu/9353000/1/j9vvik7m1c3gyxp/vk4exsggptu4.

[3] https://www.era.europa.eu/content/set-specifications-3-etcs-b3-r2-gsm-r-b1_en.

[4] http://app.ontorail.org:8060/ontorailWiki/index.php/Main_Page.

needs to be formally implemented in order to preserve a safety property. For this reason implementing a refinement link at the level of a SysML diagram would have a practical added value. As mentioned in the Directive (EU) 2016/798 of the European Parliament, in order to be allowed to operate a train system, an authorization has to be received by a National Safety Agency (NSA). For this reason, various safety experts need to be convinced by a NSA-notofoed society (there are called Nobo: notified body) that the system is safe. Using standard SysML railway objects to express system safety mechanisms seems to be relevant. When models of the norm are assessed by system experts and formally proved, they can be used to produce executable using tooled certified processes (for instance, the process may be built within the Atelier B ecosystem). This is clearly an efficient strategy to avoid design and programming errors.

3   Related Work

Several architecture modeling languages have been proposed to reason about complex systems. [24] proposes a SysML-based methodology to model Mechatronic systems. These systems are characterized by synergic interactions between their components from several technological domains. These interactions enable the system to achieve more functionalities than the sum of the functionalities of its components considered independently. However, synergic and multidisciplinary design approaches with close cooperation between specialists from different disciplines is required. Therefore, SysML is identified as a support to this work, because it is a general purpose multi-view language for systems modeling. This combination consists in extending SysML using profiles to cover all AADL concepts and is called Extended SysML for Architecture Analysis Modeling (ExSAM). This approach allows to design high-level architectures of complex systems. However, these approaches are semi-formal and based on graphical modeling whereas formal verification and validation of system specifications are necessary for complex system design, particularly for critical systems.

Paper [16] proposes a MDE based approach for modeling and verifying railway signaling systems. This approach consists in model-to-model transformation to generate Event-B model from UML class diagrams profiled with safety and railway concepts. After that, a textual Event-B code is automatically generated using model-to-text transformation. The proposed approach allows to formally verify the safety of railway signaling systems based on model checking and animator tool. Despite these approaches provide formal specifications, they do not consider high-level architectures. In fact, they focus only on the structural parts of a system and non-functional constraints such as temporal or safety ones. Adding to that, these approaches do not consider the behavioral parts of the system, neither its decomposition into system/sub-systems in a high level architecture. [32] presents an approach that defines how a precise and concise domain specific language can be used for writing abstract scenarios in a style that can be easily understood by domain experts (for validation purposes) as well as designers (for behavioral verification). Therefore, they proposed two alternative approaches to use scenarios during formal modeling: a method for refining scenarios before the model is refined so that the scenarios guide the modeling, and a method for abstracting scenarios from concrete ones so that they can be used to test early refinements of the model. More precisely scenarios are described by state-machine diagrams and the way to refine an abstract scenario of a system is to introduce the state-machine diagrams of the sub-systems into the states of the state-machine diagram of the system. Thus, the model of a complex system with many sub-systems, can become not very easy to read and understand.

The CHESS Toolset [18,23] proposes an MDE based approach for cross-domain modeling of industrial complex systems. It uses UML, SysML and MARTE modeling languages and separation of concerns achieved to address a particular aspect of the problem through the specification of well-defined design views. This tool allows to map design models into multiple language targets, and property description, verification, preservation and dependability through a dedicated UML profile. FUML [26] is a subset of UML restricted to class and activity diagrams. Despite these approaches support HLA models based on SysML or UML and allow formal verification and property preserving, they do not offer mechanisms to design model decomposition and refinement, which are particularly well suited to HLA design.

To conclude, the graphical modeling approaches cited before do not allow to model high-level architectures of systems and their system/sub-systems hierarchy. They do not provide formal specifications to be verified formally to guarantee their consistency. On the other hand, formal specification approaches do not provide graphical modeling to be understood by domain experts.

4   The Proposed Approach

The framework of the approach is adapted to complex safety critical projects where several kinds of stakeholder profiles participate. Thus, the method needs to be multi-views: graphical, so that high-level architectures can be validated by railway domain experts, and formal, to verify their consistency as well as security and safety properties. The method aims at defining all components in a layering hierarchy defining the system/sub-systems relationships. Therefore, our approach is based on Model-Driven-Engineering approach and contains a three-step process as shown in Fig. 1: high-level architecture graphical modeling, model transformation and formal verification of the generated Event-B specifications.

The first step "High-level architecture graphical modeling" consists in modeling high-level architectures using SysML diagrams. In the AFT project, SysML has been chosen in concert with domain experts and four kinds of SysML diagrams have been selected: Package diagrams, Block Definition Diagrams, State-Machine Diagrams and Sequence Diagrams.

The second step "Model transformation and Event-B generation" consists in mapping high-level architecture models into Event-B models. To conduct this transformation, a set of transformation rules has been defined, which maps elements of a subset of the meta-models of SysML into elements of the meta-model

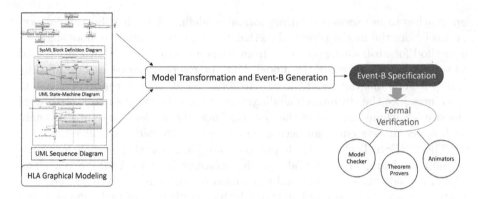

Fig. 1. The proposed approach

of Event-B. These meta-models are already defined but they do not cover all AFT modeling requirements. Therefore, they have been adapted.

Finally, a formal verification step is applied on the generated Event-B specifications using the Event-B tools (provers, model-checker and animator). In this way, design errors can be detected and invariant violation can be discovered.

Our previous work [15] details the modeling process and a deep description of the implemented translation rules.

4.1 High-level Architecture Graphical Modeling

High-level architecture is a layered hierarchy of sub-systems that interact together to satisfy parent system goals. To represent this hierarchy, new packages are designed for each sub-system. Each package is composed of a set of diagrams:

- A BDD (Block Definition Diagram) contains the sub-systems of a system as *Blocks* and associations which link them to their parent system.
- A State-Machine Diagram, one for each sub-system of the BDD, specifies the different states defining its behavior and the transitions between these states.
- A Sequence Diagram represents the behavior of the current system, the interactions between its sub-systems and how they cooperate to satisfy the objectives of the parent system.

The main objective of these models is to be transformed to Event-B models. As refinement is an Event-B fundamental concept to master complexity, we have proposed to add it in our SysML models. Therefore we have defined a new profile, called **Refinement**, on Sequence Diagrams. This profile allows to define refinement links between the behavior of sub-systems and the behavior of their parent system. It defines a stereotype called **Refines_Message** with an attribute **Refined_Message**. More precisely, the stereotype can be applied on a message exchanged between sub-systems to specify that it refines a message of the parent system as exemplified in Fig. 2. Diagram 1 describes the sequence diagram of component "RS" of type "Railway System" with a message "EnableSystem". Diagram 2 shows a message ("Activate") exchanged between "Driver" and "ATOoverETCSGoA2", sub-components of "Railway System". This message refines "EnableSystem", as precised in Part 3.

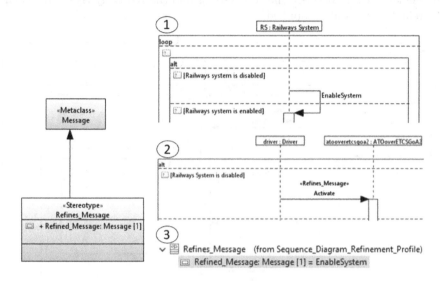

Fig. 2. Sequence diagram refinement profile

We have defined three levels in the architecture of the case study. Figure 3 presents the first one, corresponding to the main system called **Railway System**. It includes the state diagram with two states, **disabled** and **enabled** and the transitions between these states. The behavior of the **Railway System** system is described in the sequence diagram.

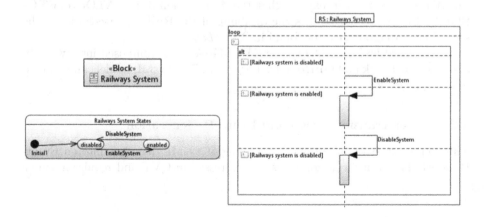

Fig. 3. First layer of the ATO over ERTMS high-level architecture

In the second layer, the **Railway System** is decomposed into two sub-systems, the **ATOoverETCSGoA2** sub-system and the **driver**. **ATOoverETCSGoA2** is activated/deactivated by the driver, thus enabling the **Railway System**. The sequence diagram of Fig. 4 describes the interactions between the **driver** and the **ATOoverETCSGoA2**. In order to model the refinement link between the sub-systems and the **Railway System** system, the refinement profile is applied.

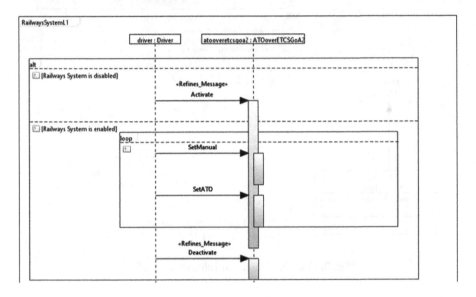

Fig. 4. Extract of the sequence diagram of the second layer

Activate refines message **EnableSystem** of the first layer sequence diagram to express that the activation of the **ATOoverETCSGoA2** by the **driver** implies the enabling of the **Railway System**. Message **Deactivate** refines message **DisableSystem** to express that the deactivation of the **ATOoverETC-SGoA2** by the **driver** implies the disabling of the **Railway System**. All the second layer diagrams can be found in [14], *"Layer 1"*.

In the third layer, the **ATOoverETCSGoA2** is decomposed into two sub-systems: the **Track** and **OnBoard** sub-systems. The SysML model can be found in [14], *"Layer 2"*.

4.2 Model Transformation and Event-B Generation

This step consists of an automatic mapping of SysML diagrams into an Event-B model. The transformation rules are expressed in QVT and require a source

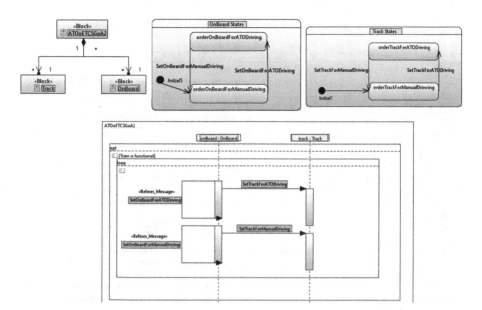

Fig. 5. Example of Generated Event-B specification

meta-model and a target one. The SysML source meta-models are elaborated from the OMG specification [29] with local adaptations discussed with the domain expert partners of the project. The Event-B target meta-model is conform to the Event-B notation used in AtelierB. The detailed specifications of these meta-models are represented in our previous work [15]. A set of 34 rules with around 700 lines of code have been implemented to map source elements into target elements.

The Event-B generation step allows to product a textual specification from the generated models of the previous step. This step uses Acceleo [25], a template-based technology allowing to automatically produce any kind of source code from any data source available in EMF format. Figures 5 and 6 shows an example of a generated Event-B specification that represents the structural and dynamic part of the sub-system **ATOoverETCSGoA2**. Figure 6 presents two parts, the context "ATOoverETCSGoA2_CONT" which defines the structural part and the machine "ATOoverETCSGoA2" defining the dynamic part. Here, we give some transformation examples:

– BDD blocks "Track" and "OnBoard" (framed in blue) are transformed into two context sets "Track" and "OnBoard" and two variables "onboardState" and "trackState".
– The variable "atooveretcsgoa2State" (framed in pink) which represents the parent block "ATOoETCSGoA2" is coming from the refined machine "ATOoETCSGoA2_Interface".
– "ATOoETCSGoA2_Interface" is the machine generated from the system/sub-systems decomposition applied on the "RailwaysSystemL1" machine.

SYSTEM
ATOoverETCSGoA2_CONT
SETS
OnBoard;
Track;
TrackStates;
OnBoardStates
CONSTANTS
onboard,
track,
orderOnBoardForATODriving,
orderTrackForManualDrinving,
orderOnBoardForManualDriving,
orderTrackForATODriving
PROPERTIES
onboard ∈ OnBoard ∧
track ∈ Track ∧
Track ={track} ∧
OnBoard ={onboard} ∧
orderOnBoardForATODriving ∈ OnBoardStates ∧
orderTrackForATODriving ∈ TrackStates ∧
orderTrackForManualDrinving ∈ TrackStates ∧
orderOnBoardForManualDriving ∈ OnBoardStates ∧
orderTrackForManualDrinving ≠
orderTrackForATODriving ∧
orderOnBoardForManualDriving ≠
orderOnBoardForATODriving ∧
TrackStates ={orderTrackForATODriving,
orderTrackForManualDrinving} ∧
OnBoardStates ={orderOnBoardForATODriving,
        orderOnBoardForManualDriving}
END
■■■■■■■■■■■■■■■■■■■■■■■■■■■■■■■■■■■
REFINEMENT
ATOoverETCSGoA2
REFINES
ATOoverETCSGoA2_Interface
SEES
ATOoverETCSGoA2_CONT,
Railways System L1_CONT,
Railways System L0_CONT
VARIABLES
onboardState,
trackState,
atooveretcsgoa2State
INVARIANT
onboardState ∈ OnBoard → OnBoardStates ∧
trackState ∈ Track → TrackStates
INITIALISATION
onboardState :∈ {onboard} → OnBoardStates ∥
trackState :∈ {track} → TrackStates ∥

atooveretcsgoa2State :∈ {atooveretcsgoa2} →
ATOoverETCSGoA2States
EVENTS
SetTrackForATODriving =
SELECT
onboardState(onboard)=orderOnBoardForATODriving ∧
trackState(track)=orderTrackForManualDrinving
THEN
trackState(track):=orderTrackForATODriving
END ;
SetTrackForManualDriving =
SELECT
onboardState(onboard)=orderOnBoardForManualDriving ∧
trackState(track)=orderTrackForATODriving
THEN
trackState(track):=orderTrackForManualDrinving
END ;
SetOnBoardForManualDriving ref SetManual=
SELECT
onboardState(onboard)=orderOnBoardForATODriving ∧
atooveretcsgoa2State(atooveretcsgoa2)=ATODriving
THEN
onboardState(onboard):=orderOnBoardForManualDriving ∥
atooveretcsgoa2State(atooveretcsgoa2):=manualDriving
END ;
SetOnBoardForATODriving ref SetATO=
SELECT
onboardState(onboard)=orderOnBoardForManualDriving ∧
atooveretcsgoa2State(atooveretcsgoa2)=manualDriving
THEN
onboardState(onboard):=orderOnBoardForATODriving ∥
atooveretcsgoa2State(atooveretcsgoa2):=ATODriving
END
END

Fig. 6. Example of Generated Event-B specification

– State-machine diagrams "OnBoard States" and "Track States" defining subsystems behaviors (framed in green) are transformed to sets "OnBoardStates" and "TrackStates".

- States of the state-machine diagram, such as "orderOnBoardForATODriving" of the state-machine diagram "OnBoard States", are mapped into constants.
- Sequence diagram lifelines (framed in yellow) such as "onBoard" are transformed to constants.
- Sequence diagram messages (framed in purple) such as "SetTrackForATO-Driving" are mapped to events in the machine.

The complete Event-B specification can be found in [13].

4.3   Formal Verification

AtelierB provers are used to perform verification and the ProB model checker is used to animate execution scenarios.

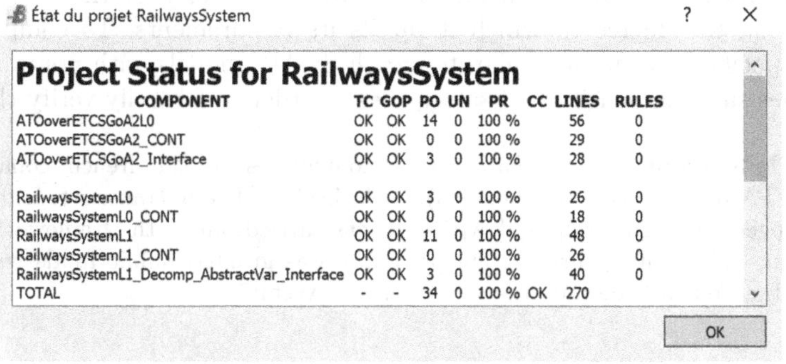

État du projet RailwaysSystem   ?   ✕

Project Status for RailwaysSystem

COMPONENT	TC	GOP	PO	UN	PR	CC	LINES	RULES
ATOoverETCSGoA2L0	OK	OK	14	0	100 %		56	0
ATOoverETCSGoA2_CONT	OK	OK	0	0	100 %		29	0
ATOoverETCSGoA2_Interface	OK	OK	3	0	100 %		28	0
RailwaysSystemL0	OK	OK	3	0	100 %		26	0
RailwaysSystemL0_CONT	OK	OK	0	0	100 %		18	0
RailwaysSystemL1	OK	OK	11	0	100 %		48	0
RailwaysSystemL1_CONT	OK	OK	0	0	100 %		26	0
RailwaysSystemL1_Decomp_AbstractVar_Interface	OK	OK	3	0	100 %		40	0
TOTAL	-	-	34	0	100 %	OK	270	

OK

Fig. 7. Status of the generated Event-B specification

Figure 7 summarises the status of the AtelierB project corresponding to the generated Event-B specification. The verification of the consistency of the formal specification required to discharge 34 proof obligations. These proofs are of type invariant preservation, non-deterministic action feasibility and well-definedness. They were all proved automatically (100%). The columns of the table are: **TC**, for "type checking", to indicate that formal model components are well defined, **GOP**, for "generation of proof obligations", to indicate that proof obligations are well generated. **PO**, for "proof obligations", presents the number of generated proof obligations for every formal model component. **UN** for "unproved" presents the number of unproved proof obligations of each element. Finally, the column **PR** presents the percentage of discharged proof obligations.

5   Conclusion

This paper proposes a model-based approach for modeling and verifying high-level architectures of complex systems, particularly railway systems. These complex systems are composed of interconnecting sub-systems that exchange information. Therefore, following the recommendations of the 50126 norm, we propose a multi-view approach, starting with graphical modeling of high-level architectures to represent the layered hierarchy of system/sub-systems of the main system and a set of model transformation rules which generate Event-B formal specifications. To conduct this transformation, an adaptation of SysML and Event-B meta-models corresponding to AFT requirements and domain experts needs have been proposed. The approach is illustrated by a case study of a project of railway norm. The SysML models have been validated by domain experts whereas the generated formal specification has been proved successfully using AtelierB and ProB so that the consistency of the system architecture is ensured. In the considered use case, it means that all the safety goals ensured by the norm are respected.

Work in progress aims at building alignment links between high-level architectures and system requirements to ensure the quality of the system that depends on the degree to which it fulfills its requirements. To complete our formal specification, we also plan to enrich SysML models with non-functional properties such as security and safety ones in order to formally verify them.

Acknowledgement. This research work contributes to the french collaborative project TFA (autonomous freight train), with SNCF, Alstom Transport, Hitachi Rail STS, Capgemini Engineering and Apsys. It was carried out in the framework of IRT Railenium, Valenciennes, France, and therefore was granted public funds within the scope of the French Program "Investissements d'Avenir".

References

1. The autonomous train program. https://railenium.eu/train-autonome/
2. CSM-RA: Guide for the application of the commission regulation on the adoption of Common Safety Method on Risk Evaluation and assessment. European Railway Agency (2017)
3. En50126-1: Railway Applications - The specification and demonstration of reliability, availability, maintainability and safety (RAMS) - Part 1: Generic RAMS Process (2017)
4. En50126-2: Railway Applications - The specification and demonstration of reliability, availability, maintainability and safety (RAMS) - Part 2: Systems approach to safety (2017)
5. Abrial, J.R.: Event model decomposition. Technical report/ETH. Department of Computer Science 626 (2009)
6. Abrial, J.R.: Modeling in Event-B: system and software engineering. Cambridge University Press (2010)
7. Abrial, J., Butler, M.J., Hallerstede, S., Hoang, T.S., Mehta, F., Voisin, L.: Rodin: an open toolset for modelling and reasoning in Event-B. Int. J. Softw. Tools Technol. Transf. **12**(6), 447–466 (2010). https://doi.org/10.1007/s10009-010-0145-y
8. Abrial, J.R., Hallerstede, S.: Refinement, decomposition, and instantiation of discrete models: application to Event-B. Fund. Inform. **77**(1–2), 1–28 (2007)
9. AtelierB: Atelier B Tool. https://www.atelierb.eu/en/atelier-b-tools/

10. Barendrecht, P.: Research project report
11. Behjati, R., Yue, T., Nejati, S., Briand, L., Selic, B.: Extending SysML with AADL concepts for comprehensive system architecture modeling. In: France, R.B., Kuester, J.M., Bordbar, B., Paige, R.F. (eds.) ECMFA 2011. LNCS, vol. 6698, pp. 236–252. Springer, Heidelberg (2011). https://doi.org/10.1007/978-3-642-21470-7_17
12. Bon, P., Dutilleul, S.C., Bougacha, R.: ATO over ETCS: a system analysis. In: 18th International Conference on Railway Engineering Design and Operation (COMPRAIL 2022) (2022)
13. Bougacha, R.: A holistic approach for modeling railway systems on the ATO over ERTMS case study: Event-b specification. https://github.com/RacemBougacha/Railway-System/tree/main/Event-B%20Specification
14. Bougacha, R.: A holistic approach for modeling railway systems on the ATO over ERTMS case study: high-level architecture models. https://github.com/RacemBougacha/Railway-System/tree/main/High-Level%20Architecture
15. Bougacha, R., Laleau, R., Collart-Dutilleul, S., Ayed, R.B.: Extending SysML with refinement and decomposition mechanisms to generate event-b specifications. In: Aït-Ameur, Y., Crăciun, F. (eds.) Theoretical Aspects of Software Engineering, pp. 256–273. Springer International Publishing, Cham (2022). https://doi.org/10.1007/978-3-031-10363-6_18
16. Bougacha, R., Wakrime, A.A., Kallel, S., Ayed, R.B., Dutilleul, S.C.: A model-based approach for the modeling and the verification of railway signaling system. In: ENASE, pp. 367–376 (2019)
17. Butler, M.: Decomposition structures for Event-B. In: Leuschel, M., Wehrheim, H. (eds.) IFM 2009. LNCS, vol. 5423, pp. 20–38. Springer, Heidelberg (2009). https://doi.org/10.1007/978-3-642-00255-7_2
18. Cicchetti, A., et al.: Chess: a model-driven engineering tool environment for aiding the development of complex industrial systems. In: Proceedings of the 27th IEEE/ACM International Conference on Automated Software Engineering, pp. 362–365 (2012)
19. Collart-Dutilleul, S.: Conclusion. In: Collart-Dutilleul, S. (ed.) Operating Rules and Interoperability in Trans-National High-Speed Rail, pp. 231–233. Springer, Cham (2022). https://doi.org/10.1007/978-3-030-72003-2_9
20. Hoang, T.S., Iliasov, A., Silva, R.A., Wei, W.: A survey on Event-B decomposition. Electronic Communications of the EASST 46 (2011)
21. Lagay, R., Adell, G.M.: The autonomous train: a game changer for the railways industry. In: 2018 16th International Conference on Intelligent Transportation Systems Telecommunications (ITST), pp. 1–5. IEEE (2018)
22. Lecomte, T., Deharbe, D., Prun, E., Mottin, E.: Applying a formal method in industry: a 25-Year trajectory. In: Cavalheiro, S., Fiadeiro, J. (eds.) SBMF 2017. LNCS, vol. 10623, pp. 70–87. Springer, Cham (2017). https://doi.org/10.1007/978-3-319-70848-5_6
23. Mazzini, S., Favaro, J.M., Puri, S., Baracchi, L.: Chess: an open source methodology and toolset for the development of critical systems. In: EduSymp/OSS4MDE@ MoDELS, pp. 59–66 (2016)
24. Mhenni, F., Choley, J.Y., Penas, O., Plateaux, R., Hammadi, M.: A sysml-based methodology for mechatronic systems architectural design. Adv. Eng. Inform. 28(3), 218–231 (2014)
25. Musset, J., et al.: Acceleo user guide, vol. 2. http://acceleo.org/doc/obeo/en/acceleo-2.6-user-guide.pdf (2006)

26. OMG: Object management group, semantics of a foundational subset for executable UML models (FUML). https://www.omg.org/spec/FUML/1.5/About-FUML/
27. OMG: Object management group. meta object facility (MoF) 2.0 core specification. https://www.omg.org/spec/MOF/2.0/About-MOF/ (2006)
28. OMG: Object management group. meta object facility (MoF) 2.0 core specification. OMG Document AD/97-08-14, 1997 (2006)
29. OMG: OMG systems modeling language, version 1.3. https://www.omgsysml.org/ (2012)
30. ProB: The ProB animator and model checker. https://prob.hhu.de/
31. Schmidt, D.C.: Model-driven engineering. Comput. IEEE Comput. Soc. **39**(2), 25 (2006)
32. Snook, C., Hoang, T.S., Dghaym, D., Fathabadi, A.S., Butler, M.: Domain-specific scenarios for refinement-based methods. J. Syst. Architect. **112**, 101833 (2021)

How IT Infrastructures Break: Better Modeling for Better Risk Management

Benjamin Somers[1,2]($\boxtimes$) (iD), Fabien Dagnat[1] (iD), and Jean-Christophe Bach[1] (iD)

[1] IMT Atlantique, Lab-STICC, UMR 6285, 29238 Brest, France
benjamin.somers@imt-atlantique.fr
[2] Crédit Mutuel Arkéa, 29480 Le Relecq-Kerhuon, France

Abstract. IT infrastructures break. Whether it be computer attacks or software, human or hardware failures, IT safety and security risk is present in many technical and organizational domains. Risk management is therefore essential to ensure infrastructure resilience, compliance with legal and contractual requirements and a better knowledge of what causes what. But risk management is hard to automate, sometimes because criteria are subject to human appreciation, sometimes because of an incomplete or wrong knowledge of the infrastructure itself. And this latter factor has become more evident with the advent of modern cloud-native architectures: complex and dynamic infrastructures make risk assessment difficult. In this article, we propose an approach based on infrastructure modeling to help automate the risk assessment process for IT infrastructures. Instead of focusing first on hazard analysis, our approach attempts to consider (most of) such an analysis as a consequence of infrastructure modeling. By deciding to focus on the infrastructure modeling itself and by involving as many of the company's stakeholders as possible in the process, we intend to make risk assessment more collaborative and thorough, by taking advantage of everyone's expertise.

Keywords: Distributed Infrastructures · Infrastructure Modeling · Risk Assessment

1 Introduction

Over the past few decades, the presence of IT in critical infrastructures has been continually on the rise [22]. This has allowed for unprecedented growth in various business sectors, but has brought its share of risk into the equation. From a few computers with monolithic software, IT infrastructures have evolved towards data centers with several thousands of servers running interacting microservices. These interactions themselves are becoming increasingly complex [24] as the design of such infrastructures follows a tendency towards abstraction. From bare metal to virtual machines, from physical networks to virtualized fabrics, from local storage to distributed datastores, risk is more and more difficult to assess [19] as there is a clear break between physical and virtual infrastructures.

S. Kallel et al. (Eds.): CRiSIS 2022, LNCS 13857, pp. 169–184, 2023.
https://doi.org/10.1007/978-3-031-31108-6_13

On top of these highly dynamic virtual infrastructures lie reconfigurable software packages. Components not known before runtime (such as dynamic libraries) are used to build software which now rely heavily on external services. As IT gets more and more ubiquitous, we observe a multiplication of entry points, inducing a much larger attack surface [12]. Assessing the risk requires to combine together information collected from a large number of stakeholders, not always willing to share.

Risk management is not something to be taken lightly: sometimes, lives depend on the very systems being studied [34]. So methods such as FTA and FMEA [28], HAZOP [14] or STPA [18] have been devised in that regard. In parallel, the various industries have been developing safety and security regulations to guide such risk analyses, whether in aerospace [29] or IT [10]. Finally, as IT services have multiplied, *Service-Level Agreements* (SLAs) have emerged and various certifications have been introduced to increase customer confidence and guarantee a certain quality of service [13].

But to be able to certify such infrastructures, one has to understand their components (technical, such as computers, and also human) and their interactions. It can be done with the help of modeling frameworks from the enterprise modeling communities (such as RM-ODP [1] or Archimate [31]) to the formal methods communities (such as Alloy [17] or Petri nets [23]) to software and network engineering communities (such as UML [25] or OMNeT++ [32]).

In this article, we advocate a collaborative approach to risk management for IT infrastructures based on better modeling of such infrastructures. To this end, we present the theoretical background of our study in Sect. 2. Section 3 proposes a set of methods to support risk management in distributed infrastructures. In Sect. 4, we show an example with the advantages and limitations of our technique. Finally, the article finishes with a conclusion in Sect. 5.

2   Related Work

In this section, we present the scientific context of our study, in the fields of risk management and infrastructure modeling. Our work attempts to unite the different methods presented here without changing the approaches and tools already in place: a federation of models respecting the expertise of each actor.

2.1   Risk Analysis

The ISO 31000 standard [16] defines risk management as a five-step process. First, the context of the study has to be defined: *what* the system is, *when* it is considered, *where* it is, *who* is involved, *why* and *how* the study is being done. The next three steps are what the standard refers to as the risk assessment step. It consists first of all of identifying risks and their causes and impacts. Then, a qualitative and quantitative risk analysis is carried out to assess likelihoods, confidence levels and magnitude of consequences. The last step of risk assessment is its evaluation, to compare the results and make decisions. Finally, the risk treatment phase addresses risks by modifying risk sources, likelihoods, consequences or simply abandoning the activity that led to it. In this work, we focus on the first two steps of the process (context and risk identification).

Several implementations of risk management have been developed, such as *Fault Tree Analysis* (FTA), *Failure Mode and Effects Analysis* (FMEA), *Hazard and Operability study* (HAZOP) or *System-Theoretic Process Analysis* (STPA). There are also risk management methods aimed at information security [2] which implement the ISO 27005 standard [15], more focused on IT risk, such as *EBIOS Risk Manager* (EBIOS-RM).

FTA [28] is a top-down approach: top events are first identified and their causes are recursively analyzed and combined using boolean logic gates. Individual causes are put in OR gates and collective causes are put in AND gates (with care taken to verify the independence of the causes). It is a deductive approach carried out by repeatedly asking: how can this event happen and what are its causes?

In contrast, FMEA [28] lists only single failures, even though they have no high-level impact. FMEA is a bottom-up, inductive method used to identify low-level failures and study their impacts on the higher levels. FTA and FMEA are often used together thanks to their opposite views, but are very time-consuming to apply thoroughly, therefore the analyses are often incomplete [8].

HAZOP [14] works quite differently. It uses standardized questions and words to investigate on possible deviations from a design intent. The technique is a qualitative way to assess complex processes and focuses on structured discussions. In some cases, this format may however provide a false sense of security by being too guided [6].

These bottom-up methods use a divide and conquer approach: they analyze separately each part to provide a synthetic assessment for the system. But interactions between such parts and dynamic behaviors may be overlooked [30].

STPA [18] is a systems approach to hazard analysis. Instead of focusing on failures, it focuses on the losses of control being the real cause of accidents. It is a top-down method to study functional control instead of physical components.

EBIOS-RM [3] proposes a cyclic approach for risk management. The approach consists of five workshops identifying high level, textual risk scenarios and their resolutions with security measures.

Some methods are more suitable for certain domains and we believe that it is important to let different actors in the IT infrastructure choose which ones they want to exploit. As mentioned in [4], a collaborative approach is key, and we believe that federating these approaches is beneficial to the domain.

2.2 Infrastructure Modeling

The ISO 31000 standard emphasizes that risk management should be a collaborative endeavor including several domains of expertise to properly define and evaluate risks. This is where we think that infrastructure modeling can be used.

Many languages and representations exist to describe IT infrastructures, from hardware to software, including networks and processes. A datacenter can be described with rack diagrams, illustrating the layout of servers and network components. A piece of software can be represented as UML diagrams [25], to show its structure and the different interactions at work, or can be described by its code. A network topology can be seen as a mathematical object (such as a graph), described with switch configurations, or as code with *Software-Defined Networking* [20].

However, these languages are mostly static description languages and do not always adapt to the changing structures of modern IT infrastructures. Such languages are particularly adapted to their respective domains [9], but they are sometimes not very understandable by external parties. From the perspective of risk analysis, we believe that we can bring together different technical fields through model federation [11].

3   Guided Risk Management for IT Infrastructures

Over the years, IT infrastructures have evolved from the "traditional" model. Even though so-called legacy systems are still in use in some critical businesses, virtualization has brought a completely different paradigm. Traditionally, software components are directly deployed on physical nodes. This guarantees stability in space (services do not "move" to another place), in quantity (no frequent increase or decrease in the number of nodes), in resources (hardware is not frequently replaced) and network (the topology does not significantly change) over time. A simplified deployment, where functional components are directly mapped to physical servers, is shown on Fig. 1. Risk analysis here is not much different from what is done in other sectors (although the domain is more prone to component reuse), but it is important to update it as the infrastructure evolves.

Virtualized infrastructures, and more recently cloud infrastructures keep these guarantees of stability for a much shorter period of time (sometimes hours or even minutes). Although instantaneous risk studies are possible, guaranteeing a zero deviation between the studied infrastructure and the real one at any time seems unrealistic. The risk analysis may take longer than the period during which the infrastructure is stable and some infrastructure reconfiguration algorithms are unpredictable or non-deterministic. Moreover, the deployment on these infrastructures (shown on Fig. 2) is more complex than on traditional ones due to the additional abstraction layer. There is indeed a clear separation between the virtual infrastructures (how VMs "see" one another) and the physical ones (where VMs are located). While the deployment of functions on hardware was *one-to-one* (one functional component per machine) or *many-to-one* (several functional components on the same machine), it is now common to have *one-to-many* (distributed functional component) and *many-to-many* (distributed functional assemblies) deployments. Risk analysis also becomes more complex, as there are now three models (logical, deployment and physical) on which the analysis can be done.

In the rest of this section, we describe what we refer to as the *risk cycle* and present three methods of risk analysis in the context of IT infrastructures.

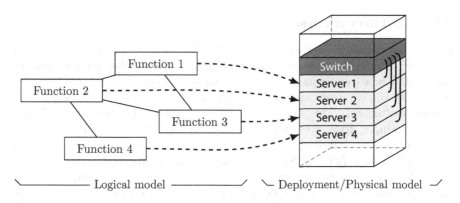

Fig. 1. Traditional IT infrastructure, where the deployment model generally corresponds to the physical model

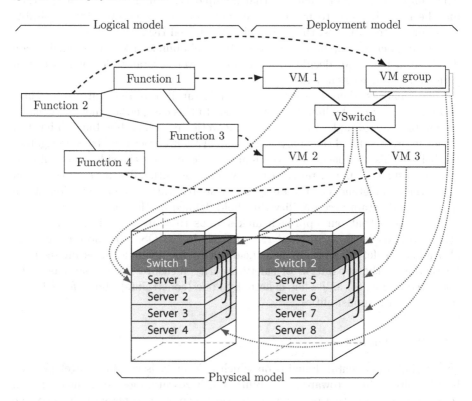

Fig. 2. Modern cloud infrastructure, where there is a clear separation between the virtual and the physical infrastructures

3.1 Side-Effect Analysis

IT infrastructures are subject to risks. Regulatory bodies, whether they have statutory or advisory powers, provide requirements to follow for adequate risk coverage. These requirements are then implemented or translated into constraints by the company and these constraints can have an effect, beneficial or adverse, on the risk. This is what we call the *risk cycle* (represented on Fig. 3).

For example, to address the risk of credit card fraud, the Payment Card Industry Security Standards Council proposed the *Payment Card Industry Data Security Standard* (PCI DSS). Depending on the company, these requirements translate into various constraints on the IT infrastructure. For example, PCI DSS sub-requirement 9 (restricting physical access to cardholder data) may be implemented by encrypting the staff's hard drives and deploying a corporate policy prohibiting removable media. These constraints have a direct effect on the risk. An example of an adverse effect is that if employees cannot use USB sticks, they may be more inclined to use insecure sharing services, or even try to disable their corporate antivirus, thus increasing the initial risk.

As another example, to address the availability risk for a single-node database, a team can decide to distribute it over several nodes, which can in turn lead to a consistency risk.

The analysis then continues recursively until the risks are sufficiently addressed or cannot be handled any further. In this case, either they are deemed acceptable (for example, the system is theoretically vulnerable, but too hard to attack in practice) and the analysis can end, or their causes need to be mitigated. We believe this approach to be original, as it focuses on the side effects of constraints instead of parts, processes or systems. Additionally, its stop condition is not the completeness of the analysis *per se*, but rather the diminution of the risk below a certain acceptability threshold defined by the company.

We believe that our approach makes steps that are sometimes implicit in other methods (such as residual risk analysis in EBIOS-RM) more explicit. It also adds a safety dimension in a field where the main focus is on security. Furthermore, the separation of safety/security measures into what has to be done (requirements) and what is actually done (constraints) allows for a better separation of responsibilities.

3.2 Part Analysis

Unlike the fundamental domains on which risk analysis was first developed, IT is culturally inclined towards reusability. For hardware, most systems deal with some form of computing power, fast and slow memory and network. Most of the components are also readily available, off-the-shelf [27]. For software, the growing acceptance of open source over the years has led to the creation of many software products that reuse open source libraries, with their fair share of risk [5].

IT infrastructures can thus be made of thousands of components provided by hundreds of actors (companies, communities or single developers). Analyzing all these individual parts is impossible in a reasonable amount of time, as software

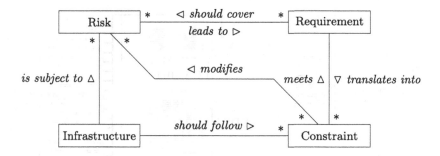

Fig. 3. The risk cycle

and hardware are sometimes seen as a black box (*e.g.* Hardware Security Modules and proprietary firmware) and are regularly replaced or updated.

In such infrastructures, it could prove useful to include the employees in the process of risk assessment. For example,

- Software developers understand the functional interactions between different elements of the software infrastructure and are able to describe precisely with their tools such an architecture;
- Datacenter "smart hands" are hardware experts who know what the servers are made of, in which bay of which datacenter specific machines are, and they have tools for these specific needs;
- Network engineers understand the network topology of the infrastructure, they configure business-critical hardware and, again, have tools and representations to assist their work.

All these actors perform, in their way, infrastructure modeling. Benefiting from such expertise and tools would be a way to involve more people and cover more domains in the risk assessment process. But even with that, the knowledge of the infrastructure may still not be exhaustive and a compromise needs to be found: the risk should be analyzed as best as possible, despite the inaccuracies and lack of knowledge inside the company.

However, knowledge does not need to come only from the company itself. Manufacturers and external developers have indirectly great responsibilities within the company and we believe that a common interchange format for risk analyses could be of great benefit. It could indeed lead towards a more systematic risk analysis that respects the expertise (the actors should "know best") and the responsibilities (if a system breaks, it would be easier to identify who is at fault) of each stakeholder. The individual components of the infrastructure could then be federated in an FMEA-like analysis, particularly well adapted to study the parts of a system. If a software developer or a hardware manufacturer discovers a vulnerability, they can easily update their risk analysis, which in turn updates the risk analysis of a company using these products, without any intervention from them. This approach is a work in progress.

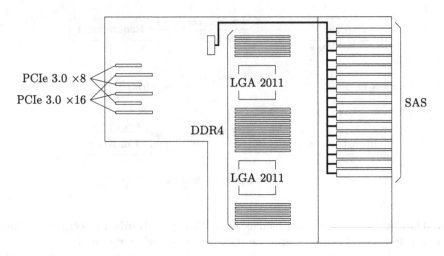

Fig. 4. Typical server motherboard, with memory (DDR4) and expansion card (PCIe 3.0) slots, CPU sockets (LGA 2011) and drive trays (SAS)

3.3 Assembly Analysis

Composite hardware, such as motherboards, often have clearly distinct slots for distinct components. In other words, given the risk of a motherboard malfunction, there is a requirement for hardware compatibility, and one of the constraints chosen to implement this requirement is the presence of different sockets. This is illustrated on Fig. 4.

However, this sole constraint is often not sufficient to eliminate the risk. Old PCIe expansion cards may not function properly on modern hardware, because of deprecation or standard incompatibilities. In addition, the very way of assembling the components on the motherboard has an impact. For example, the layout of the RAM modules can be very constrained on some motherboard models. That is why manufacturers release technical guides on how to build the systems.

Similarly, a piece of software may require a connection to a database, and the communication protocol will identify a type of database. However, if the database engine version is not adequate, the software may fail. This is why software vendors provide installation and deployment guides.

As shown in the two previous paragraphs, components assembled together sometimes exhibit properties that none of the individual components have, this is why both bottom-up and top-down approaches to risk analysis are used. Here again, we could benefit from a common risk interchange format, because actors could perform analyses on the hardware they manufacture, using for example FTA or STPA. If a large-scale infrastructure is suitably modeled, these analyses could be reused in an automated analysis of the whole infrastructure.

4   Case Study: A Cloud Infrastructure

We illustrate in this section how the combination of the above techniques help assess the risk. As risk analysis is an iterative process, our examples are not meant to be comprehensive.

Let us apply these three methods on a fictional European banking company, processing financial transactions and handling client information. The company opted for a private cloud-based architecture for all of its new projects. This cloud infrastructure is linked to the company's legacy systems and communicates with interbank and payment networks. But this is only a part of the its network flows: the company manages a fleet of several thousands of *Point of Sale* (POS) terminals and *Automatic Teller Machines* (ATM) that need a safe and secure connection. On top of that, it provides *Business-to-Business* (B2B) services to other companies wishing to offer banking solutions to their clients.

4.1   Requirements

Because of its activities, the company is subject to various requirements. We have classified some of them below[1] into two categories and four subcategories:

- External
  - Regulatory and legal, with:
      (R1) *General Data Protection Regulation* (GDPR) [10], governing the use and collection of personal information,
      (R2) PCI DSS [26], stating how cardholder data can be used and stored;
  - Contractual, with
      (R3) payment processor requirements [21,33], applying financial penalties in case of non-compliance with quality standards,
      (R4) SLAs with its business clients, enforcing adherence to various availability and quality criteria;
- Internal
  - Functional:
      (R5) the services have to "work reasonably well";
  - Technical:
      (R6) the services have to "be properly secured".

Each of these requirements can be expressed with varying levels of detail. On one side, there are very specific requirements, such as (R3), with clearly defined quantitative criteria. On another side, there are requirements that call for a more human appreciation, such as (R2). Finally, some requirements need to be further refined by domain experts, such as (R5).

---

[1] They are chosen randomly to illustrate concretely our approach.

4.2 Infrastructure Model

Logical Model

Let us now focus on the infrastructure itself before undertaking the risk assessment. A synoptic diagram is shown on Fig. 5. This cloud infrastructure is composed of four zones:

– A *Demilitarized Zone* (DMZ) consisting of public-facing services, such as
  • web servers, for the company's main websites and open banking APIs for its B2B services,
  • authoritative DNS servers, to ensure the proper resolution of the company's domain names,
  • mail servers, for its day-to-day communication needs;
– A regular backend, for most of its business operations, with, among others,
  • databases (primary and secondary LDAP and SQL servers) for its queryable data,
  • business software (customer relationship management and enterprise resource planning software) for its management activities,
  • in-house software for its core processes;
– A PCI DSS backend, for its electronic payment activities, with
  • card processing software,
  • sensitive cardholder and transaction databases;
– A VPN for the network access of its ATMs.

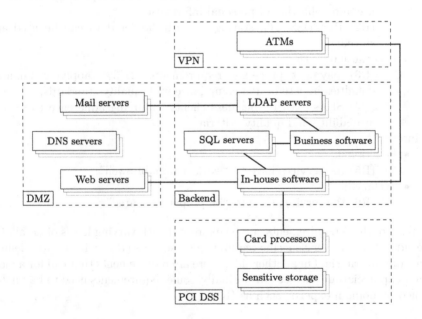

Fig. 5. Infrastructure zones

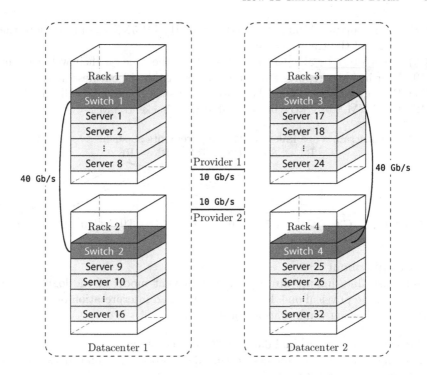

Fig. 6. Physical infrastructure

Physical Model

Every cloud infrastructure eventually relies on a physical one. The company owns two datacenters in two different locations and allocated 32 servers (16 in each datacenter) for its private cloud. These servers are distributed in several rooms, as shown on Fig. 6 and both data centers are connected via two separate network links from two providers.

4.3   Constraints

From Requirements

Considering the infrastructure described above, the requirements (R1) to (R6) can be broken down into the following constraints (the terms in small capitals are defined in [7]):

(C1) Users MUST be able to access their personal data;

(C2) Personal information MUST be securely stored;

(C3) Access to personal data MUST be subject to strong authentication;

(C4) Non-PCI DSS server MUST NOT access PCI DSS databases directly;

(C5) Non-PCI DSS VM MUST NOT be collocated with a PCI-DSS one;

(C6) PCI-DSS VMs MUST run on PCI-DSS nodes;

(C7) 99.9% of transactions MUST be processed within 3 s;

(C8) Open banking APIs MUST NOT return HTTP 5XX errors for more than
      0.01% of the transactions;
(C9) Users MUST be able to connect 99.7% of the time on their web account;
(C10) User incident reports MUST be handled within 12 business hours;
(C11) Primary and secondary database nodes SHOULD NOT be collocated;
(C12) DMZ VM MUST NOT be collocated with backend VMs.

These constraints are linked to the requirements as such:

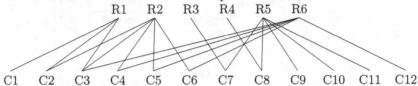

... to Deployment

These constraints impact directly the deployment model of the logical infrastructure on the physical one. For example, from an interpretation of C2, we can
derive the following configuration constraints:

(C2α) Disks storing personal data MUST be encrypted;
(C2β) Physical access to servers hosting disks storing personal data MUST be
restricted to authorized personnel;
(C2γ) Data flows carrying personal data MUST be encrypted.

As another example, the following constraints can be chosen to provably satisfy
(under the hypothesis that the switches have a perfect VLAN isolation) C4:

(C4α) PCI DSS databases MUST be on their own VLAN;
(C4β) Other logical components MUST NOT be on this VLAN;
(C4γ) PCI DSS VMs MAY access the PCI DSS databases VLAN;
(C4δ) Non-PCI DSS VMs MUST NOT access this VLAN.

4.4   Risk

Side-Effect Analysis
From the constraints, the following hazards can for example be identified :

(C1) ⟨ (H1) Personal data can be stolen from users if their machines get
            infected;
         (H2) Personal data can be stolen from users if their passwords get
            stolen;

(C3) ⟨ (H3) Personnel losing a physical factor cannot do their work;
         (H4) Users losing a physical factor cannot access the services in
            case of an emergency;

(C7) ── (H5) The company accepts transactions that should be rejected;
(C10) ── (H6) Time constraints put pressure on the employees.

From there, the company needs to update its requirements. (H1) is considered out of the scope of the company and (H2) is already covered by (C3). (H5) is a hazard difficult to balance. On the one hand, in case of a network congestion and during peak hours, transaction times increase and the issuing bank risks paying penalties if the transactions time out. On the other hand, the company may be tempted to automatically accept some transactions, but may then be liable in case of a fraudulent payment, and therefore reimburse the payment out of his own funds. Finally, the company does not have the internal skills to handle (H6) and needs to outsource them.

(H3) —— (R7) The company must deal with lost or stolen authenticators;
(H4) —— (R8) Emergency services must be offered to clients;
(H6) —— (R9) Time pressure on employees must be handled.

The company then has to implement the requirements with constraints and do the recursive side-effect analysis again until it ends. It should be noted that the boundaries between requirements and constraints is blurred. The distinction is not always useful, but we consider here that constraints generate side-effects on risks, while requirements are rules independent of the infrastructure.

Part Analysis

The company has deployed a *Configuration Management Database* (CMDB) that provides information about hardware (brands, models, locations), OSes, services and their configurations. The CMDB pulls its information from several domain-specific models continuously updated by hand or automatically. To diagnose hardware-related problems, the company can fetch the relevant manuals from its CMDB, but often needs to contact the manufacturer directly. The incident analysis must therefore be outsourced, as the company does not have a sufficiently broad knowledge on the inner workings of such hardware.

Providing incident (and, to take a proactive approach, risk) analysis tools would be an interesting move from the manufacturer, as it would save time for itself and the company. We also believe that it could give more confidence in the reliability of its products.

Assembly Analysis

A common risk assessment referential could also allow the company to reuse and share experience on the interactions of cloud infrastructure components: datacenters, hypervision clusters or distributed software have specific properties that their components do not have. Datacenters present risks for the environment and the population. Clusters behave differently depending on their sizes and the voting algorithms they implement. A piece of distributed software may have sub-optimal performance if one of its nodes is operational but shows a degraded capacity.

An example of a generic referential entry for hypervision clusters that the company could use is shown on Table 1. It would ideally be parsable by a computer and should be able to interface with the various infrastructure models.

Table 1. Extract of a risk referential entry for hypervision clusters

Component	Hazard	Criteria	Likelihood	$\cdots$
Hypervision Cluster	CPU cache can leak to a collocated VM	VMs are paravirtualized	Moderate	
		VMs are fully virtualized	Low	
	Resource exhaustion	Over-allocation of resources	Very high	
	Badly distributed database	Two database nodes located on the same physical node	Moderate	$\cdots$
	Saturation of the internal hypervision network	Two nodes communicating heavily while not located the same physical node	Moderate	
		$\cdots$		

4.5   Lessons Learned

We illustrate in this example how our approach can help business to perform a more thorough risk analysis. We advocate that, in the spirit of modern software development, such analyses should be shared and be interoperable. In the context of dynamic and increasingly distributed infrastructures, automating IT risk analysis could help ensure greater security and safety, where manual analyses, although potentially more advanced, are more suited to static systems.

5   Conclusion and Future Work

In this article, we have shown, through an example of cloud infrastructure, how risk analysis on modern IT architectures differs from the domains where it is traditionally used, such as avionics or railway systems. Such analyses cannot be comprehensive because of the dynamic nature of IT infrastructures. Additionally, knowledge is limited by the lack of detailed understanding of several hardware or software elements that make them up. The big picture of a company on the other hand can be obtained through rigorous infrastructure modeling. Federating all these views is not the quest for *the* perfect risk analysis for such infrastructures, but rather the search for *a* better analysis, one that gives the company a sufficient degree of confidence and helps it identify previously unforeseen risk scenarios.

The strategies presented in this article are not yet implemented, because they rely on local risk analyses from manufacturers and developers. The work is already done in part in user manuals, but the lack of a common risk interchange format motivates us to establish a risk referential to start the effort. This is a work in progress. On top of that, we are developing a modeling language for IT infrastructures, in order to link together local infrastructure models and risk analyses for computer-assisted risk management on such infrastructures.

References

1. Reference Model of Open Distributed Processing (RM-ODP). http://rm-odp.net/
2. Abbass, W., Baina, A., Bellafkih, M.: Using EBIOS for risk management in critical information infrastructure. In: 5th World Congress on Information and Communication Technologies, pp. 107–112 (2015). https://doi.org/10.1109/WICT.2015.7489654
3. Agence Nationale de la Sécurité des Systèmes d'Information: EBIOS Risk Manager (2019). https://www.ssi.gouv.fr/uploads/2019/11/anssi-guide-ebios_risk_manager-en-v1.0.pdf
4. Alturkistani, F.M., Emam, A.Z.: A review of security risk assessment methods in cloud computing. In: Rocha, Á., Correia, A.M., Tan, F.B., Stroetmann, K.A. (eds.) New Perspectives in Information Systems and Technologies, Volume 1. AISC, vol. 275, pp. 443–453. Springer, Cham (2014). https://doi.org/10.1007/978-3-319-05951-8_42
5. Anthes, G.: Open source software no longer optional. Commun. ACM **59**(8), 2949684 (2016) https://doi.org/10.1145/2949684
6. Baybutt, P.: A critique of the Hazard and Operability (HAZOP) study. J. Loss Preven. Process Indust. **33**, 52–58 (2015). https://doi.org/10.1016/j.jlp.2014.11.010
7. Bradner, S.O.: Key words for use in RFCs to Indicate Requirement Levels. RFC 2119 (1997). https://www.rfc-editor.org/info/rfc2119
8. Cristea, G., Constantinescu, D.: A comparative critical study between FMEA and FTA risk analysis methods. IOP Conf. Ser. Mater. Sci. Eng. **252**, 012046 (2017). https://doi.org/10.1088/1757-899x/252/1/012046
9. van Deursen, A., Klint, P., Visser, J.: Domain-specific languages: an annotated bibliography. SIGPLAN Notices **35**(6), 352035 (2000). https://doi.org/10.1145/352029.352035
10. European parliament and council of the European union: general data protection regulation (2016). https://eur-lex.europa.eu/legal-content/EN/TXT/PDF/?uri=CELEX:32016R0679
11. Golra, F.R., Beugnard, A., Dagnat, F., Guérin, S., Guychard, C.: addressing modularity for heterogeneous multi-model systems using model federation. In: Companion Proceedings of the 15th International Conference on Modularity (MoMo2016). ACM (2016). https://doi.org/10.1145/2892664.2892701
12. Hannousse, A., Yahiouche, S.: Securing microservices and microservice architectures: a systematic mapping study. Comput. Sci. Rev. **41**, 100415 (2021). https://doi.org/10.1016/j.cosrev.2021.100415
13. He, J., Sun, L.: A Review on SLA-Related Applications in Cloud Computing. In: 2018 1st International Cognitive Cities Conference (IC3) (2018). https://doi.org/10.1109/IC3.2018.00027
14. International Electrotechnical Commission: IEC 61882:2016 – Hazard and operability studies (HAZOP studies) - Application guide (2016). https://webstore.iec.ch/publication/24321
15. International Organization for Standardization: ISO 27005:2018 – Information technology - Security techniques - Information security risk management (2018). https://www.iso.org/standard/75281.html
16. International Organization for Standardization: ISO 31000:2018 – Risk management - Guidelines (2018). https://www.iso.org/standard/65694.html

17. Jackson, D.: Software abstractions: logic, language, and analysis. The MIT Press, second edn. (2011)
18. Leveson, N.G., Fleming, C.H., Spencer, M., Thomas, J., Wilkinson, C.: Safety assessment of complex, software-intensive systems. SAE Int. J. Aerospace **5**(1), 233–244 (2012). https://doi.org/10.4271/2012-01-2134
19. Lv, J., Rong, J.: Virtualisation security risk assessment for enterprise cloud services based on stochastic game nets model. IET Inf. Secur. **12**(1), 0038 (2018). https://doi.org/10.1049/iet-ifs.2017.0038
20. Masoudi, R., Ghaffari, A.: Software defined networks: a survey. J. Netw. Comput. Appli. **67**, 016 (2016). https://doi.org/10.1016/j.jnca.2016.03.016
21. Mastercard: transaction processing rules (2021). https://www.mastercard.us/content/dam/public/mastercardcom/na/global-site/documents/transaction-processing-rules.pdf
22. Merabti, M., Kennedy, M., Hurst, W.: Critical infrastructure protection: a 21st century challenge. In: 2011 International Conference on Communications and Information Technology (ICCIT) (2011). https://doi.org/10.1109/ICCITECHNOL.2011.5762681
23. Murata, T.: Petri nets: Properties, analysis and applications. Proceed. IEEE **77**(4), 24143 (1989). https://doi.org/10.1109/5.24143
24. Neville-Neil, G.: I Unplugged what? Commun. ACM **65**(2), 3506579 (2022). https://doi.org/10.1145/3506579
25. OMG: Unified Modeling Language (UML), Version 2.5.1 (2017). https://www.omg.org/spec/UML/2.5.1
26. Payment card industry security standards council: payment card industry data security standard (2022). https://www.pcisecuritystandards.org/documents/PCI-DSS-v40.pdf
27. Rose, L.C.: Risk management of COTS based systems development. In: Cechich, A., Piattini, M., Vallecillo, A. (eds.) Component-Based Software Quality. LNCS, vol. 2693, pp. 352–373. Springer, Heidelberg (2003). https://doi.org/10.1007/978-3-540-45064-1_16
28. SAE International: ARP4761 – Guidelines and methods for conducting the safety assessment process on civil airborne systems and equipment (1996). https://www.sae.org/standards/content/arp4761/
29. SAE International: AS9100D – Quality management systems - requirements for aviation, space, and defense organizations (2016). https://www.sae.org/standards/content/as9100d/
30. Sulaman, S.M., Beer, A., Felderer, M., Höst, M.: Comparison of the FMEA and STPA safety analysis methods–a case study. Software Qual. J. **27**(1), 349–387 (2017). https://doi.org/10.1007/s11219-017-9396-0
31. The Open Group: ArchiMate ® 3.1 Specification. https://publications.opengroup.org/c197
32. Varga, A., Hornig, R.: An overview of the OMNeT++ simulation environment. In: Proceedings of the 1st International Conference on Simulation Tools and Techniques for Communications, Networks and Systems & Workshops. Simutools 2008, ICST (Institute for Computer Sciences, Social-Informatics and Telecommunications Engineering) (2008)
33. Visa: Visa core rules and visa product and service rules (2022). https://bb.visa.com/content/dam/VCOM/download/about-visa/visa-rules-public.pdf
34. Yates, A.: A framework for studying mortality arising from critical infrastructure loss. Int. J. Crit. Infrastruct. Protect. **7**(2), 100–111 (2014). https://doi.org/10.1016/j.ijcip.2014.04.002

IoT Security Within Small and Medium-Sized Manufacturing Companies

Johannes Beckert[✉], Teo Blazevic, and Alexander Dobhan

Technical University of Applied Sciences Würzburg-Schweinfurt, 97421 Schweinfurt, Germany
{Johannes.Beckert,Alexander.Dobhan}@thws.de

Abstract. Digitization of production is on the strategic agenda of many companies across the globe. The term IoT (Internet of Things) is meanwhile common for small and medium-sized companies (SMEs). Along with the technical innovations, especially in the environment of cloud based IoT solutions, the topic of IoT security is gaining outstanding importance. This paper presents a pre-study and investigation of the experience, awareness, activities, and knowledge regarding IoT security among SMEs. Despite of the limited numbers of respondents (29) the results of the research show that while SMEs are aware of IoT security threats, they also lack the knowledge to protect themselves against all possible attack vectors.

Keywords: IoT Security · Attack vectors · IoT

1 Introduction

Digitization of production is on the strategic agenda of many companies across the globe. The term IoT (Internet of Things) is meanwhile common for medium-sized companies. In general, IoT is a paradigm, where objects in the real world have a unique digital address and are interacting with each other through a wireless or wired connection to create new services (Patel 2016). Along with the technical innovations, especially in the environment of cloud based IoT solutions and smart factories, the topic of "IoT security" in general is gaining outstanding importance (WEF 2022). Nevertheless, when starting an IoT project, the security of the systems is often neglected in favor of focusing on functionality (Vogt 2016). More and more SMEs are starting to implement IoT technologies in their value chains as well as other technics synonymous with Industry 4.0 (Malik 2021). Therefore, IT and IoT are becoming more intertwined, and security is of the utmost importance in this field. In addition to the classic IT world, the IoT infrastructure includes new types of devices such as wearables or physical production machines, which are connected to the classic IP-based IT infrastructure or cloud-based services. With the ever-increasing digitization of objects and processes within the companies, new vulnerabilities and exploits are available to any person who wants to deal with damage to the implemented IoT systems (Singh 2021). To combat these new vectors of attack, organizations should gather *experience*, show *awareness*, take *activities*, and possess the *knowledge* to assure they are well protected from any attackers they might encounter. In general, the Oxford

S. Kallel et al. (Eds.): CRiSIS 2022, LNCS 13857, pp. 185–190, 2023.
https://doi.org/10.1007/978-3-031-31108-6_14

Advanced Learner's Dictionary defines *experience* as "the knowledge and skill that you have gained through doing something for a period of time". Experiences increase people's awareness of possible threats arising. From this perspective, *awareness* can be seen as the perception of possible dangers. Furthermore, awareness leads to *activities* and a behavior change, which afterward should protect the individual or organization from these threads based on the *knowledge* each of them got (Hänsch 2014). While many large corporations can leverage their capital to invest in the necessary knowledge and activities to secure themselves, smaller companies are often strapped for cash, constantly evaluating where their next budget should be allocated (Heidt et al. 2019). Therefore, this pre-study, which is embedded in a wider research initiative, questions, where especially SMEs stand in this current situation and how well they are prepared for the challenges ahead to protect their IoT environments. Even though the number of respondents (29) is very limited, we believe the results are interesting and contributes to IoT Security within SMEs. In future the study will be combined with further research results to get an in-depth understanding in IoT security within SMEs. In addition to other studies that were conducted in IoT security like Neshenko et al. (2019) or Zhao (2020), which in general focus on IoT attack vectors, this research paper especially provides insights into the current situation of manufacturing-based SMEs and their strategies for tackling IoT security. For this purpose, the research subcategorizes the process of evaluating into four intertwined parts: experience, awareness, activities, and knowledge.

Our hypotheses toward these categories are:

H1: The majority of small and medium-sized manufacturing companies have experience with implementing IoT infrastructure. (*Experience*).

H2: Most small and medium-sized manufacturing companies are aware of the risk of an attack on their IoT infrastructure. (*Awareness*).

H3: The majority of small and medium-sized manufacturing companies are taking activities to protect their IoT infrastructure. (*Activities*).

H4: The knowledge of all possible dangers in connection with IoT attacks is available within small and medium-sized manufacturing companies. (*Knowledge*).

2 Research Methodology

Quantitative research in form of a survey was used to gain an understanding of the IoT security situation in manufacturing-based SMEs and to prove our hypothesis H1-H4. The survey consists of twelve questions, which are formulated as closed questions. Question one relates to the number of employees to determine whether the company is a SME or whether it falls outside our grid. For the study, the target group of interest was manufacturing SMEs. The literature differed from 100 to 500 employees to define SMEs (Aybar-Arias 2003). The concentration on manufacturing businesses was done because IoT will be implemented more and more within the production process (Jung et al. 2021). The selection of companies was narrowed down according to the criteria "small and medium-sized" and "manufacturing". Question 2 deals with the role of the respondent within the company. Questions 3 and 4 focus on the experience of the company implementing IoT technics and suffering damages from IT attacks in general. Question 5 asks for the estimation of how likely the company thinks an attack on the IoT infrastructure is and addresses the awareness. Questions 6 till 11 concern the activities carried out by the company, like investing in security solutions, using internal or external staff, planning of improvements, repeat training of the employees, implementing an emergency plan or hacking itself to learn how vulnerable the own infrastructure is. With question 12, the research evaluates if the knowledge of these companies allows them to be protected themselves from attacks on their systems by referencing a scientific IoT attack classification from Deogirikar (2017) and Farsi (2020). 150 companies were contacted during December 2021. As a result, 29 answers have been recorded by questionnaire, which is a response rate of 19,3% of all companies questioned.

3 Data and Findings

This paper highlights the results based on a survey questioning SMEs regarding IoT security. We hypothesized; that the majority of small and medium-sized manufacturing companies have *experience* with implementing IoT infrastructure (H1) and that most companies are *aware* of the risk of an attack on their IoT infrastructure (H2). Further, we assumed that the majority of companies are taking security *activities* to protect their IoT infrastructure (H3). At least we assumed that the *knowledge* within the companies is available for all possible dangers in connection with IoT attacks (H4).

3.1 Screening

13 out of 29 Companies (44.83%) had less than 50 employees, 7 companies (24.14%) had between 51 and 250 employees. 3 (10,34%) companies had between 251 and 500 employees. Due to the definition of small and medium-sized companies, all companies that exceed a size of 500 employees are initially left out of the further analysis. The answers of 6 companies out of 29 companies - which is 20.69% - have been removed from the further analysis due to their company size. 15 of the 23 respondents, which is 65.22%, are company managers or similar. 21.74% (5) are administrators, who administrate the IoT solution. Further 8.7% (2) are end-users, which are dealing with the IoT environment in their daily business. One respondent (4.35%) could not match any of the offered categories.

3.2 Experience

The question "Do you have IoT systems in use in your company?" was used to identify if the company has experience with IoT technologies. 69.57% (16) of the companies have already implemented some form of IoT systems and a further 13.04% (3) stated that they are planning to implement such technologies. Within the result set, 4 respondents (17.39%) answered, that they are not using IoT environments and that they are not planning to use them in the future. Due to these circumstances, these four answers are excluded in the following, because the questions are referencing the IoT systems within the companies. The question "Have you ever suffered damages from IT attacks in general?" examined whether companies have already been attacked. 26.32% (5) of the companies stated, that they already have been attacked and suffered damages. 21.05%

(4) stated that they "do not know" if they have been attacked. 52.63% (10) answered "No". Our hypothesis H1 was hereby confirmed. It can be said that the majority gathered experiences with IoT technologies. In addition to that, over 26% of the companies have even suffered damage by IT attacks in general.

3.3 Awareness

With the question "Do you think small and mid-sized companies are prone to attacks on the IoT infrastructure?" we are looking at the extent to which companies are aware of the resulting risk of an attack on the IoT systems. From the data we have gathered, our hypothesis H2 was confirmed. It can be extracted that more than 84% (16) of the companies are aware that SMEs are vulnerable to an attack on their IoT infrastructure. The majority of the companies realize that they are a possible target for attacks.

3.4 Activities

Our hypothesis H3 was confirmed, but it can be noted that the situation towards activities to protect the IoT infrastructure differs within the respondent group. 57,89% (11) stated that the costs for implementing IoT security in comparison to the overall IT costs are "medium". However, almost 21% (4) of the respondents also stated that the costs were "low" (15.79%) or "very low" (5.26%). Only 21.05% (4) stated they are "high". It can be observed that nearly the half (around 47.37%, 9) of the companies work with a combination of internal employees and external partners. 36.84% (7) cover their IT security completely internally. Further 15.79% (3) of the respondents have completely outsourced their IT security. It is very pleasing to see that 57.89% (11) of the respondents stated that they have plans for improving their IoT security. However, over 42.1% (8) also indicated that they have no further plans for improvement. The evaluation showed that in 21.05% (4) of the companies surveyed, IoT security training only takes place every two to three years and in 36,84% (7) not at all. Less than the half (42.1%) are trained once within a year. Furthermore, the survey revealed that 36.84% (7) do not have an emergency plan and 68.42% (13) mentioned that they had not tried to hack themselves. This leads to the assumption that many companies do not even know where their vulnerabilities lie. Only 15.79% tried to hack their IoT infrastructure to learn how vulnerable it is.

3.5 Knowledge

The survey revealed that the knowledge of all possible dangers in connection with IoT attacks is not available in all small and medium-sized manufacturing companies. (cf. Figure 1). In that way, our hypothesis H4 was not confirmed. The results have shown that there are vectors, which are well known as "Viruses & Worms", "Phishing Attacks" or "DoS Attackes". In many other vectors of attack like "Sinkhole Attacks", "Node Tampering", Cryptanalysis Attacks, "Side-channel Attacks" or "Malicious Node Injection" there are still very large deficits to be worked through. This can be an indication to catch up to acquire knowledge and protect oneself better.

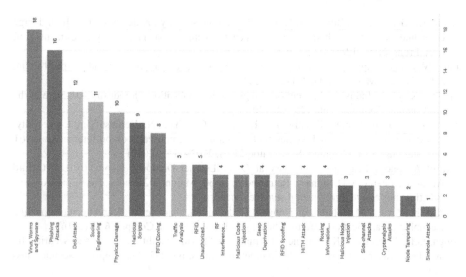

Fig. 1. Question 12: "Mark all IoT security attacks you are familiar with."

4 Conclusion and Further Research

This paper investigated the experience, awareness, activities, and knowledge of SMEs regarding IoT security. The paper showed that IoT technologies are quite common even within small and medium-sized manufacturing companies. Further, it pointed out that the majority of SMEs is aware of attacks on their IoT infrastructure. However, it disclosed that the companies differ in the scope and depth of the implementation of security measures. Furthermore, the survey also revealed that most companies are currently not covering all IoT security-related perspectives to secure their IoT infrastructure. This offers a high potential to expand knowledge regarding IoT attack vectors and improve the situation within small and medium-sized manufacturing companies. Regarding our study, it needs to be stated that in our future research, the sample of the survey will be expanded to verify the findings presented. Furthermore, we are going to analyze the interferences between each survey question to identify dependencies between respondent answers.

References

Aybar-Arias, C., Casino-Martinez, A., & Lopez-Gracia, J.: Capital structure and sensitivity in SME definition: a panel data investigation. Available at SSRN 549082 (2003)

Deogirikar, J., Vidhate, A.: Security attacks in IoT: a survey. In: 2017 International Conference on I-SMAC (IoT in Social, Mobile, Analytics and Cloud) (I-SMAC), pp. 32–37. IEEE (2017)

Farsi, M., Daneshkhah, A., Hosseinian-Far, A., Jahankhani, H. (eds.): IT, Springer, Cham (2020). https://doi.org/10.1007/978-3-030-18732-3

Hänsch, N., Benenson, Z.: Specifying IT security awareness. In: 2014 25th International Workshop on Database and Expert Systems Applications, pp. 326–330. IEEE (2014)

Heidt, M., Gerlach, J.P., Buxmann, P.: Investigating the security divide between SME and large companies: how SME characteristics influence organizational IT security investments. Inf. Syst. Front. **21**(6), 1285–1305 (2019)

Jung, W.K., et al.: Appropriate smart factory for SMEs: concept, application and perspective. Int. J. Precis. Eng. Manuf. **22**(1), 201–215 (2021)

Malik, P.K., et al.: Industrial Internet of Things and its applications in industry 4.0: State of the art. Comput. Commun. **166**, 125–139 (2021)

Neshenko, N., Bou-Harb, E., Crichigno, J., Kaddoum, G., Ghani, N.: Demystifying IoT security: an exhaustive survey on IoT vulnerabilities and a first empirical look on Internet-scale IoT exploitations. IEEE Commun. Surv. Tutor. **21**(3), 2702–2733 (2019)

Oxford Advanced Learner's Dictionary at OxfordLearnersDictionaries.com. (o. D.). Oxford Advanced Learner's Dictionary. Retrieved from 30. March 2021. https://www.oxfordlearne rsdictionaries.com/definition/english/experience_1

Patel, K.K., Patel, S.M.: Internet of Things-IOT: definition, characteristics, architecture, enabling technologies, application & future challenges. Int. J. Eng. Sci. Comput. **6**(5) (2016)

Singh, G.P., Bangotra, P.K.: Internet of Things (IoT): vulnerability, attacks, and security. In: Wireless Sensor Networks and the Internet of Things, pp. 247–262. Apple Academic Press (2021)

Vogt, A., Landrock, H., Dransfeld, H.: Industrie 4.0/IoT vendor benchmark 2017: an analysis by Experton Group AG. An ISG Business, Munich, German (2016)

WEF: IoT security: How we are keeping consumers safe from cyber threats. (2022, 28. February). World Economic Forum (2022). https://www.weforum.org/impact/iot-security-keeping-consumers-safe/

Zhao, B., Ji, S., Lee, W. H., Lin, C., Weng, H., Wu, J., Beyah, R.: A large-scale empirical study on the vulnerability of deployed IoT devices. IEEE Trans. Depend. Secure Comput. **19**, 1826–1840 (2020)

An Incentive Mechanism for Managing Obligation Delegation

Liang Chen[1(✉)], Cheng Zeng[2], and Stilianos Vidalis[1]

[1] Department of Computer Science, University of Hertfordshire, Hatfield, UK
{l.chen26,s.vidalis}@herts.ac.uk
[2] Central Southern China Electric Power Design Institute, Wuhan, China
zc5793@csepdi.com

Abstract. Many modern information systems use a policy-based approach to manage sensitive information and availability of services. Obligations are essential part of security policies, which specify what actions a user is obliged to perform in the future. One interesting feature of obligations is unenforceable, that is, the system cannot guarantee that each obligation will be fulfilled. Indeed, obligations go unfulfilled for a variety of reasons. For example, a user may have family emergency that leads her having little time to discharge assigned obligations. We argue that delegation of obligations can be regarded as a means of providing opportunity for obligations to be discharged. However, this opportunity will be wasted if users who received delegation do not fulfil the obligations eventually. In this paper we propose a mechanism that incentivises users to accept and fulfil obligations for others by rewarding users credits. The amount of credits can be earned depends on their trust score, which reflects precisely how diligent of individuals in fulfilling obligations in the past. Users are motivated to raise up their trust scores by fulfilling obligations for others, in order to earn more credits in the future. We run experiments in a simulated multi-agent systems to evaluate our approach, which turns out that delegation with incentives achieves the best outcome in terms of the number of obligations being fulfilled.

1 Introduction

Obligation and authorisation are essential building blocks to form security policies [14], which define the correct behaviour of an information system. A system adopting this type of policy-based approach to governing agents' behaviour is called normative multiagent systems [3]. Obligations in such systems define what activities have to be performed by whom and when, and these obligatory actions are integral part of the control procedures in many organisations. For example, a course leader is obliged to submit a course assessment report to an external examiner at least three days before exam board meeting. As the example illustrates, the system can determine whether and when the obligation is fulfilled, but cannot force the course leader to submit the report on time. In other words, the system cannot ensure that obligations can always be fulfilled, but instead it

S. Kallel et al. (Eds.): CRiSIS 2022, LNCS 13857, pp. 191–206, 2023.
https://doi.org/10.1007/978-3-031-31108-6_15

should give every *opportunity* for obligations to be discharged, in order to ensure the correct operation of a system.

One of such opportunities to allow a user to delegate her assigned obligations to others. We refer to the user who performs a delegation as a "delegator", and the user who receives a delegation as a "delegatee". Indeed, there are a number of organisational motives behind the delegation of an obligation [13]. For example, a user may have been assigned a few obligations which need to be fulfilled at similar sort of deadline. However, due to other work commitments, it would be desirable for the user to delegate some of the obligations to others who has similar competence but have less constraints. There has been some work on delegation of obligations, most of which focuses on operational semantics for delegation and mechanisms for monitoring the fulfilment of delegated obligations [13], as well as identifying responsibilities among the users who involved in the delegation of obligations [2]. While allowing the occurrence of delegation provides an opportunity for delegator's assigned obligations to be discharged, it is not clear that why delegatee would be willing to fulfil obligations for others unless there is an incentive for them to do so. If delegatees eventually leave the delegated obligations going unfulfilled, all complexities from managing the delegation become unnecessary. The question of how to incentivise delegatees to discharge delegated obligations, to the best of our knowledge, has not yet been adequately investigated. Such considerations are the focus of this paper. More specifically, the contributions of this paper are as follows:

- We introduce a simple trust computation method on the basis of the Beta distribution to compute trust score of users, reflecting their performance on fulfilling obligations. We discuss a number of possible ways of updating trust score for the delegator and delegatee when a delegated obligation is fulfilled or violated. The discussion confirms the best possible way to update trust in order to incentivise delegtees to fulfil obligations.
- We further propose a credit rewarding scheme that rewards delegatee credits for fulfilling obligations, but the amount of credits can be rewarded is determined by her trust score. From the delegator's perspective, he needs to pay credits to the delegatee on her efforts to fulfilling the delegated obligation, thus the scheme avoids the situation where users are always seeking to delegate their assigned obligations to others.
- When a delegated obligation arises in the system, we define a set of eligibility criteria for delegatees to bid for the obligation. We also define a number of possible risk preferences a delegator may take in terms of choosing a delegatee, since the chosen delegatee has uncertainty of whether to fulfil the delegated obligation. We also explore the incentive mechanism in the face of cascaded delegation of obligations.
- We run experiments in a simulated multi-agent systems to evaluate our models. The results reveal that the proposed incentive mechanisms promote users being more diligent in fulfilling obligations.

In the next section we describe relevant background materials on the Beta distribution and obligation properties.

2   Background

2.1   The Beta Distribution

Let X be a continuous random variable that has a Beta distribution [10] with two parameters α and β, where $\alpha > 0$ and $\beta > 0$. Then the *probability density function* of X can be expressed as:

$$f(x|\alpha, \beta) = \frac{x^{\alpha-1}(1-x)^{\beta-1}}{B(\alpha, \beta)}, \tag{1}$$

where $0 \leqslant x \leqslant 1$, and $B(\alpha, \beta)$ is a Beta function that can be defined in terms of the factorial functions when α and β are positive integers:

$$B(\alpha, \beta) = \frac{(\alpha-1)!(\beta-1)!}{(\alpha+\beta-1)!}. \tag{2}$$

The *probability expectation value* of the Beta random variable X is given by:

$$E(X) = \frac{\alpha}{\alpha + \beta}. \tag{3}$$

The standard beta distribution uses the interval range $[0, 1]$, which is ideal for modelling probabilities, particularly for experiments with only two outcomes, "success" and "failure". Also, the beta distribution is a *conjugate prior* to the binomial likelihood in Bayesian analysis. It means, after running more experiments, we can compute the posterior simply by adding the number of success and failure to the existing parameters α, β respectively, rather than multiplying the likelihood with the prior distribution. We will take this approach to model users' probability of fulfilling obligations which always have two outcomes, satisfied and violated.

2.2   Defining Obligations

There exists a number of policy languages being designed for specifying obligation policies. The most common approach is to use the temporal logic to capture time constraints associated with obligations [7,15]. However, we take an approach that is similar to [5,9], which defines a simple data structure capturing the essential components of an obligation.

We assume the existence of a clock, whose ticks are indexed by the natural number $\mathbb{N}$. A *time interval* $i = [t_1, t_2]$, where $t_1, t_2 \in \mathbb{N}$ and $t_1 < t_2$, is the set $\{t_1 \leqslant t \leqslant t_2\}$. We define an obligation *obl* as a tuple (u, a, i), where u is a user, a is an action, i is a time interval during which u is obliged to take action a. At a particular point of time t, an obligation $obl = (u, a, [t_s, t_e], c)$ may be in one of three states: active, satisfied, or violated. We say *obl* is *satisfied* if u has fulfilled the obligation (performed action a) at t and $t \in [t_s, t_e]$. We say *obl* is *violated* if the obligation has not been fulfilled, but t_e has passed ($t > t_e$). We say *obl* is *active* at t if it is neither satisfied nor violated.

It is important to keep the system always in a *desirable* state where no obligations go violated. However, since the system cannot enforce users to fulfil obligations, some obligations may go violated. What the system can do is to monitor the status of the obligation (e.g., whether it has been violated at some point of time) and to use reward and blame mechanisms to incentivise users to fulfil obligations. In the next section we introduce the concept of *obligation trust* for every user, which represents an user' trustworthiness in fulfilling obligations.

3   An Incentive Scheme for One Hop Delegation

3.1   Obligation Trust

Our approach to computing obligation trust for a user is based on the *evidence* the system has observed regarding the user's performance on fulfilling obligations in the past. The evidence we have is a sequence of good (satisfaction of an obligation) and bad (violation) experiences with that user. These experiences can be used to estimate the probability that the user will make obligations being satisfied in the future. We employ the Beta probability density function to transform the sequence of values of the binary variable representing good and bad experiences to a static probability distribution representing the user's obligation trust.

Formally, let H^{obl} be a history of obligation stratification events, whose members are the form of (u, obl, s), where $s \in \{\mathsf{satisfied}, \mathsf{violated}\}$, representing that the status s of obligation obl is caused by user u. Let r_u represent the observed number of obligations that are satisfied by u and let s_u represent the observed number of obligations that are violated by u. Then we set $\alpha = r_u + 1$ and $\beta = s_u + 1$, and follow Eqs. 1, 2 and 3 to compute obligation trust of an user u as:

$$P_{obl}(u)(r_u, s_u) = \frac{r_u + 1}{r_u + s_u + 2}, \tag{4}$$

where $r_u \geqslant 0$ and $s_u \geqslant 0$. It can be seen that the initial value for $P_{obl}(u) = 0.5$ when $r_u = s_u = 0$, but it will be updated as new evidence appears in the history H^{obl}. When r_u and s_u are obvious from context, we will simply write $P(u)$ for $P_{obl}(u)(r_u, s_u)$.

3.2   Delegating Obligations

In many situations, a user needs to delegate her assigned obligations to someone else, so that the obligations can be discharged by others rather than left to be violated. Let us first introduce delegation protocol, and its resulting data structures. We write $\mathsf{deleg}(obl, W)$ to denote a *delegation request*, meaning that the responsible user appearing in obligation obl requests to delegate it to some user w in the group W. The delegation request $\mathsf{deleg}(obl, W)$ will be evaluated by running a protocol and resulted in a delegatee w being chosen. We informally describe how the protocol works as follows:

1. A user u starts off broadcasting a delegation request $\text{delg}(obj, W)$ to a group of users W in the system. This group of users, for example, have similar competence level or job responsibilities within an organisation.
2. On receipt of the delegation announcement, each user $w \in W$ who wishes to put themselves forward will evaluates it with respect to their own schedule. If w is eligible to bid, w will submit her current obligation trust $P(w)$ to u;
3. Based upon several such bids being received in response to the announced delegation, u selects the most appropriate user to be assigned with the obligation obj.
4. Finally, u sends an award message to the successful bidder w, and also informs others whose bids were not successful.

In Sect. 4, we elaborate on how each user w assesses the eligibility against her own schedule, and how u makes a choice when multiple bids are received.

Following a successful running of the delegation protocol, we assume that the delegatee w is agreed to discharge the delegated obligation, while the delegator still remains as a responsible user for the obligation. We call delegatee w as an *obligated user* for the delegated obligation. We introduce a data structure, namely *delegated obligation*, that records an user-obligation assignment that arises from a delegation request being evaluated. A delegated obligation obl_d extends obl tuple with one additional element w, that is $obl_d = (u, a, i, w)$, where w is a user obligated to take action a during the time period i, whereas u is the original user taking responsibility for the fulfilment of obl_d. Specifically, suppose that a delegation request $\text{deleg}(obl, W)$ is evaluated at time t, then this results in updating obl as obl_d, where $obl_d = (u, a, (t + 1, t_e), w)$. It is reasonable to assume that u is no longer able to fulfil obl_d once it is generated, and only w can. As we discussed in Sect. 4, the user u may take some penalty if obl_d goes violated, thus keeping u in the data structure provides convenience for linking it to H^{obl}.

4   Incentivising Schemes

4.1   Updating Obligation Trust

We now explore how to incentivise users to discharge delegated obligations when delegations described above occur in the system. In such cases, it is not straightforward to give an appropriate assignment of blames or rewards to individuals who are involved in the delegation process.

Given a delegated obligation obl_d, there are two users involved: delegator u and delegatee w. We introduce two *weighting functions* $f_r : \{u, w\} \to [0, 1]$ and $f_s : \{u, w\} \to [0, 1]$, where $f_r(u) + f_r(w) = 1$ and $f_s(u) + f_s(w) = 1$. With the weighting function f_r, the full positive update value of 1 is distributed among users u and w. The function f_s serves the negative update among u and w in an analogous fashion. More specifically, given a delegated obligation obl_d and weighting functions f_r and f_s, we update r and s for users u and w as follows:

$$(r_u, s_u) = \begin{cases} (r_u + f_r(u), s_u) & \text{if } obl_d \text{ is satisfied} \\ (r_u, s_u + f_s(u)) & \text{otherwise} \end{cases} \tag{5}$$

$$(r_w, s_w) = \begin{cases} (r_w + f_r(w), s_w) & \text{if } obl_d \text{ is satisfied} \\ (r_w, s_w + f_s(w)) & \text{otherwise} \end{cases} \tag{6}$$

The two weight functions provide great flexibility on designing a number of possible ways of updating r and s for both users u and w to different degrees. Let us now discuss four cases that respond to incentivising w to fulfilling obl_d.

Case 1. The first extreme case is that w is only user taking responsible for the fulfilment outcome of obl_d. More specifically, if w satisfies obl_d, the system counts it as one positive evidence added to r_w ($f_r(w) = 1$), and there is no update on r_u ($f_r(u) = 0$). On the other hand, if w violates obl_d, then the negative evidence is only added to s_w ($f_s(w) = 1$), not to s_u ($f_s(u) = 0$). It means u transfers the responsibility of fulfilling obl_d to w when the delegation succeeds. This may be acceptable to w, as w takes advantage of this to "repair" her positive evidence. However, as the system get evolved, when w sees herself not be able to fulfil obl_d, she may choose to further delegate it to someone else, as she do not want to be penalised with the negative evidence being incremented. We will explore the situation of cascaded delegation in Sect. 5.

Case 2. The second feasible case also does not hold u and w equally responsible for the fulfilment outcome of obl_d. Unlike the first case, if w violates obl_d, then the system counts it as one negative evidence added to s_u ($f_s(u) = 1$), while s_w ($f_s(w) = 0$) remains unchanged. Like the first case, if obl_d is satisfied, one positive evidence is added to r_w only ($f_r(w) = 1$ and $f_r(u) = 0$). This case possesses two appealing characteristics:

- User w is incentivised to satisfy obligations for others, because this helps to repair its obligation trust score by increasing its r_w value;
- If u decides to delegate an obligation to others, then u needs to choose an *appropriate* user so as to ensure that s_u would not increment.

Note that this case is not without its problems. It may lead u to only delegate obl_d to someone w who she knew, because, for any stranger w, there is no negative impact on w's trust score if obl_d goes violated. In other words, the incentive for w to fulfil obligations for others is weak in this case.

Case 3. We now look at a case that divides the weight evenly between u and w, holding them equally responsible for the fulfilment of obl_d, that is $f_r(u) = f_r(w) = f_s(w) = f_s(u) = 0.5$. If w satisfies obl_d, $r_u = r_u + 0.5$ and $r_w = r_w + 0.5$. Likewise, if w violates obl_d, $s_u = s_u + 0.5$ and $s_w = s_w + 0.5$. However, someone may argue that this case leads u being unfairly rewarded: u may never fulfil obligations for herself or others, but her obligation trust is still increasing due to all obligations for which she is responsible are being fulfilled by others.

Case 4. We can rectify the unfairness of case 3 by adjusting the weighting function that gives one positive evidence to w ($f_r(w) = 1$) while obl_d is discharged by w. If obl_d goes violated, u and w are equally penalised by adding 0.5 to their s parameters ($f_s(w) = f_s(u) = 0.5$). Of course, we can slide a bit more negative weights on either direction - towards w or u, for example, setting $f_s(u) = 0.6$ and $f_s(w) = 0.4$. However, the principle is that both u and w should be blamed if obl_d is violated.

Following the discussion of four cases, we believe that the weights setting at Case 4 is the most appropriate one in terms of incentivising w to fulfil obl_d.

4.2   Earning Reward Credits

In essence, the four cases being discussed focus on the ways of updating *obligation trust* for users involved in the fulfilment of delegated obligations. However, it is not clear why a user who has high or full obligation trust is willing to accept a delegated obligation and discharge it within a deadline. This in fact leads to a more fundamental question: What is user's obligation trust used for?

Before addressing this question, let us extend the structure of obligation to include an element, called *reward credit*. That is, $obl = (u, a, i, c)$, where $c \in \mathbb{R}$ is *reward credit* associated with obl. It means, when obl is fulfilled by u, u is rewarded with the credit c. Of course, u would not receive c if obl goes unfulfilled. For ease of exposition we consider c to be a *constant* for every obligation.

We then take some ideas from the Principal-Agent model [8] to propose an incentive mechanism that utilises each user's obligation trust. If a user decides to delegate one of her assigned obligations to someone else, she has to pay delegatee some of the reward credit associated with the obligation. Likewise, if a user is willing to take some effort to fulfil an obligation for others, her effort should be paid off by some credit from the obligation. Our basic idea is that a user whose obligation trust is high can charge relevantly more credits, while user whose trust score is low receives relevantly less credits.

Formally, suppose that a delegated obligation obl_d is discharged by user w and c is a reward credit associated with obl_d, w's payoff (or "utility") is $\pi = c \times P(w)$, where $P(w)$ is w's obligation trust. This serves an incentive for users to fulfil obligations for others not only to earn credits but also to bring up their trust score in order to earn more credits in the future. From delegator u's point of view, u's payoff (or "profit") is the difference between the credit c associated with obl_d and the credit paid to delegatee w, that is $\phi = c - \pi$. A user w, for example, has a full trust score ($P(w) = 1$) can earn the whole credit c, thus there is no payoff left for u.

For simplicity, we assume that u is rational with an objective of choosing a delegatee w to maximise her payout ϕ. Choosing a user w who has the least trust score indeed maximises ϕ, but has a high risk that obl_d will go violated, leading to losing credit c completely and her obligation trust being reduced. Let us look at a simple example to examine the possible choices of u in more details. Given a delegated obligation obl_d whose reward credit is $c = 100$, there are three users w_1, w_2, w_3 eligible to accept obl_d, where $P(w_1) = 0.2$, $P(w_2) = 0.6$, $P(w_3) = 0.3$.

Hence u can earn payoff $\phi_{w_1} = 80$, $\phi_{w_2} = 40$ and $\phi_{w_3} = 70$ by choosing w_1, w_2 and w_3 respectively. In other words, u has probability of 0.2 of earning 80 credits by delegating obl_d to w_1; 40 credits with probability of 0.6 by delegating obl_d to w_2; 70 credits with probability of 0.3 by delegating obl_d to w_3.

With this example, which user w_1, w_2 or w_3 should u delegate obl_d to? We define three types of delegator u with respect to their *risk preference* when choosing w:

- *Risk-averse delegators*: This type of user u prefers to take a low uncertainty on whether delegated obligations will be satisfied, thus she always choose a delegatee w whose trust score is high but with a low return of payoff (credits). This type of u would choose w_2 as a delegatee for the example above.
- *Risk-seeking delegators*: This type of user u is willing to take a greater uncertainty on the obligation fulfilment in exchange for the potential of higher return of credits. In other words, u would choose w with least trust score in order to receive the highest payoff. A risk-seeking u would choose w_1 as a delegatee.
- *Risk-average delegators*: This type of user u is seeking a choice that achieves a great balance between return of credits and likelihood of obtaining the return. Taking the example above, u first calculates $\frac{1}{3}\sum_{i=1}^{3}(\phi_{w_i} \times P(w_i)) = 20.33$ and then chooses w_3 whose value $\phi_{w_3} \times P(w_3) = 21$ is closest to 20.33.

In Sect. 6, we run experiments to evaluate the performance of earning credits by the three types of delegators.

4.3   Eligibility of Delegatees

With the credit reward scheme introduced above, delegators would only wish to delegate obligations to others when they are legitimate to do so, because, compared with discharging obligations themselves, they are worse off in terms of earning credits by letting others fulfil their obligations. However, from the delegatee's perspective, they may wish to earn as much credits as they can by fulfilling obligations for others. When a delegation request for an obligation arises in the system, the system may want to restrict who are the eligible users to bid for accepting the obligation. We certainly want to exclude a user who already has a large number of active obligations whose deadlines clashed with the one at request.

We introduce a mechanism that establishes a schedule for each user in the system in terms of their assigned obligations. A *schedule* of a user w is a kind of look-up table that is indexed by time clocks. When an obligation is assigned to w, its fulfilment deadline t_e is marked in the schedule. Figure 1 shows an example of schedule for w where there is two obligations whose deadline is at t_4, four obligations at t_8, and five obligations at t_{10}.

We also implement a *restricted window* of size n on the schedule, where n indicates the number of time clocks the system would look at, in order to determine how busy w is within the window. Then we can define a threshold

h: The system may say that w is not eligible to accept more obligations if the number of marks within the window n exceeds h. This tends to encode rules such that "you cannot work more than h hours in the next n days". Take the example in Fig. 1, suppose that $h = 11$ and $n = 7$, when an obligation obj arises in the system at t_4, user w is not allowed to bid obj, because her current active obligations within the current window $n = 7$ (shown in dotted boarder in Fig. 1) reaches the threshed $h = 11$.

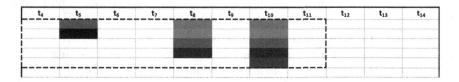

Fig. 1. A schedule for w at t_4

Having defined criteria assessing whether a user is eligible to accept a delegated obligation, we now in a position to confirm the computation for Step 2 of the delegation protocol introduced at Sect. 3.2. We can also see that how u chooses a delegatee w at Step 3 of the protocol depends upon their risk preference on earning credits.

5   Cascaded Delegation of Obligations

There are some situations where the obligated user w may wish to further delegate obl_d to a third user who is better qualified to fulfil obl_d. Take the example of Fig. 1, user w, at t_6, may realise that she is no longer able to discharge one of her previously awarded obligations, whose deadline is at t_{10}, and then she sends out a delegation request for the obligation in the system at t_6. Such a *delegation chain* is formed when an obligation is delegated from one user to another, who in turn delegates the obligation to a third user, and so on. We model the delegation chain by generalising the data structure of delegated obligations as $obl_d = (u, a, (t_s, t_e), c, (w)_{i=1}^{k})$, where $(w)_{i=1}^{k}$ is a sequence of users with the index running from $i = 1$ to $i = k$. For example, $obl_d = (u, a, (t_s, t_e), c, (w)_{i=1}^{3})$, where $(w)_{i=1}^{3} = (w_1, w_2, w_3)$ and w_3 is the *fourth* user in the delegation chain, since the first user in the chain would always be the originator u. Note that, given $obl_d = (u, a, (t_s, t_e), c, (w)_{i=1}^{3})$, t_s is the time obl_d awarded to w_3, which should *not* be close to t_e yet, otherwise w_3 would not have sufficient time to fulfil it. When it is clear from the context, we also write $dc = (u, w_1, \ldots, w_k)$ to denote a delegation chain.

Let us now examine whether we need to adjust the incentive mechanism in face of delegation chain. The first one is about how to update obligation trust for users appearing in a delegation chain. From the perspective of incentivising users to fulfil obligations, we believe that it is sensible to update our trust in these users to various degrees, in order to reflect that a particular outcome of obligation fulfilment (satisfied or violated) should not reflect equally on all the users' responsibilities for this outcome, and therefore on their trustworthiness. More specifically, we apply the full weights 1 to the last user who discharged the obligation. If the obligation goes violated, we apply an increasing proportion of weight along the delegation chain. For example, the last user in the chain receives the most negative weight added to her s evidence parameter, while the originating user (the first one in the chain) is given least negative weight. Given a delegation chain $dc = (u, w_1, \ldots, w_k)$, and $v_j \in dc$ where j denotes a position in the sequence dc, we compute the negative weight added to s_j as $\frac{2 \times j}{|dc|^2 + |dc|}$, where $|dc|$ is *size* of the delegation chain dc. Given $obl_d = (u, a, (t_s, t_e), c, (w)_{i=1}^3)$, it may not be possible for the originating user u to know in advance that w_1 will sub-delegate obl_d to w_2, and in turn w_1 would not know w_2 will sub-delegate obl_d to w_3. Thus it may not fair to penalise u equally as the last user w_3 who failed to fulfil obl_d. In other words, users at the back of chain who are willing to bid the obligation should bear more responsibilities for fulfilling it.

Withe respect to earning reward credits by users in the delegation chain, we take our previous approach that a delegator needs to pay delegatee's effort in fulfilling obligations. However, the amount of reward credits available to earn decreases along the delegation chain. Take an example of a delegation chain shown in Fig. 2, where w_3 can only earn 12 credits ($P(w_3) \times c_2$) despite her trust score is high ($P(w_3) = 0.8$), that is because w_2 herself only has 15 credits to give away, and this 15 credits is what she earned from c_1 ($P(w_2) \times c_1$). The best position here is u who can earn 70 credits if the obligation is eventually fulfilled by w_3. We can see that c_2 is relevantly low, which means it does not have much credits to earn in c_2, and thus may be difficult to attract anyone to bid for fulfilling the obligation. This is reasonable because it indirectly forces w_2 to fulfil the obligation as a priority, rather than sub-delegating it. Unless there exists someone w_3 who only cares about increasing her obligation trust, not on how much credits she can earn from fulfilling the obligation.

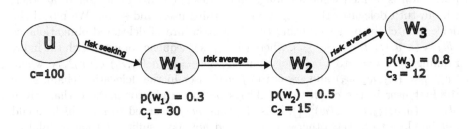

Fig. 2. An example of a delegation chain

When comes to risk perception of users in the delegation chain, our scheme provides great flexibility. That is, each user in the chain is free to take their own decision on how to choose a delagatee w. The decision can be made on the basis of their perception of which risk preference (risk-averse, risk-seeking, or risk-average) is the most appropriate one at a particular position of the chain. This results in a delegation chain where various risk preferences are adopted by users along the chain. Let us revisit the example in Fig. 2, where u took a risk-seeking approach for choosing w_1 in order to maximise her credit return 70, while w_1 took a risk-average approach when choosing w_2. User w_2 tends to choose someone w_3 who is most likely to fulfil the obligation by taking the risk-averse approach. We will be running experiments to confirm the performance of obligation fulfilment when allowing such a flexible cascaded delegation versus one-hop delegation only.

6 Evaluation

6.1 Experimental Setup

We develop a simulated multi-agent system to run experiments for evaluating our approach described above. Each experiment generates 100 users, which is first split into three groups with roughly equal in size: 33 risk-seeking users, 33 risk-averse users and 34 risk-average users. The system generates 3000 obligations every 50 time ticks. Each obligation is randomly assigned to one of the 100 users, and its fulfilment window $t_e - t_s$ is different, ranging from minimum 30 time ticks to maximum 80 time ticks. We also classified the 100 users into another three groups with respect to their *profile* of managing obligations: *diligent, potential* and *unmotivated*. Table 1 provides an interpretation of the three profiles. For example, users belonging to the potential profile, at every time tick, take 40% chance of executing active obligations (including system assigned and delegated obligations), 30% chance of requesting to delegate an obligation, and 30% chance of not taking any action. We allocate the same probability 0.3 of requesting a delegation to all the three profiles, which reflects the fact that every user has the same opportunity to delegate obligations to others. With the settings, the system now has in total *nine* types of users representing different behaviour in terms of fulfilling obligations and choosing delegatees.

Table 1. User behaviour at every time tick

Profile ID	Fulfilling Obligations	Delegating Obligations	Doing nothing
Diligent	0.6	0.3	0.1
Potential	0.4	0.3	0.3
Unmotivated	0.2	0.3	0.5

We implement a communication protocol between users for managing the delegation protocol defined in Sect. 3.2. This communication protocol runs in parallel to each possible action taken by a user defined in Table 1. It takes 3 time ticks to run from announcing a delegation request to confirming a successful bidder. Every user is always participating in bidding at every time tick as long as she is eligible to bid. We set up the eligibility criteria as the restricting window n as 40 time ticks and the threshold h as 15, which means a user is not allowed to bid if her active obligations exceed 15 within the next 40 time ticks. We also implement the approaches described in (Sects. 4.1 and 5) to update obligation trust and compute credits for one-hop delegation as well as cascaded delegation.

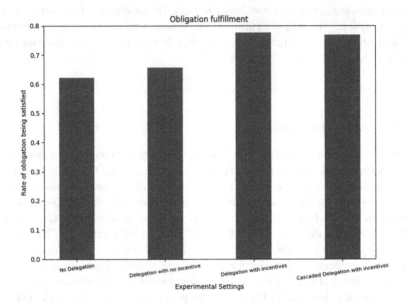

Fig. 3. A comparison for obligation fulfilment

6.2   Results

We run the settings for 4500 time ticks, which generates 270, 000 obligations. Figure 3 compares the results on the percentage of obligations being fulfilled with respect to the following four cases:

– *No delegation*: With this case, we turn off all the computations that involve with delegation. For example, a diligent user would now, at every time tick, have the probability of 0.6 to fulfil an obligation and probability of 0.4 being idle. Figure 3 shows that 62% obligations are satisfied in this case.

– *Delegation with no incentive*: This case considers the opportunity of allowing delegation to occur but users behaviour as defined in Table 1 do not get change (static) over the 4500 time ticks, even though their trust scores and associated credits are dynamic. The results in Fig. 3 confirms our expectation that a slight increase of obligation fulfilment rate to 66% due to the opportunity of delegation, but still 34% obligations being violated because of no incentive for users to change behaviour.

- *Delegation with incentives*: This case implements our incentive mechanisms within the experimental settings. Basically, the likelihood of each user to fulfilling obligations should get increase over the time because of the incentive to increasing their credits. There are many ways to realise this vision – we take a simple way in which, for each user, the ratio of increasing the likelihood at the next time tick depends on the number of delegated obligations being awarded currently. It means, if a user is dedicated to take responsibility to fulfilling obligations for others, then the system should provide an opportunity by increasing the probability for her to do so. Figure 3 illustrates a significant effect of the incentive mechanism on the number of obligations being satisfied (reaching 78%).
- *Cascaded delegation with incentives*: This case relaxes the restriction on the one-hop delegation to support all the features of cascaded delegation introduced in Sect. 5. A user, at every time tick, has 30% chance of choosing to further delegate an obligation that has been previously delegated to her, provided that the obligation has reasonable fulfilment window remaining (we set at least 40% of the original window as a condition). With the incentive mechanism employed, Fig. 3 shows another great result (77%) on the percentage of obligations being fulfilled.

Our experiments produce a rich set of data capturing the behaviour of nine different types of users with respect to fulfilling and delegating obligations. An interesting one is the dynamic change of trust score, as shown in Fig. 4, which reveals that our incentive scheme indeed takes effect. For the delegation with no incentive case, the trust score tends to *constant* over the time, which is consistent with the static profile defined in Table 1. However, with incentives employed, we can see that users' trust score gradually increases over the time, particularly obvious for those users belonging to unmotivated group.

7   Related Work

There has been considerable research on the frameworks for modelling and managing obligations. However, to the best of our knowledge, no previous work has studied incentive mechanisms for fulfilling obligations in the presence of delegation. In this section we are going to review the existing work that are most closely related to ours and highlight the novelty of our contributions.

Firstly, there exists a sizeable body of work on exploring interactions between authorisation and obligations. Irwin *et al.* [6,9,12] formally study the problem of maintaining *accountability* for system states when there exist dependencies between obligations, that is, one or more obligations provide necessary privileges or resources to enable the fulfilment of other obligations. A state is said to be accountable if the only reason for obligations going unfulfilled is due to user's negligence rather than a lack of necessary authorisation or resources. In order to focus on incentive schemes for discharging obligations for others, we assume that actions in the obligations are not subject to access control, and thus they can always be fulfilled. Of course, one of interesting future work is to model and

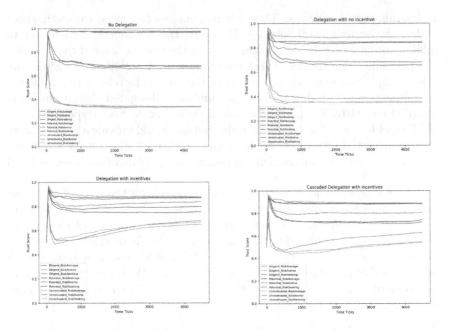

Fig. 4. The dynamic change of users' trust score over 4500 time ticks

analyse the accountability problem in our framework. Also there has been some work to structure incentives that motivate users to fulfil obligations in access control systems. For example, Chen *et al.* [5] look at a number of ways of applying obligations to account for the risk incurred by granting access requests. Like ours, they proposed incentives for users to fulfil obligations but the incentives are about granting users with risky access or restricting users from future access. Baracaldo and Joshi [1] use obligations as a means to deter insider attacks. Basically, one of conditions determining whether to grant an access request is to evaluate how trustworthy of the requester in fulfilling an obligation resulting from granting the access. Similar to ours, their approach to computing a trust value for each user is based on user's historical performance of fulfilling obligations, but their computation model is more complex to account for strategic malicious users who adapt its behavioural pattern to earn a high trust value.

Another strand of work closed to ours is delegation of obligations or tasks. Schaad and Moffett [13] identify the delegation of obligations as a recurring phenomenon in an organisation context and propose policy constructs in Alloy to deal with delegation operations and reviews. Specifically, when a subject delegates an obligation to another subject, the delegating subject loses its assignment to the obligation but a new review obligation is created and assigned to her as a means to account for the delegated obligation. Unlike ours, their work does not address how to incentivise and monitor subjects to fulfil their assigned obligations. Ben-Ghorbel-Talbi *et al.* [2] use a logical method to define different kinds of responsibilities when delegation of obligations is occurred, including functional responsibility, causal responsibility, liability and sanctions. However, there is no study of complexity in terms of managing and reasoning with these responsibilities when a large number of delegation operations are granted and some of which may result in conflicting responsibilities. Norman and Reed [11] present the use of the Hamblin logic capturing a responsibility-based semantics of delegation, which provides a rich account of how responsibility is transferred, acquired and discharged during and after delegation. In particular, their theoretical model is able to capture the case of a task being delegated to a group and to analyse the consequent responsibilities of each of the parties involved in the group. This inspires us to consider how to incentivise users in a group to work in a collaborative manner to discharge a delegated group obligation. Burnett and Oren [4] evaluate a number of different weighting strategies which are used to update trust for individuals involved in a delegation chain. Unlike our work, none of their strategies tends to incentivise users to executing tasks.

8   Concluding Remarks

In this paper we argue that one effective means of managing obligation fulfilment is via delegation of obligations. We propose a protocol for managing the delegation process that involves with announcement, bidding and awarding steps. We further develop a model that combines trust update with a credit rewarding scheme to incentivise users to fulfil delegated obligations. We also explore how the incentive mechanism can be extended to the case where cascaded delegation of obligations occurs. We run experiments to evaluate our models in a simulated multi-agent system. The results showed that, with respect to the number of obligations being fulfilled, delegation with incentives outperforms the other two settings: no delegation, and delegation with no incentive.

One immediate future work is to further examine our experimental data to define a number of appropriate ways of implementing the incentive schemes (incentivising users to earn credits), and to compare their fairness and effectiveness on reducing obligations being violated. Another interesting direction is to investigate the interaction with authorisation when delegation of obligation occurs. For example, when John delegates an obligation of preparing the quarterly sales report to Charlie, Charlie may not have permission to view the sales database. Who should grant the authorisation to Charlie: the system or John? What are the security implications for doing so? We would like to take a formal approach to study the balance between authorisation and obligation fulfilment.

References

1. Baracaldo, N., Joshi, J.: Beyond accountability: using obligations to reduce risk exposure and deter insider attacks. In: Proceedings of the 18th ACM Symposium on Access Control Models and Technologies, pp. 213–224 (2013). https://doi.org/10.1145/2462410.2462411

2. Ben-Ghorbel-Talbi, M., Cuppens, F., Cuppens-Boulahia, N., Métayer, D.L., Piolle, G.: Delegation of obligations and responsibility. In: Proceedings of the 26th IFIP TC 11 International Information Security Conference, pp. 197–209 (2011). https://doi.org/10.1007/978-3-642-21424-0_16

3. Boella, G., van der Torre, L.W.N., Verhagen, H.: Introduction to normative multiagent systems. Comput. Math. Organiz. Theory **12**(2–3), 71–79 (2006). https://doi.org/10.1007/s10588-006-9537-7

4. Burnett, C., Oren, N.: Sub-delegation and trust. In: Proceedings of the 11th International Conference on Autonomous Agents and Multiagent Systems, pp. 1359–1360 (2012)

5. Chen, L., Crampton, J., Kollingbaum, M.J., Norman, T.J.: Obligations in risk-aware access control. In: Proceedings of the 10th Annual International Conference on Privacy, Security and Trust, pp. 145–152 (2012). https://doi.org/10.1109/PST.2012.6297931

6. Chowdhury, O., Pontual, M., Winsborough, W.H., Yu, T., Irwin, K., Niu, J.: Ensuring authorization privileges for cascading user obligations. In: Proceedings of the 17th ACM Symposium on Access Control Models and Technologies, pp. 33–44 (2012). https://doi.org/10.1145/2295136.2295144

7. Dougherty, D.J., Fisler, K., Krishnamurthi, S.: Obligations and their interaction with programs. In: Proceedings of the 12th European Symposium On Research In Computer Security, pp. 375–389 (2007). https://doi.org/10.1007/978-3-540-74835-9_25

8. Holmstrom, B., Milgrom, P.: Multitask principal-agent analyses: incentive contracts, asset ownership, and job design. J. Law Econ. Organiz. **7**, 24–52 (1991)

9. Irwin, K., Yu, T., Winsborough, W.H.: On the modeling and analysis of obligations. In: Proceedings of the 13th ACM Conference on Computer and Communications Security, pp. 134–143 (2006). https://doi.org/10.1145/1180405.1180423

10. Keeping, E.S.: Introduction to statistical inference. Dover Publications, New York (1995)

11. Norman, T.J., Reed, C.: A logic of delegation. Artif. Intell. **174**(1), 51–71 (2010). https://doi.org/10.1016/j.artint.2009.10.001

12. Pontual, M., Chowdhury, O., Winsborough, W.H., Yu, T., Irwin, K.: Toward practical authorization-dependent user obligation systems. In: Proceedings of the 5th ACM Symposium on Information, Computer and Communications Security, pp. 180–191 (2010). https://doi.org/10.1145/1755688.1755711

13. Schaad, A., Moffett, J.D.: Delegation of obligations. In: Proceedings of the 3rd International Workshop on Policies for Distributed Systems and Networks, pp. 25–35 (2002). https://doi.org/10.1109/POLICY.2002.1011290

14. Twidle, K.P., Dulay, N., Lupu, E., Sloman, M.: Ponder2: a policy system for autonomous pervasive environments. In: Proceedings of the 5th International Conference on Autonomic and Autonomous Systems, pp. 330–335 (2009). https://doi.org/10.1109/ICAS.2009.42

15. Xu, C., Fong, P.W.L.: The specification and compilation of obligation policies for program monitoring. In: Proceedings of the 7th ACM Symposium on Information, Computer and Communications Security, pp. 77–78 (2012). https://doi.org/10.1145/2414456.2414501

Virtual Private Network Blockchain-based Dynamic Access Control Solution for Inter-organisational Large Scale IoT Networks

Rahma Trabelsi[1]([✉]) [iD], Ghofrane Fersi[1] [iD], and Mohamed Jmaiel[1,2] [iD]

[1] ReDCAD Laboratory, National School of Engineers of Sfax, University of Sfax, B.P. 1173, 3038 Sfax, Tunisia
rahma.trabelsi@redcad.org
[2] Digital Research Center of Sfax, B.P. 275, Sakiet Ezzit, 3021 Sfax, Tunisia

Abstract. Access control management in IoT environment faces big challenges. Unfortunately, it is hard to implement current access control standards on smart objects due to the complexity of access control solutions and the limited capacities of IoT devices. The problem becomes harder when these IoT devices belong to different organisations and need to interact together frequently. In the last few years, blockchain technology has been widely used in inter-organisational access control solutions for IoT. In fact, this technology can ensure an efficient and distributed access control. However, the existing solutions require lot of time and resources. In this paper, we provide a solution for a secure access control management in inter-organisational IoT networks based on blockchain and Virtual Private Network (VPN) technology. To optimize the resources and the time needed for access control, the IoT devices that belong to different organisations and cooperate frequently are added to the same VPN. The access control is ensured per VPN using blockchain. The experimental results of our proposed approach have shown the efficiency of our proposed approach in offering a secure, real-time response, decentralized, scalable and lightweight access control solution.

Keywords: IoT · Security · Access control · Blockchain · Virtual Private Network

1 Introduction

The rapid proliferation in IoT systems has a double edged weapon. Effectively, it has widened their applications range, but it has engendered new security issues. Effectively, the increase of the number of IoT devices and their ubiquity led to an increasing number of cyber attacks. Several solutions [29–33] have been proposed to overcome this limit and ensure the required security. However, the efficiency of these solutions are limited. In fact, various attacks such as Deny of service (DoS), Distributed deny of service (DDoS) and Man in the middle (MITM) are

S. Kallel et al. (Eds.): CRiSIS 2022, LNCS 13857, pp. 207–222, 2023.
https://doi.org/10.1007/978-3-031-31108-6_16

still very common and frequent attacks. Unauthorized access is one of the most important sources of such attacks [34,35]. This problem becomes harder when the IoT devices belong to different organisations.

Hence, proposing an efficient access control scheme will have an important role on the reduction of these attacks. The first solutions that have been proposed are centralized [16–18] which results on single point of failure. Then, there are some solutions that have integrated the blockchain in access control process in order to avoid centralization and ensure high level of security [4–7]. However these solutions present a major limit. Effectively, in these proposed researches in each time a given object wanting to access to an object that belongs to a different organisation, is compelled to have the access permission from the blockchain that processes through dedicated smart contracts a fine grained verification according to the different attributes of the demanding object to decide whether to grant or revoke access. Such strategy is not practical when there are too many interactions and collaborations between nodes belonging to different organisations because the time and resources consumption will be increased since there will be a huge number of requests that should be approved by blockchain.

Our proposed approach overcomes these limits by conceiving a new distributed access control system based on blockchain and virtual private network technology named VPNBDAC. The principle contribution of this approach is to reduce access to the blockchain when it comes to frequent communications between the different objects that belong to different organizations. Effectively, in VPNBDAC, the objects that interact and access frequently the resources and data of each other are put in the same VPN. The frequence degree from which these objects are put in the same VPN is specified by the network administrator depending on the application needs. The belonging criteria for each VPN are managed by blockchain smart contracts. Once a node fulfills the requirements to join a given VPN, it has an access to the resources of the nodes belonging to the same VPN even if they do not belong to the same organisation. In other words, the integration of the concept of VPNs reduces the complexity of the access right policy, which in turn incurs a reduction in terms of energy and cost. The blockchain stores access rights policies and virtual network configuration. It manages the membership of virtual network and the conditions to be a member. Our proposed contribution offers an access control solution that ensures:

- Decentralization and Distribution: Avoid single point of failure.
- Scalability: An IoT system connects a huge number of devices. Our system can handle the growing amount of devices and can manage their access control efficiently.
- Dynamicity: Access right can be changed over the time according to defined criteria.
- Time response: Access right request time is reduced.

The remainder of this paper is organized as follows: Sect. 2 presents the background. Section 3 gives a brief review on state of the art in access control for IoT systems. Section 4 illustrates the details of the proposed VPNBDAC system. Then, Sect. 5 explains the implementation of the prototype. The experimental results and evaluation are discussed in Sect. 6. Finally, the conclusion, current limitations and future direction are discussed in Sect. 7.

2   Background

Since our proposed contribution is based on blockchain and VPN, we give in this section an overview of these two technologies.

2.1   Blockchain

The blockchain [20] has been recognized as a distributed digital ledger with robust consensus mechanism. The blockchain is a sequence of blocks. Each block points on the previous block. And this what makes it difficult to tamper. Blockchain has the ability to revolutionize IoT with an open, trusted, and auditable sharing platform, where any information exchanged is reliable and traceable. It offers [21]:

- Decentralization: The decentralized aspect of blockchain can eliminate any single points of failure which improves the fault tolerance. Using blockchain, devices can interact with each other without the involvement of any intermediary.
- Distribution: Blockchain as it is a distributed ledger technology, has the ability to store and distribute device information.
- Immutability: Data in the blockchain cannot be altered.
- Scalability: Blockchain technology can control the collection and processing of data of a large number of IoT devices.
- Anonimity: It is possible to interact with a general address. Personal information are not necessary to add a transaction.
- Security High Performance: Blockchain technology utilizes advanced security compared to other platforms.

2.2   Virtual Private Networks (VPN)

Principe and Definition. Virtual Private Network (VPN) is a communication environment with a controlled access. VPN creates a secure connection between the users of this network. VPN network relies on a protocol called the "tunneling protocol". This protocol makes it possible to circulate information in an encrypted way from one end of the tunnel to the other. The principle of tunneling consists of building a virtual path between the sender and the recipient. Its strategy consists on encrypting all traffic from point A (the device) to point B (the VPN server) and creating a mask of privacy that all the traffic is passed through. Thanks to this mask, attackers cannot attack IoT devices because they cannot see them in any way to get access [14].

Characteristics. A VPN system must be able to implement the following functionalities:

- User authentication: Only authorized users should be able to identify themselves to the virtual network.
- Address management: Every client in the network must have a private and confidential address.
- Data encryption: During transport on the public network, data must be protected by effective encryption.
- Key management: Encryption keys for client and server must be able to be generated and regenerated.

3 Related Work

We give in this section a general overview of the basic access control models in IoT as well as the most recent works that have studied the inter-organisational access control in IoT systems.

3.1 Basic Access Control Model in IoTs

There are various access control methods and solutions proposed to address IoT security challenges. Access policies can rely on several different models to evaluate an access request and decide whether the request is or not authorized. The most known models are the following: [1–3]

- DAC (Discretionary Access Control) [24]: In this model, only the object owner has the responsibility of defining rights of each subject on the object. DAC mechanism controls are defined by user identification with supplied credentials during authentication.
- MAC (Mandatory Access Control) [25]: In this model, only the administrator has the right of defining rights. Access decision is taken by the security system.
- RBAC (Role Based Access Control) [22]: RBAC is a role or rule based access control. It is considered more "real" access control model. In fact, access is based on user's job function within organization. In other words, RBAC is a model of access control to an information system in which each access decision is based on the role to which the user is associated. Users performing similar functions can be grouped under the same role and the access is given according to this role.
- ABAC (Attribute based Access Control) [23]: In ABAC model, accesses are allowed based on the notion of attributes. With ABAC, dynamically changing attributes, such as time of day and location, can be accommodated in access control decisions.

To recapitulate, traditional access control models like MAC, DAC and RBAC do not take into account additional parameters such as resource information and dynamic information. So in order to provide a more flexible mechanism, the ABAC model was proposed, in which authorization decisions are based on attributes that the user has to prove. The Table 1 presents different access control models. The ABAC model offers a fine grained access control solution but the solution based on ABAC model is complex to implement and it consumes a lot of time and energy.

Table 1. Different access control model

AC model	Policy evaluation criteria	Applicability to IoT
DAC [24]	Subject's identifier	Extensively used because it is simple to implement but it is static
MAC [25]	Subject's access to a security label	This model is not suitable for IoT domain
RBAC [22]	Subject's role	This model is very used in IoT domain but RBAC defines access in a static manner
ABAC [23]	Subject's attributes (dynamic ones)	The most suitable for IoT scenarios as it can support flexible attributes

3.2 Inter-organisational Access Control Solution Overview

Most of IoT networks connect several application domains: smart health, smart home, smart living, smart transport, public safety, etc. These different organisations need to cooperate with each other. This cooperation needs communication which must be efficient and secure. For this reason, several researches proposed an access control mechanism between organisations. These researches can be divided into two types: classical solutions and blockchain-based solutions.

Classical Solutions. Authors in [16] implemented a centralized RBAC model and defined an extension of it. This extension adds an exception situation. When the user is aware of an exception situation he can request permission from administration. RBAC benefits are not sufficient to meet the needs of large organizations. For this reason, the authors in [17] proposed an integration of the ABAC and RBAC model. This model retains the flexibility offered by ABAC while maintaining the RBAC advantage of easier administration. Based on attributes type, a role is allocated to the client. Before deciding the policy, the priority-based condition is also evaluated for making fine-grained decisions. These two approaches are centralised by the administrator.

The authors in [18] introduce a new adaptive XACML scheme that extends the typical XACML by integrating access code generation and verification for heterogeneous distributed IoT environments. This approach is secure and fine-grained but it is not scalable.

Blockchain-based Solutions. To ensure user-driven access, transparency and pseudonymity, the authors in [4] proposed a distributed access control framework based on Bitcoin technology named FairAccess. In this approach, a resource owner defines access policies in the beginning through a GrantAccess transaction. After that, the system generates a Token and sends it to the requester. The requester sends its request with the Token to the blockchain network. And a GetAccess transaction will be verified by the blockchain. The authors proposed an extension named FairAccess 2.0 [26]. In this work, they introduced a Smart-Contract called a PolicyContract which is a representation of an access control policy defined by a Resource owner, to manage access over one of his resources. This work intend to overcome some FairAcess's limits. They offer a fine-grained solution since they adopt an ABAC model. Contrary to our solution, FairAccess suffers from some limits. First, obtaining access licenses requires long time due to the necessity of contacting the owner of the resource for each new access request or for each token expiration. Second, this model is complex to manage and adapt. Whereas, the access request management in our proposed solution is simple since the complexity of the implementation of the smart contract is reduced and there is only a need to verify the belonging to the same virtual network to make a decision. The authors in [5] employed an identity-based capability token management strategy named BlendCAC, which introduces the concept of smart contract for registration, propagation and revocation of the access authorization using private Ethereum technology. This work presents a blockchain-based decentralized access control system where IoT devices interact directly with the blockchain and are always connected. This work has some limitations. First of all, the delegation act may cause permission leakage resulting in an unauthorized access. Second, this model needs larger computation and storage overhead because IoT device is a node in the blockchain. The lightweight nature of the devices is not taken into consideration. We have overcome these limits in our approach. Effectively, we respected the limited capacities of IoT device and the delegated tasks to these devices are very light. The IoT device is not a node in blockchain but it can interact with the blockchain via the management point that is directly connected to the blockchain.

The authors in [6] introduced the concept of dynamic access rights using smart contracts based on Ethereum. This work consists of multiple access control contracts (ACCs) that are responsible for validating access permissions, one judge contract (JC) which is responsible for judging the misbehaving activities of the subject, and one register contract (RC) which is used to save all the system entities. In this framework, each ACC provides one access control method for a subject-object pair, which implements both static access right validation based on predefined access control policies and dynamic access right validation by checking the behavior of the subject. The authors in [7] proposed an ABAC framework for smart cities by using private Ethereum. The proposed framework consists of one Policy Management Contract (PMC) which is responsible for the storage and management of the ABAC policies, one Subject Attribute Management Contract (SAMC) which is used to store the attributes of subjects, one

Object Attribute Management Contract (OAMC) which is used to store the attributes of objects and one Access Control Contract (ACC) which is responsible for controlling the access requests from the subjects to the object. They defined the policy as a combination of a set SA of subject attributes, a set OA of object attributes, a set A of actions and a set C of context information. For simplicity, they use start time and end time as an attribute for establishing a dynamic access control. The evaluation shows that this approach is not suitable for large scale IoT network because it is very complex and expensive in terms of time and resources. Our proposed VPNBDAC offers a time-efficient access-control for resource-constrained devices.

In all the previous works, each access request goes through blockchain and this consumes time and energy. Our contribution overcomes these limits by introducing a virtual private network technology. Members of the same virtual network can communicate together without connection to blockchain. This allows us to save time and resources. Table 2 shows a detailed comparison of inter-organisation blockchain based solution. As depicted in this table, our proposed VPNBDAC is the only approach that offers at the same time dynamicity and scalability with offering a reduced response delay and reduced complexity. This is thanks to the fact that our proposed system is based on ABAC model to establish the first access and after that, the access control model is VPN-based.

Table 2. Access control in inter-organisation blockchain based solution

Solution	Model	Technology	Smart Contract	Dynamicity	Scalability	Real Time	Complexity
FairAccess [4]	OrBac	Bitcoin	No	No	Yes	No	+++
FairAccess 2.0 [26]	ABAC	Etherum	Yes	No	Yes	No	+++
BlendCAC [5]	CapAC	Etherum	Yes	No	No	Yes	+
Sc-Based AC [6]	-	Etherum	Yes	Yes	No	No	++
ABAC for SmartCities [7]	ABAC	Etherum	Yes	Yes	No	No	+++
Proposed VPNBDAC	ABAC and VPN-based	Etherum	Yes	Yes	Yes	Yes	+

4   VPNBDAC for Large Scale IoT Network

Our approach aims to minimize the security risks of unauthorized access in large scale IoT environment. This solution guarantees access control management between different distributed organizations. In order to address the issues of the previous works, we manage access control between different IoT networks through blockchain and VPN technology. In each organisation, there are some members that interact actively and frequently with other members in other organisations. For example, as depicted in Fig. 1, a doctor A in the organisation 1, accesses frequently to the data collected from Patient's P sensors that belong to organisation 2. Also, the nurse B, belonging to organisation 3, has frequent accesses and communications with doctor A and Patient P'. If each access is controlled separately, this would lead to on extra resource usage in the addition to the excessive time spending.

Our basic idea is to form Virtual Private Networks. Each VPN is made up of actors that interact frequently together. In our example, Doctor A from organisation 1, Patient P from organisation 2 and nurse B form organisation 3 form a VPN. In this way, instead of controlling access per actor, our approach controls the access per VPN. Hence, in VPNBDAC each member can be a member of one or multiple VPNs and each resource owner specifies the access rights for each VPN according to a dedicated smart contract. Membership to a given VPN is ensured according to a specific smart contract as well. In order to ensure dynamicity, the resource owner can revoke an access right if he detects a misbehaviour. He only has to update his smart contract.

In this way, our contribution minimizes the complexity of the management of access rights and optimizes time and energy consumption.

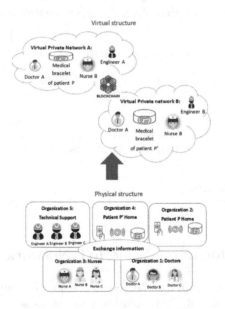

Fig. 1. Proposed VPNBDAC architecture

4.1 Actors

The principal actors in our system are:

- A resource owner (RO) who defines new policies. In this work, RO can grant access per Virtual Network (VN).
- The resource (Res) to which we want to perform an action. It is not directly connected to the Blockchain.
- A requester (Rq) who requests access to resource. In this work, RQ can also request to be member in virtual network.
- The management point (MP) which is connected directly to blockchain. It is responsible for exchanging information between organizations and the communication between organisation members and blockchain.

4.2   Smart Contract and Transactions

In order to ensure fine grained, distributed and dynamic access control, VPNBDAC uses blockchain. Each access-related activity is ensured via smart contracts. In this work, we have implemented three smart contracts.

The first smart control is access control management smart contract ACM_SC which is responsible of managing VPN access control. In ACM_SC, we store access rights for each virtual network. This smart contract will be executed when the RO grants or revokes access rights.

This contract contains GrantAccess transaction, GetAccess transaction and RevokeAccess transaction.

- GrantAccess transaction: In this system, a RO defines access control policies per VPN. For example, the patient who is the resource owner of a camera as well as bio-medical sensors allows the action ≪ access camera ≫ for VPN A (made up of doctor A, Patient P and nurse B). Each new defined access generates a grant access transaction.
- GetAccess Transaction: The requester requests a connection to a resource. A getaccess transaction will be sent to the blockchain. For the first connection, the blockchain verifies if the requester belongs to the same virtual network as the resource. For later connections, the requester and the resource are in the same virtual private network so they can communicate directly.
- RevokeAccess transaction: The RO can revoke access by introducing the access and select the virtual network to whom he wants to remove access. A revokeAccess transaction will be executed and the access will be removed.

The second smart contract is virtual network access control smart contract (VNAC_SC) which is responsible of managing virtual network members. It will be executed when the management point adds or deletes a member from VN.

- AddMemberToVN transaction: The MP is responsible of managing VPN membership. If a member confirms the conditions of subscription to a virtual network, the MP will add this member to adequate VPN.
- DeleteMemberFromVN transaction: If the MP detects a member misbehaviour, the member will be banned from access. And a DeleteMemberFromVN transaction will be executed.

The third smart contract is attribute based access control management Smart contract (ABACM_SC). This smart contract is responsible of managing the attributes of each virtual network.

- AddAttributesToVN transaction: To be a member of a virtual network, it is necessary to have specific attributes. These attributes will be defined by the management point.
- BeMemberOfVN transaction: If the requester requests to be a member of a virtual network, the (ABACM_SC) will be executed. It checks if the requester's attributes matche the VPN attributes.

For more clarification, Algorithm 1 describes the authorization process. This process begins with the definition of an access right. When a requester wants to perform an action, a getAccess transaction will be executed and verify if the requester fulfills the conditions to have an access.

Algorithm 1 : Authorization process

//In order to add an access to a resource for a virtual network, we call addRight method
write = contract.grantAccess ("idResource","virtualNetwork","action");
//In order to perform we call getRight method and this one returns the action to be performed
read = await contract.getAccess("idResource","virtualNetwork");
if (read=="requested action")
console.log("Access is approved");
redirect to information page ;
else console.log("access is denied ");

---

5   Implementation of the Prototype

As a "proof of concept", we have established an initial implementation and execution of our approach. Our proposed VPNBDAC can be used for a variety of IoT applications. To demonstrate the efficiency of the proposed solution, we consider as a typical use case the following scenario: A patient wears a medical bracelet: MAXREFDES103 Health Sensor Band that measures the oxygen saturation and heartbeat. The functioning of the bracelet and its interaction with blockchain is summarized in the Fig. 2. Since the patient is the resource owner of this bracelet, he can give access to a group of people that belong to different organisations. This group is represented by a VPN. For example, he can give a read access to virtual network made up of some doctors and nurses.

As we have explained in the previous section, the management point is responsible of managing VPN members. Hence, the overall system consists of five major components

- Resource: In this case, the resource is the medical bracelet.
- Resource owner: is the owner of medical bracelet. He manages access using a mobile application.
- Requester: any user who wants to access to the medical bracelet's data. This will be done using a mobile application.

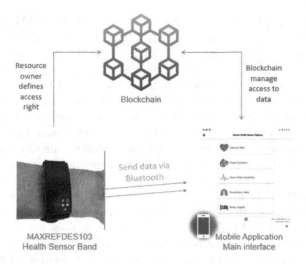

Fig. 2. Proposed scenario: Bracelet's functioning and interaction with blockchain

- Management Point: In this work, the MP is a laptop application which manages VPN members.
- Ethereum Public Blockchain: This work is implemented using Ropsten which is an ethereum public blockchain for test.

The VPNBDAC system includes two graphical interfaces one for the resource owner and the second for the requester. These interfaces are based on Android and the programming language is JAVA. To interact with Smart contract developed with Solidity [8], we use Web3j library [9]. The management point interacts with Smart Contract through a JS application. Also, a configuration is required. First of all, an ETH node was deployed using Infura [10]. Second, we should create a wallet. For that, we used Metamask [11] which is crypto wallet and gateway to blockchain apps.

6 Performance Evaluation

In order to evaluate the performance of VPNDBAC solution, we have compared its execution time as well as its cost with other related works. The Table 3 depicts the required time for data insertion. As shown, VPNDBAC offers reasonable data insertion time thanks to its very simple smart contracts. Figures 3 and 4 depict the time needed from sending access request to getting decision for different access-control solutions. In the Fig. 3, our proposed approach is compared to other blockchain-based solutions. And in Fig. 4, our proposed VPNBDAC is compared to other access control solutions that are not blockchain based. It is clear from these figures that VPNBDAC offers the lowest time needed from sending a request to getting a response even in comparison with solutions without blockchain. This can be explained by the fact that the implementation of

ABAC such as Smart Contract-Based Access Control [6], ABAC in RFID Systems [12], BEAAS [13], Distributed ABAC for IoT [14] or RBAC model using smart contract is very complex since they need to do a fine grained verification to each role or attribute in each access request which consumes time and energy. In our work, the verification process in blockchain is light thanks to the simplicity of the smart contract. Unlike the ABAC and RBAC approaches, the smart contract just checks if the requester is member of a virtual network or not to establish the first connection to a resource. For later connections, the objects which belong to the same virtual network can communicate directly. BlendCAC uses a capability-based access control. The implementation of this model is simple. For this reason, the access request time is small and almost equal to ABAC and RBAC without blockchain. However, in this approach the IoT device is a node in blockchain which requires a high consumption in terms of energy. Also BlendCAC builds a static access control solution, it does not ensure dynamicity. ABAC and RBAC without blockchain solutions offer an acceptable response time but since they did not integrate blockchain, the level of security is low. Our approach is more secure since it is a blockchain based solution.

Table 3. Comparison of data insertion time

	Data Insertion
ABAC in RFID Systems [12]	between 12225 ms and 40646 ms
BEEAS [13]	addUser 1276.59 ms
	addUserAttribute 1220.03 ms
	addAttributePossible Values 1349.40
	addUserAttribute ValuePair 1157.66
Proposed VPNBDAC	addMemberToVLAN 1824 ms
	addrightToVLAN 2188 ms
	AddAttributesToVN 890 ms

The users need to pay some money to deploy smart contracts on the blockchain and execute the ABIs of these contracts. The Fig. 5 displays the cost of our approach compared to other solutions. We notice that the cost of our application is very reasonable in spite of having three smart contracts thanks to the simplicity and efficiency of their implementation. The authors in [12] adopt an ABAC model hence the implementation of the smart contract is complicated compared to our solution. As a result, the cost of this solution is high. The cost of RBAC and CapAC model is acceptable compared to ABAC model but they do not ensure a fine-grained control. Our approach is fine-grained since we build the virtual networks according to eligible attributes.

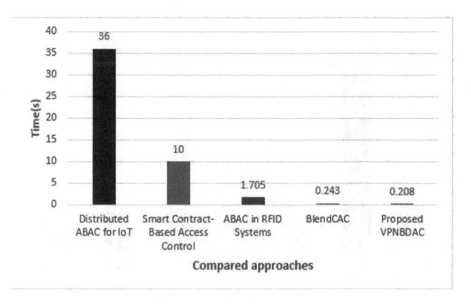

Fig. 3. Comparison of time needed from sending access request to getting decision with other blockchain based solution

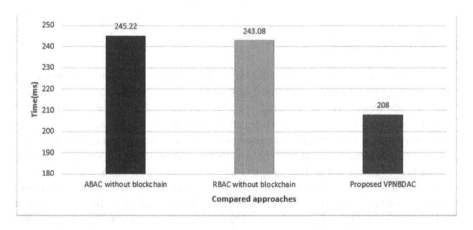

Fig. 4. Comparison of time needed from sending access request to getting decision with non-blockchain based solution

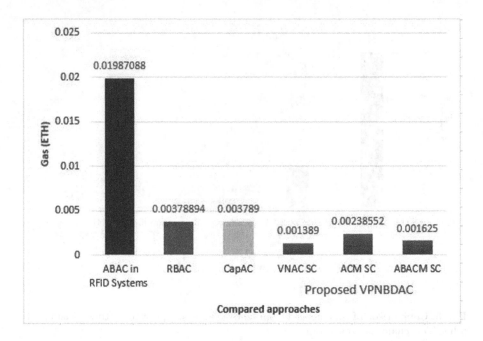

Fig. 5. Cost Evaluation

7   Conclusions

In this paper, we proposed VPNBDAC, a VPN blockchain-based solution for access control in inter-organisational IoT. The main idea is to gather members that interact frequently in a virtual private network. The settings of different VPN are managed by blockchain. A public Ethereum blockchain network was constructed to implement the proposed solution and evaluate its feasibility and cost in terms of money and time. The results have shown that this work is feasible to achieve distributed and fine-grained IoT access control. Also it is efficient in terms of cost and time. Our ongoing and future work is focused on improving our proposed system by adding more dynamicity. Access right can be changed over the time according to defined criteria. The management point will be responsible for checking if the behaviour of the requester is normal or abnormal. And this will be ensured by machine learning algorithms which aim to detect malicious behaviour. We will grant and revoke access according to the score or reputation of the requester after behaviour's analysis.

References

1. Ouaddah, A., Mousannif, H., Ait Ouahman, A.: Access control models in IoT: the road ahead. In: IEEE/ACS 12th International Conference of Computer Systems and Applications (AICCSA), pp. 1–2 (2015). https://doi.org/10.1109/AICCSA. 2015.7507090

2. Bertin, E., Hussein, D., Sengul, C., Frey, V.: Access control in the Internet of Things: a survey of existing approaches and open research questions. Ann. Telecommun. **74**, 375–388 (2019). https://doi.org/10.1007/s12243-019-00709-7

3. Qiu, J., Tian, Z., Du, C., Zuo, Q., Su, S., Fang, B.: A survey on access control in the age of internet of things. IEEE Internet Things J. **7**(6), 4682–4696 (2020). https://doi.org/10.1109/JIOT.2020.2969326

4. Ouaddah, A., Elkalam, A., Ouahman, A.: FairAccess: a new blockchain-based access control framework for the Internet of Things: FairAccess: a new access control framework for IoT. Security and Communication Networks, 9 (2017). https://doi.org/10.1002/sec.1748

5. Xu, R., Chen, Y., Blasch, E., Chen, G.: BlendCAC: a blockchain-enabled decentralized capability-based access control for IoTs. In: IEEE International Conference on Internet of Things (iThings) and IEEE Green Computing and Communications (GreenCom) and IEEE Cyber, Physical and Social Computing (CPSCom) and IEEE Smart Data (SmartData), pp. 1027–1034 (2018)

6. Zhang, Y., Kasahara, S., Shen, Y., Jiang, X., Wan, J.: Smart contract-based access control for the internet of things. IEEE Internet Things J. **6**(2), 1594–1605 (2019). https://doi.org/10.1109/JIOT.2018.2847705

7. Zhang, Y., Sasabe, M., Kasahara, S.: Attribute-based access control for smart cities: a smart contract-driven framework. IEEE Internet Things J. **8**(8), 6372–6384 (2021)

8. https://docs.soliditylang.org/en/v0.8.11/ . Accessed Jan 2022

9. https://docs.web3j.io/4.8.7/ . Accessed Jan 2022

10. https://infura.io/ . Accessed Jan 2022

11. https://metamask.io/ . Accessed Jan 2022

12. Figueroa, S., Arrizabalaga, S.: An attribute-based access control model in RFID systems based on blockchain decentralized applications for healthcare environments. Computers **8**(3), 57 (2019)

13. Kumar, R., Palanisamy, B., Sural, S.: BEAAS: blockchain enabled attribute-based access control as a service. In: IEEE International Conference on Blockchain and Cryptocurrency (ICBC), pp. 1–3 (2021)

14. Yutaka, M., Zhang, Y., Sasabe, M., Kasahara, S.: Using Ethereum blockchain for distributed attribute-based access control in the internet of things. In: 2019 IEEE Global Communications Conference (GLOBECOM) (2019)

15. Hunko, M., Ruban, I., Hvozdetska, K.: Securing the Internet of Things via VPN technology. Comput. Inf. Syst. Technol. (2021)

16. Bouadjemi, A., Abdi, M.K.: Towards an extension of RBAC model. Int. J. Comput. Dig. Syst. **10**, 1–11 (2020)

17. Thakare, A., Lee, E., Kumar, A., Nikam, V.B., Kim, Y.-G: PARBAC: priority attribute based RBAC model for azure IoT cloud. IEEE Internet Things J., 1–1 (2020)

18. Riad, K., Cheng, J.: Adaptive XACML access policies for heterogeneous distributed IoT environments. Inf. Sci. **548**, 135–152 (2021). https://doi.org/10.1016/j.ins.2020.09.051

19. Pinjala, S.K., Sivalingam, K.M.: DCACI: a decentralized lightweight capability based access control framework using IOTA for internet of things. In: 2019 IEEE 5th World Forum on Internet of Things (WF-IoT) (2019)

20. Reyna, A., Martín, C., Chen, J., Soler, E., Díaz, M.: On blockchain and its integration with IoT, challenges and opportunities. Future Gener. Comput. Syst. **88**, 173–190 (2018)

21. Abdelmaboud, A., et al.: Blockchain for IoT applications: taxonomy, platforms, recent advances, challenges and future research directions. Electronics **11**, 630 (2022)

22. Ferraiolo, D., Kuhn, D.R., Chandramouli, R.: Role-Based Access Control. Artech House, London, UK (2003)

23. Park, J.S., Sandhu, R.: Smart Certificates: extending X.S09 for secure attribute services on the web. In: National Information Systems Security Conference, pp. 337–348 (1999)

24. Ricci, R.G., Mesiar, R.: Multi-attribute aggregation operators. Fuzzy Sets Syst. **181**(1), 1–13 (2011)

25. Manzano, L.G., Fuentes, J.M., Pastrana, S., Lopez, P.P., Encinas, L.H.: PAgIoT-privacy-preserving aggregation protocol for internet of things. J. Netw. Comput. Appl. **71**, 59–71 (2016)

26. Bellaj, B., Ouaddah, A.: FairAccess 2.0: a smart contract-based authorization framework for enabling granular access control in IoT. Int. J. Inf. Comput. Secur. **15**, 18–48 (2021)

27. https://github.com/samuelxu999/Blockchain_dev/CapbilityToken/contracts/RBACToken.sol

28. https://github.com/samuelxu999/Blockchain_devCapbilityToken/contracts/CapACToken.sol

29. Zhu, S., Setia, S., Jajodia, S.: LEAP+: efficient security mechanisms for large-scale distributed sensor networks. ACM Trans. Sens. Netw. **2**(4), 500–528 (2006). https://doi.org/10.1145/1218556.1218559

30. Choi, T., Acharya, H.B., Gouda, M.G.: The best keying protocol for sensor networks. In: Pervasive and Mobile Computing 9.4, pp. 564–571 (2013)

31. Chen, W.: An IBE-based security scheme on Internet of Thing. In: 2012 IEEE 2nd International Conference on Cloud Computing and Intelligence Systems, pp. 1046–1049 (2012). https://doi.org/10.1109/CCIS.2012.6664541

32. Chatzigiannakis, I., Pyrgelis, A., Spirakis, P.G., Stamatiou, Y.C.: Elliptic curve based zero knowledge proofs and their applicability on resource constrained devices. IEEE Eighth Int. Conf. Mobile Ad-Hoc Sens. Syst. **2011**, 715–720 (2011). https://doi.org/10.1109/MASS.2011.77

33. Yang, Y., Liu, X., Deng, R.H., Li, Y.: Lightweight sharable and traceable secure mobile health system. IEEE Trans. Dependable Secur. Comput. **17**(1), 78–91 (2020)

34. Ouaddah, A., Mousannif, H., Abou Elkalam, A., Ait Ouahman, A.: Access control in IoT: Survey & state of the art. In: 2016 5th International Conference on Multimedia Computing and Systems (ICMCS), pp. 272–277 (2016)

35. Qiu, J., Tian, Z., Du, C., Zuo, Q., Su, S., Fang, B.: A survey on access control in the age of internet of things. IEEE Internet Things J. **7**(6), 4682–4696 (2020). https://doi.org/10.1109/JIOT.2020.2969326

Pseudonym Swapping with Secure Accumulators and Double Diffie-Hellman Rounds in Cooperative Intelligent Transport Systems

Hannes Salin$^{(\boxtimes)}$ (iD)

Swedish Transport Administration, Borlänge, Sweden
`hannes.salin@trafikverket.se`

Abstract. The notion of pseudonym certificates is used for anonymity and privacy of vehicles in Cooperative Intelligent Transport Systems. Due to attacks where an adversary can link a certain vehicle to a geographical bounded area or usage of services, there is a need to protect the vehicle's real identity, but at the same time being able to prove its existence at a later stage due to auditing. We propose a pseudonym swapping protocol aligned with a new security architecture where signature keys are stored in both a typical secure hardware module and in a secure accumulator that provides proof for key validity. We propose minor adjustments to the current ETSI standard to include such secure setup and provide a comparative proof of concept implementation between two variants of secure accumulators.

Keywords: Cryptographic Accumulator · Pseudonym Swapping · C-ITS · Privacy

1 Introduction

Intelligent Transport Systems (ITS) are information and communication technologies for connected and intelligent infrastructure, where vehicles, sensors, traffic management equipment, pedestrians and other moving and stationary nodes are included [1]. The main goal for an ITS system is to provide traffic management services, safety enhancements and other types of smart functions that enable traffic efficiency and safety. Cooperative Intelligent Transport Systems (C-ITS) is a subset of ITS and in particular the collection of technologies and standards that enables communication and cooperation between two or more connected entities within an ITS eco-system, e.g. vehicles and roadside units [2]. One key component in such architecture is the Vehicle-to-Vehicle (V2V) and Vehicle-to-everything (V2X) communication technologies.

Although a promising and still very developing area of research and innovation, several challenges are still unsolved or not yet harmonized, especially within the privacy and security domain of C-ITS; in particular interoperability, public

S. Kallel et al. (Eds.): CRiSIS 2022, LNCS 13857, pp. 223–238, 2023.
https://doi.org/10.1007/978-3-031-31108-6_17

key infrastructure (PKI) scalability, pseudonym reusage policies and revocation methods [3–5]. Many of these issues are directly related to V2X and V2V communication protocols and architectures. Several ongoing European C-ITS initiatives are currently investigating and evaluating different solutions where above mentioned challenges are included, e.g. the C-ROADS and NordicWay 3 [6,7]. The main driver towards the development and deployment of (C)-ITS within the European Union is the Directive 2010/40/EU [1], which most of the mentioned initiatives stem from. Government agencies, academia and the automotive industry collaborate in several instances to drive the research forward [2,6–8].

Privacy concerns need to be handled; it should not be allowed to track an individual via the vehicle's traveling path(s) or inclusion of cooperative computations and data sharing in ITS-related functions or resources [9]. For these reasons (and further elaborated in detail in Sect. 1.1 and Sect. 4.1) the notion of *pseudonyms* have been introduced. The main goal is that a vehicle should not reveal its canonical (true) identity during communication and data transfer, but at the same time allow for an authority to verify that canonical identity if needed. Hence, pseudonym management is an integral part of a C-ITS architecture and must be handled with care and harmonization in mind. Also, with more and broader networking capacities and progress in autonomous driving, such collaborative environments must be able to distinguish dishonest entities from trustworthy ones [3–5], therefore a solid trust model is of greatest importance.

1.1 Pseudonyms in Cooperative Intelligent Transport Systems

The ETSI standards [10,11] specify different types of safety messages for V2X communication, e.g. the Cooperative Awareness Messages (CAM) and Decentralized Environmental Notification Messages (DENM) in particular. None of these C-ITS messages are encrypted, thus the content must be carefully considered. Encryption for these types of messages are not suitable since many different nodes may need to receive them fast (CAM messages are broadcast) and encryption adds a layer of computations that will affect the performance [12]. However, CAM messages are signed by the sender. The content of CAM messages are divided into mandatory and optional data. Vehicle position, direction and speed are examples of such data that can be included, which also are of high importance since alteration or faulty data could imply critical safety issues [3–5,12]. For this reason alone, it is crucial that the identity of the sender is trusted and valid. On the other hand, privacy for the vehicle's identity and location is also needed, and for this the notion of pseudonyms is a potential solution.

If the identity is private via pseudonymization, it must still be accountable [9]. The unlinkability property ensures that an identity can be used in multiple resources or functions within the ITS eco-system without an internal or external observer being able to track that. Furthermore, according to the ETSI standards, the canonical identity, i.e. the real immutable identity of the vehicle, cannot be transferred between any ITS stations via ITS safety messages [9]. Several proposals in the ETSI standards for how to handle pseudonym renewal and change, refer to [13] for pseudonym swapping as an alternative. This method is for vehicles that are close to each other, within a certain geographical boundary and allows for pseudonym exchange. Such a method would then confuse an adversary that tracks a vehicle by identity, since the pseudonyms are refreshed regardless if an actual swap occurred or not between two vehicles. For this reason each vehicle will have (and build up) a pool of pseudonyms to use over time, and similarly revoke and discard already used ones. One main concern for that method is that it may become difficult to reveal the link between a pseudonym and the canonical identity (if required by external authorities). Finally, although ETSI addresses and gives several different proposals for pseudonym change mechanisms [14], there are not yet any final standardization decisions made for explicit pseudonym management.

1.2 Problem Statement

For C-ITS scenarios where a cluster of vehicles connect into a dynamic network, a VANET, we need to provide adequate privacy and anonymity (via un-linkability of a vehicle's identity and location) at the same time where an external auditor can verify the canonical identity at any given time stamp. Moreover, when storing private pseudonym signature keys in the vehicle, if an adversary is able to compromise the key storage module, it may alter or replace keys, hence we need a mitigation feature. We explore the usage of cryptographic accumulators to create a verification layer when signing a critical safety message, i.e. a key validation mechanism that also serves as an intermediate revocation function when surrounding certificate authorities are not available.

1.3 Contribution

- We propose a secure pseudonym storage and swapping method with double Diffie-Hellman rounds and cryptographic accumulators for efficient key verification.
- We provide a proof of concept implementation of two variants for comparison: RSA-based [15] and pairing-based [16] accumulators respectively.
- We propose how to adjust current ETSI standard trust model to incorporate an accumulator-based pseudonym swapping architecture.

2 Related Work

Several different pseudonym change (management) strategies have been proposed [12,17–20]. The primary goal of such a strategy is to determine how and when vehicles should initiate and execute a change (or update) of their pseudonyms. Indeed the strategy must impose the unlinkability and anonymity properties. However, except pseudonymization approaches, several other methods have been proposed for addressing the privacy concerns, e.g. group signatures [12]. Hybrid variants of group signatures and pseudonym changing strategies have also been considered [12]. These strategies are sensitive to the compromising of the group manager that knows all the identities of the group members. Boualouache et al. propose a pseudonym management framework called PRI-VANET [21] which builds on geographical vehicular location privacy zones where entering vehicles will assess the need for pseudonym updating. The solution is focused on the mathematical modeling for computing the privacy zones based on traffic density and vehicle's demand on entering.

Several European pilot projects have approached the pseudonym management differently [14,22], e.g. the PRESERVE project used 120 s intervals for every pseudonym change, the SCOOP@F project where a pool of pseudonyms is updated after a fixed number of messages are sent (and signed), and the C2C-CC project which uses segmentation of the roads and distance-based calculations to decide how and when pseudonyms should be updated.

For swapping based protocols, several solutions have been proposed. Eckoff et al. propose an identity diffusion protocol using a time-slotted variant of the pseudonym pool, allowing for a temporal based swapping where both currently used and future pseudonyms can be exchanged between vehicles [13]. Primary focus is on the temporal-based algorithms for initiating the swapping, and the actual swap is assumed to use a typical data transfer using cryptography as proposed in WAVE [23]. X. Li et al. proposes a pseudonym swapping protocol called PAPU, based on generalized differential privacy, noted pseudonym indistinguishability [24]. Their protocol uses a Road Side Unit (RSU) for calculating the necessary prerequisites before a swap, e.g. driving similarity, and from a pool of participating vehicles' pseudonyms, a pseudonym assignment process starts. The main focus is on the probability calculations of when to initiate the swapping; the swap procedure itself is not detailed. In contrast, Yang et al. proposed a scheme [20] based on dynamic pseudonym swap zones that allows for pseudonym swapping within that temporary zone, and where the current pseudonym and corresponding key-pair for the vehicle's are exchanged in a secure session detailed in a swapping scheme. Among the swapping vehicles there is only one that is real and the others are fictitious in order to confuse an attacker. The pseudonyms are derived onboard each vehicle using a specific key for that purpose, and each new pseudonym is a keyed hash using the previous pseudonym as input, thus constituting a hash chain of pseudonyms.

3   Preliminaries

For our proposal we need a set of cryptographic primitives: a pairing scheme, a signature scheme and an accumulator scheme. We only give an informal definition of a pairing: let $\hat{e} : \mathbb{G}_1 \times \mathbb{G}_2 \to \mathbb{G}_\tau$ be a bilinear map with bilinearity, non-degeneracy and computability properties [25]. The tuple $\{\hat{e}, \mathbb{G}_1, \mathbb{G}_2, \mathbb{G}_\tau, g_1, g_2, p\}$ is then an instantiation of a pairing over secure groups $\langle g_1 \rangle = \mathbb{G}_1, \langle g_2 \rangle = \mathbb{G}_2$ and $\mathbb{G}_\tau$, and a prime p. The provably secure BLS signature scheme [26] is based on pairings; to create a signature over message m we compute $\sigma = \mathcal{H}(m)^{\mathsf{sk}}$ with a secret key sk and a secure hash function $\mathcal{H}$ that maps to elements of $\mathbb{G}_1$. Verification of σ is done by checking $\hat{e}(\sigma, g) \stackrel{?}{=} \hat{e}(\mathcal{H}(m), \mathsf{pk})$ using public key pk.

The Diffie-Hellman (DH) key exchange protocol [27] relies on the Diffie-Hellman hardness assumption:

Definition 1 (Diffie-Hellman assumption). *Let $\mathbb{G}$ be a secure group with generator g. Then for any probabilistic polynomial-time adversary $\mathcal{A}$ it is hard to compute g^{ab} given g^a and g^b for some $a, b \in \mathbb{Z}$.*

A cryptographic accumulator consists of a set of algorithms with the main purpose of proving set-memberships: for element a in set A, a prover can provide a proof that $a \in A$ without revealing any information about the elements or the set. The proof is called a witness. We introduce two different type of accumulators, one proposed by Benaloh and de Mare [15], and one by Nguyen [16]:

Definition 2 (Benaloh and de Mare-based accumulator). *Let p, q be strong primes and a an integer relatively prime to $pq = N$, secure under the strong RSA assumption. Then for an element x_i to be accumulated, we compute $A \leftarrow a^{x_i} \bmod N$. To extract a witness w_i for $x_i \in A$ with n elements, we compute $w_i = a^{\Pi_{j=1:j \neq i}^{n} x_j}$. To verify that $x_i \in A$ we compute $w_i^{x_i} \overset{?}{=} A$. To delete x_i we compute x_i^{-1} and run $A' \leftarrow A^{x_i^{-1}}$.*

Definition 3 (Nguyen-based accumulator). *Let $\hat{e}$ be a bilinear map over secure groups $\mathbb{G}_1, \mathbb{G}_2, \mathbb{G}_\tau$ with generators $g_1 = \langle \mathbb{G}_1 \rangle, g_2 = \langle \mathbb{G}_2 \rangle$ respectively, and p a prime. Let $t = \{\hat{e}, \mathbb{G}_1, \mathbb{G}_2, \mathbb{G}_\tau, g_1, g_2, p\}$ be a pairing instance secure under the q-Strong Diffie-Hellman Assumption. Let $s \leftarrow_\$ \mathbb{Z}_p$, then to accumulate x_i we compute $A \leftarrow g_1^{(x_i + s)}$; same s is used for all accumulated values. To extract a witness w_i for element $x_i \in A$ with n elements, we compute $w_i = g_2^{\Pi_{j=1:j \neq i}^{n}(x_j + s)}$. To verify that $x_i \in A$ we compute $\hat{e}(g_1^{x_i} g_1^s, w_i) \overset{?}{=} \hat{e}(A, g_2)$. To delete x_i we compute $(x_i + s)^{-1}$ and run $A' \leftarrow A^{(x_i + s)^{-1}}$.*

4   System Model and Architecture

4.1   C-ITS Trust Model and Architecture

This section will introduce the basic notation and relevant concepts for privacy related flows within a C-ITS and V2X/V2V architecture. The current ETSI standardization package [28] for ITS security and privacy describes a PKI architecture aligned with IEEE Wireless Access in Vehicular Environments security messaging [29]. The general trust model include the following certificate authority instances [28]:

Root Certification Authority (CA): The root certificate authority as in traditional PKI, with the primary purpose as a self-signed certificate, issues and creates trust chains for subsequent certificate authorities, e.g. the enrollment and authorization authorities.

Enrolment Authority (EA): An ITS node that by physical secure processes can establish a canonical identifier, canonical key-pair and profile information data for the vehicle to be enrolled.

Authorization Authority (AA): An ITS node that receives authorization requests and if validated correctly, the AA will return authorization tickets for the vehicles to consume, i.e. a set of temporary pseudonym certificates.

Each vehicle will have one or several pseudonym certificates (PC). These are used for signing ITS safety messages and providing an ephemeral identity for the vehicle. Establishing a secure connection between a vehicle and EA or AA within the PKI, several type of protocol stacks can be used, e.g. ITS-G5 via roadside units, cellular network links via 3G,4G or LTE, or WLAN communication via IEEE 802.11 protocols [14]. When vehicles are broadcasting CAM messages, these are signed by the PC's corresponding private key using the Elliptic Curve Digital Signature Algorithm (ECDSA) [30]. We illustrate a simplified architecture in Fig. 1 for a standard C-ITS setup.

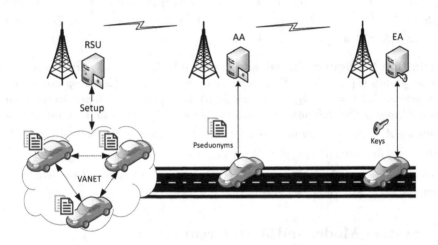

Fig. 1. C-ITS architecture with enrollment (of canonical keys) by EA, authentication and pseudonym collection via AA and a dynamic VANET in a geographical bounded area with a cluster of nearby vehicles.

4.2   Threat Model

We model our adversary $\mathcal{A}$ such that it is an active attacker that can eavesdrop any messages sent between vehicles and at time stamp t_0, just before the dynamic VANET is established, record all involved v_i's current pseudonyms (via collected signed CAM messages). We also let the adversary have the power of compromising the vehicle's secure storage memory module $\mathcal{M}$ such that it can replace, remove or insert new pseudonym keys. An successful attack by $\mathcal{A}$ would be to either alter the set of pseudonym signing keys such that a future CAM message is signed with a compromised key, or that the anonymity of a vehicle v_i is broken after a successful swap. We note however that we limit the attack to scenarios where the environment does not allow for deduction of a vehicle's identity, e.g. if there are only two vehicles v_1 and v_2, it would be trivial to identify which pseudonym is given to each vehicle after the swap.

4.3   Pseudonym Swapping System Model

We consider a set of vehicles $\mathcal{V} = \{v_1, v_2, ..., v_n\}$ that are part of the same VANET within a C-ITS eco-system. Each vehicle v_i have at least one PC $p_{i,j}$, which consists of a key-pair $\mathsf{pk}_i, \mathsf{sk}_i$ and some certificate meta-data. Moreover, each vehicle have their own canonical private and public key-pair $\mathsf{pk}_{v_i}, \mathsf{sk}_{v_i}$. A standard scenario within the model is that vehicle v_i needs to update $p_{i,j}$ such that anonymity and privacy properties are fulfilled. Moreover, we assume this happens only when neighbouring vehicles are present via means of short-range communication, within the same VANET or any other type of typical V2X protocol stack. We note that here is no need for updating $p_{i,j}$ if the vehicle is alone, thus not exposed to potential adversaries that tries to mount a tracking- or de-pseudonymization attack. Each vehicle also store and updates an accumulator z_i which holds all pseudonym secret keys. z_i can be stored in an untrusted area of the vehicle's On Board Unit (OBU) and a secure copy of the keys are preferably managed within an trusted platform module (TPM) or hardware security module (HSM); we denote such module $\mathcal{M}$. We assume any secure computations are done within $\mathcal{M}$, which also handles all pseudo random generators and signature computations. From a formal perspective all accumulator functions such as key generation, witness extraction and verification are computed in $\mathcal{M}$ and outputs *accept* or *reject* type of messages.

We note that a PC have a certain explicit structure according to the ETSI standards, referred to as a `EtsiTs103097Certificate` data structure [30], which also corresponds to the IEEE 1609.2 certificate standard. Except data such as certificate id, validity time, permissions etc., the corresponding public key is included, and by specification is of the type `EccP256CurvePoint`, i.e. a ECDSA 256 bit key. Therefore, the PC is a a tuple $p_{i,j} = (C, \mathsf{sk}_{(i,j)})$ where C is the certificate including the public key $\mathsf{pk}_{(i,j)}$. The vehicle will then both accumulate $\mathsf{sk}_{(i,j)}$ into z_i and store it in $\mathcal{M}$ as with any data (e.g. a typical keystore structure used for certificates), thus the witness $w_{i,j}$ would prove that anything signed with $\mathsf{sk}_{(i,j)}$ will only belong to the key holder of $\mathsf{pk}_{(i,j)}$ and C, due to the accumulation.

5   Pseudonym Swapping with Accumulator-Based Storage

We propose a DH double round pseudonym swapping protocol with accumulators to be used within the C-ITS system model described in Sect. 4.3. The protocol is based on the current proposed trust model from the ETSI technical specification 102 941 V1.4.1 [9], hence aligned with the C-ITS PKI architecture. The solution is delimited to cover and evaluate the PC secret key (accumulator) storage and swapping parts.

5.1 Proposed Alignment to ETSI Standard

The proposed protocol is aligned with the EtsiTs103097Certificate structure and we recommend one additional entry for the accumulator value which the PC secret key is bound to: in the certificate's Ieee1609Dot2Data entry, the optional signedData should include the accumulator value z_i as AccumulatorStorage with components AccType and AccValue which specifies if the accumulator is of type RSA (bit 0) or Paring-based (bit 1), and the actual value which is either a big integer or ECC point on curve, i.e. of type EccP256CurvePoint. These updates should be included in the ETSI TS 103 097 standard (Security header and certificate formats) [30].

5.2 Proposed Security Architecture

Vehicle v_i stores the pseudonym secret keys $\mathsf{sk}_{(i,1)}, ..., \mathsf{sk}_{(i,n_i)}$ in $\mathcal{M}$ and the accumulator $z_i = g^{\mathsf{sk}_{(i,1)} + \cdots + \mathsf{sk}_{(i,n_i)}}$ in an untrusted area outside of $\mathcal{M}$. The motivation is as follows: z_i can easily be distributed and shared among different ITS stations and EA/AA parties in order to verify v_i's pseudonyms, without leaking or sending the actual keys. Moreover, assuming $\mathcal{M}$ is compromised and one or several keys are altered, this will efficiently be detected since a witness verification for each key against the accumulator will be done before usage. This also serves as an intermediate revocation solution until the vehicle is connected to an AA again for updates to a certificate revocation list, in the case of rapid revocation of a certain signing key.

5.3 Protocol Definition and Algorithms

Algorithms for deciding when a cluster of vehicles should connect and swap PC:s have been considered specifically in [20,21,24] and will be out of scope. The primary building blocks are an accumulator, realized as a RSA-accumulator and a pairing-based accumulator for comparison, and the protocol algorithms that initiates and executes the pseudonym swapping. The protocol description consists of three algorithms, Swap, Assign and Verify. Included is also a signing procedure Sign, running a standard BLS signature [26], an encryption tuple Enc, Dec which encrypts and decrypts a stream of data, and a pseudorandom generator PRNG seeded by some secure randomness γ. In the Assign procedure an interactive DH-protocol is run between each participant in order to exchange a session key for protecting an assignment value α_i and later the pseudonym keys to be sent; this protocol is denoted DH in the algorithm description. Note that before running Swap, a pre-stage protocol is needed to setup and initialize the swapping zone where all vehicles are connected within a VANET. Given the described C-ITS trust model and architecture, we assume the following are in place before the swapping protocol initiates: The CA have distributed necessary certificates to the EA and AA. By entering a larger VANET, each v_i will execute the standard enrollment procedure with the EA and authenticate itself to the AA in order to receive the pseudonyms. From the EA the initial set of canonical keys have been created and stored securely in the vehicle's $\mathcal{M}$. The PC:s are retrieved from the AA along with corresponding secret keys and witnesses. This implies that for each set of PC:s, the corresponding witnesses are stored as well in the EA and can efficiently be distributed if needed for verification purposes at later stages. We now describe the main idea of the proposed solution and then detail each algorithm in pseudo-code. Each vehicle v_i have a secure accumulator $z_i = g^{\mathsf{sk}(i,1)\mathsf{sk}(i,2)\cdots\mathsf{sk}(i,k)}$ stored in the OBU, and the corresponding secret keys accumulated in z_i are stored in $\mathcal{M}$, i.e. k number of signing keys.

Definition 4 (Double DH Pseudonym Swap and Accumulation Protocol). *The following protocol is run when a cluster of vehicles $\mathcal{V} = \{v_1, ..., v_n\}$ are close-by, and a swapping initiates:*

- *$\mathcal{V}$ create an ad-hoc group connection in which every v_i can broadcast messages and connect to all vehicles in the group.*
- *Each vehicle sign and commit their set of pseudonyms $\mathcal{P}$ by computing a signature value using the canonical secret key sk by: $\sigma = \mathsf{Sign}(\mathcal{P}, t) = (\mathcal{H}(\mathcal{P}\|t))^{\mathsf{sk}}$ where t is the current timestamp, $\mathcal{H}$ a cryptographically secure hash function, and $\|$ the concatenation operation.*
- *Each v_i performs one DH round with each v_j where $j \neq i$, to distribute the accumulator z_i and assignment value α_i using an ephemeral DH session key $k_{i,j}$.*
- *Each v_i combine all accumulators and assign values into a master value z, and computes the assignment slot with Assign, i.e. which set of pseudonym keys each v_i will swap to. After a successful assignment all other keys and accumulators are discarded.*
- *Each v_i performs one additional DH round with all the v_j's, where v_p is the vehicle it is assigned to, and swaps with a second DH session key $k_{i,p}$.*
  For the rest of v_j's, only dummy values are sent in order to confuse an eavesdropping adversary.
- *If an authority or AA need to verify a set of PC:s for a vehicle, the Verify procedure verifies the existence and validity of a particular PC. Same procedure is run internally before signing a message to check that the key is not altered in $\mathcal{M}$.*

We propose the following algorithms for Swap and Assign, as for Verify only a membership proof computation using corresponding witness is used, therefore we do not state that as a separate algorithm description here. All accumulator- and pairing based operations are not explicitly described for simplicity. The main algorithm is called Swap which represents the main protocol where the other algorithms are sub-procedures, and Swap should be interpreted as a set of interactive procedures running between the vehicles. The primary algorithms are defined as follows (Fig. 2):

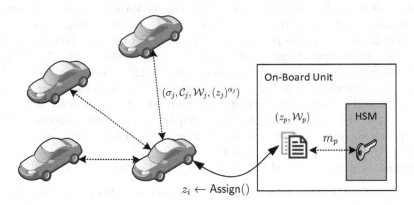

Fig. 2. Example assignment flow from one vehicle's perspective. After the double DH rounds the new z_i is assigned and corresponding secret keys m_p are stored in HSM unit $\mathcal{M}$, after the assignment procedure.

Swap($\mathcal{V}, \mathcal{W}, \mathcal{K}, \mathcal{P}, T$) This is the main procedure that needs the vehicles $\mathcal{V}$, the set of all witnesses $\mathcal{W}$, the signing keys $\mathcal{K}$, all PC:s $\mathcal{P}$ and a threshold value T that determines when to swap. The algorithm runs the complete protocol when the cluster of vehicles have decided to start swapping pseudonyms. It returns an updated, swapped set $\mathcal{P}'$ of PC:s for the vehicles to be stored within a road side unit for later auditing. Assign is a sub-procedure used by Swap.

Assign($\mathcal{V}, \mathcal{W}, \mathcal{K}, \mathcal{P}, z_1, ..., z_n, \alpha_1, ..., \alpha_n$) → ⊥/1 All vehicles share their accumulators z_i, the corresponding (encrypted) keys and witnesses (sk_i, w_i) and assignment values α_i. Ephemeral encryption keys are distributed in DH rounds between each participant, first for securely transferring each α_i, and later for the pseudonym keys. The assignment process therefore uniquely distributes keys and accumulators to all involved vehicles, and performs a final verification round afterwards. This procedure aborts if any of the steps or verification fails, otherwise returns success.

Verify($w_{i,j}, z$) → ⊥/1 This procedure verifies the existence of $\mathsf{sk}_{i,j} \in z_i$ by using the corresponding witness $w_{i,j}$, if successful it returns 1, ⊥ otherwise.

We note that the threshold value T is decided in the pre-stage protocol, e.g. it may depend on the number of vehicles, road segments or time slots [14,22]. We need a threshold in order to abort if the assignment values cannot be established since it is crucial for anonymity, i.e. the permutation cannot be known.

Algorithm 1. Swap

Require: $\mathcal{V}, \mathcal{P}, \mathcal{W}, \mathcal{K}, T$
  $s_c = 0$
  $s = \mathsf{False}$
  while $s = \mathsf{False}$ and $s_c < T$ **do**
    $s \leftarrow \mathsf{Assign}(\mathcal{V}, \mathcal{W}, \mathcal{K}, \mathcal{P})$
    $s_c = s_c + 1$
    if s = False or $s_c > T$ **then return** Error
    end if
  end while

---

6   Security Analysis

We briefly analyse the security and correctness properties of the proposed protocol. Only informal proofs are given due to space constraints, but captures the main ideas.

Theorem 1. *The sub-protocol* Assign *correctly distributes a swapping.*

Proof (Sketch of proof). Let $v_1, .., v_k$ be a set of vehicles in the swap protocol, with accumulators $z_1 = g^{\mathsf{sk}(1,1),...,\mathsf{sk}(1,n_1)}, ..., z_k = g^{\mathsf{sk}(k,1)\cdots\mathsf{sk}(k,n_k)}$ respectively. Each v_i chooses $\alpha_i \leftarrow \mathbb{Z}_p$ randomly and computes $(z_i)^{\alpha_i}$. All pairwise v_i and v_j where $i \neq j$ runs one round of the DH key exchange protocol which successively builds up to

$$z = g^{\mathsf{sk}(1,1)+...+\mathsf{sk}(k,n_k)+\alpha_1+\alpha_k}. \tag{1}$$

To clarify, for fixed vehicles v_1 and v_2, the build-up is done via the first DH round; the exchange of $k_{1,2}$ is done by v_1 chooses $x_{1,2} \leftarrow \mathbb{Z}_p$ and v_2 chooses $x_{2,1} \leftarrow \mathbb{Z}_p$. Next, they exchange $g^{x_{1,2}}$ and $g^{x_{2,1}}$, hence $k_{1,2} = k_{2,1} = g^{x_{2,1}x_{1,2}}$. Then the α_i's are shared encrypted as $(\alpha_i)^{k_{1,2}}$.

Now, to compute the assignment values, each vehicle creates a list, by computing the following values:

$$a_1 = \hat{e}(z,g) = \hat{e}(g^{\mathsf{sk}(1,1)+...+\mathsf{sk}(k,n_k)}, g)^{\alpha_1+...+\alpha_k} = \hat{e}(g^{\mathsf{sk}(1,1)+...+\mathsf{sk}(k,n_k)}, g^{\alpha_2+...+\alpha_k})^{\alpha_1} \tag{2}$$

and so on up to:

$$a_k = \hat{e}(g^{\mathsf{sk}(1,1)+...+\mathsf{sk}(k,n_k)}, g^{\alpha_1+...+\alpha_{k-1}})^{\alpha_k} \tag{3}$$

which results in $L = \{a_1, a_2, ..., a_k\}$. The reason for adding the paring operations to compute each assignment value is to bind all participants' keys, via the accumulators. Although the accumulators can be eavesdropped, the α_i's cannot, hence the assignment is now bound to the group via the secret keys and secured by the encryption of the α_i's.

Algorithm 2. Assign sub-routine

Require: $\mathcal{V}, \mathcal{W}, \mathcal{K}, \mathcal{P}$

Ensure: $\perp$ or 1

> **for** each v_i **do**
>> $\alpha_i \leftarrow$ PRNG
>>
>> $x_i \leftarrow$ PRNG
>>
>> $\sigma_i = \text{Sign}(z_i \| i)$
>>
>> **for** each v_i where $i \neq j$ **do**
>>> $k_{i,j} \leftarrow \text{DH}(g^{x_{i,j}}, v_j)$
>>>
>>> $\mathcal{W}_i = w_{(i,1)}, .., w_{(i,n_i)} \leftarrow \mathcal{W}$
>>>
>>> $\mathcal{C}_i = \alpha_i^{k_{i,j}}$
>>>
>>> send $(\sigma_i, \mathcal{C}_i, \mathcal{W}_i, (z_i)^{\alpha_i})$ to v_j
>>
>> **end for**
>>
>> $z \leftarrow z_i$
>>
>> $z' \leftarrow g$
>>
>> **for** each received $(\sigma_j, \mathcal{C}_j, \mathcal{W}_j, (z_j)^{\alpha_j})$ **do**
>>> **if** verify σ_j is successful **then**
>>>> $z \leftarrow z \cdot z_j$
>>>>
>>>> $z' \leftarrow z' \cdot z'^{\alpha_j}$
>>>
>>> **end if**
>>
>> **end for**
>>
>> $L \leftarrow \emptyset$
>>
>> **for** each $u = 1, ..., n$ **do**
>>> $a_u \leftarrow \hat{e}(z, z') = \hat{e}(g^{\sum_{l=1}^{n_l} sk_{(u,l)}}, g^{\sum_{l=1}^{n} \alpha_l - \alpha_u})^{\alpha_u}$
>>>
>>> $L[u] \leftarrow a_u$
>>
>> **end for**
>>
>> $L \leftarrow \text{Sort}(L)$
>>
>> $p \leftarrow L$ where p is the index where a_u derived from α_i is located in L
>>
>> $z_p \leftarrow z$
>>
>> Remove all $(\sigma_j, \mathcal{C}_j, \mathcal{W}_j, (z_j)^{\alpha_j})$ except from index p
>>
>> $k_{i,p} \leftarrow \text{DH}(g^{x_i}, v_p)$
>>
>> $\mathcal{C}'_i = \text{Enc}(\text{sk}_{i,1}, ..., \text{sk}_{i,n_i}) = (\text{sk}_{i,1}, ..., \text{sk}_{i,n_i})^{k_{i,p}}$
>>
>> v_i sends $\mathcal{C}'_i$ and receives $\mathcal{C}_p$
>>
>> $m_p = \text{Dec}(\mathcal{C}_p) = (\mathcal{C}_p)^{k_{i,p}^{-1}}$
>>
>> Store $(z_p, \mathcal{W}_p)$ in v_i and m_p in $\mathcal{M}$.
>
> **end for**
>
> **if** no error **then**
>> return 1
>
> **end if**
>
> return $\perp$

Next, we sort the list such that $\text{Sort}(L) = a_i < ... < a_j$. In the unlikely event that any two values are equal the protocol will abort and re-run, however if using random integers in $\mathbb{Z}_p$ for sufficiently large p such collision for n vehicles is negligible. Now, since each a_i is unique with an overwhelming probability, $\text{Sort}(L)$ can be mapped to indices, i.e. if a_i is the lowest integer it will map to index 1, thus the vehicle will discard all received z's except z_i, since for any party, it will have all separate z_i's from the DH rounds. Finally, from the second DH round, all vehicles exchange all keys: for fixed vehicles v_1 and v_2 computes x_1' and x_2' respectively, and shares the ephemeral DH key $k_{1,2}' = g^{x_1' x_2'}$. The decryption for v_1 is then $(\mathsf{sk}_{(1,1)} + ... + \mathsf{sk}_{(1,n_1)})^{g^{k_{1,2}'^{-1}}} = \mathsf{sk}_{(1,1)} + ... + \mathsf{sk}_{(1,n_1)}$.

$\square$

Theorem 2. *The* Swap *protocol provides anonymity and privacy.*

Proof (Sketch of proof). From Theorem 1 we deduce that an outside observer does not know which set of keys each vehicle will choose, since due to the discrete logarithm problem it is intractable to extract any α_i from $(\alpha_i)^{k_{i,j}}$ or any signing keys from from $(\mathcal{C}_i)^{k_{i,j}'}$. Therefore, it would be impossible to predict which v_i will swap with v_j. However, if the adversary manages to guess the swapping order correctly, the second DH round still protects the signing keys sent between two swapping nodes, hence the privacy property is not broken. Finally, since the keys are both accumulated into z_i and stored in $\mathcal{M}$, if a key is altered in $\mathcal{M}$, the adversary still needs to break the secure accumulator scheme since it verifies the key in $\mathcal{M}$ before signing, hence any attack on the keys will be detected. $\square$

7   Proof of Concept Implementation

We used the efficient MCL library with a Python wrapper [31] for the proof of concept implementation. The BLS12-381 curve was used.

Table 1. Collected timings for the different accumulator operations and fundamental crypto operations, all in milliseconds (ms).

Accumulator op.	Time (ms)	Crypto op.	Time (ms)
RSA accumulation	0.0610411	Sign	0.1831055
RSA deletion	0.0657268	Enc	0.1258850
RSA witness extraction	0.0656888	Dec	0.1261234
RSA verification	0.0623901	$\mathcal{H}$	0.0970364
Pairing-based accumulation	0.1771541	PRNG	0.0016689
Pairing-based deletion	0.1862679	**Mathematical op.**	**Time (ms)**
Pairing-based witness extraction	0.1191020	Pow in $\mathbb{G}_1$	0.1270771
Pairing-based verification	1.1851931	Inv in $\mathbb{G}_1$	0.0052452

All tests were run on a MacBook Pro, M1-chip, 1,4 GHz and each test ran for 1000 times where the average timing was noted. We collected all results of the individual procedures and operations in Table 1. Tests were run for the Assign procedure, excluding communication parts for the DH rounds, but included all computations. For a single node participating in the swapping protocol, the number of collaborative vehicles n scales linearly as shown in Fig. 3. A cluster with more than 100 vehicles that needs to swap pseudonyms seems unlikely since using the IEEE 802.11p stack for communication it is estimated to handle between 20–30 vehicles efficiently [32]. However, due to the strong linearity, a larger number of vehicles scale efficiently from a computational perspective. We also measure the performance of verifying elements, i.e. signing keys in each type of accumulator, where we conclude a large advantage for the RSA-based accumulator by Benaloh and de Mare. We note that current hardware for OBU equipment is less power-ful than the laptop used for the experiments. However, modern OBU equipment usually performs well in terms of computational power, whereas the bottlenecks are related to the wireless communication complexity [33].

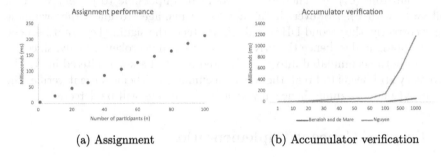

(a) Assignment   (b) Accumulator verification

Fig. 3. Scalability analysis of number of participants n, for the Assign procedure run on one node (a), and for accumulator verification on increasing number of elements (b).

8 Conclusion

From our proposed architecture and analysis we conclude that a double DH round protocol for pseudonym swapping, using parallel key management with accumulators, is feasible. With the proposed solution we provide an additional layer of key verification, i.e. that a certain signing key belongs to a pseudonym holder with efficient accumulators. Further analysis is needed for the commu-nication complexity and future research could include efficient secret shuffling methods merged with key exchange protocols to reduce the DH steps.

References

1. Council of European Union. Council regulation (EU) no 2010/40 (2010)
2. C-ITS. C-its deployment group. https://c-its-deployment-group.eu (2022). Accessed 10 May 2022
3. Hbaieb, A., Ayed, S., Chaari, L.: A survey of trust management in the internet of vehicles. Comput. Netw. **203**, 108558 (2022)

4. Giannetsos, T., Krontiris, I.: Securing v2x communications for the future: can pki systems offer the answer? In: Proceedings of the 14th International Conference on Availability, Reliability and Security, ARES '19, New York, NY, USA (2019). Association for Computing Machinery

5. Ghosal, A., Conti, M.: Security issues and challenges in v2x: a survey. Comput. Netw. **169**, 107093 (2020)

6. C-Roads. C-roads - the platform of harmonised c-its deployment in Europe. https://www.c-roads.eu (2022). Accessed: 14 May 2022

7. NordicWay 3. Nordicway 2 and nordicway 3. https://www.nordicway.net (2022). Accessed: 14 May 2022

8. C-MobILE. The c-mobile project. https://c-mobile-project.eu (2021). Accessed: 14 May 2022

9. European Telecommunications Standards Institute. ETSI TS 102 941 V1.4.1: Intelligent Transport Systems (ITS); Security; Trust and Privacy Management. https://www.etsi.org/standards (2022). Accessed: 11 May 2022

10. European Telecommunications Standards Institute. ETSI EN 302 637–3: Intelligent Transport Systems (ITS); Vehicular Communications; Basic Set of Applications; Part 3: Specifications of Decentralized Environmental Notification Basic Service. https://www.etsi.org/standards, 2014. Accessed: 15 May 2022

11. European Telecommunications Standards Institute. ETSI EN 302 637–2: Intelligent Transport Systems (ITS); Vehicular Communications; Basic Set of Applications; Part 2: Specification of Cooperative Awareness Basic Service. https://www.etsi.org/standards (2014). Accessed: 15 May 2022

12. Boualouache, A., Senouci, S.-M., Moussaoui, S.: A survey on pseudonym changing strategies for vehicular ad-hoc networks. IEEE Commun. Surv. Tutorials **20**(1), 770–790 (2018)

13. Eckhoff, D., Sommer, C., Gansen, T., German, R., Dressler, F.: Strong and affordable location privacy in VANETs: Identity diffusion using time-slots and swapping. In: 2010 IEEE Vehicular Networking Conference, pp. 174–181 (2010)

14. European Telecommunications Standards Institute. ETSI TR 103 415 V1.1.1: Intelligent Transport Systems (ITS); Security; Pre-standardization study on pseudonym change management. https://www.etsi.org/standards (2018). Accessed: 12 May 2022

15. Benaloh, J., de Mare, M.: One-way accumulators: a decentralized alternative to digital signatures. In: Helleseth, T. (ed.) EUROCRYPT 1993. LNCS, vol. 765, pp. 274–285. Springer, Heidelberg (1994). https://doi.org/10.1007/3-540-48285-7_24

16. Nguyen, L.: Accumulators from bilinear pairings and applications. In: Menezes, A. (ed.) CT-RSA 2005. LNCS, vol. 3376, pp. 275–292. Springer, Heidelberg (2005). https://doi.org/10.1007/978-3-540-30574-3_19

17. Petit, J., Schaub, F., Feiri, M., Kargl, F.: Pseudonym schemes in vehicular networks: a survey. IEEE Commun. Surv. Tutorials **17**(1), 228–255 (2015)

18. Zhong, H., Ni, J., Cui, J., Zhang, J., Liu, L.: Personalized location privacy protection based on vehicle movement regularity in vehicular networks. IEEE Syst. J. **16**(1), 755–766 (2022)

19. Deng, X., Gao, T., Guo, N., Zhao, C., Qi, J.: PCP: a pseudonym change scheme for location privacy preserving in vanets. Entropy, 24(5), (2022)

20. Yang, M., Feng, Y., Fu, X., Qian, Q.: Location privacy preserving scheme based on dynamic pseudonym swap zone for internet of vehicles. Int. J. Distrib. Sens. Netw. 15(7), 1550147719865508 (2019)

21. Boualouache, A., Senouci, S.-M., Moussaoui, S.: Privanet: an efficient pseudonym changing and management framework for vehicular ad-hoc networks. IEEE Trans. Intell. Transp. Syst. **21**(8), 3209–3218 (2020)

22. Fouchal, H., Boutehalla, R.: Comparison of pseudonym change strategies for C-its. In: 2021 IEEE Symposium on Computers and Communications (ISCC), pp. 1–6 (2021)

23. IEEE Standard for Wireless Access in Vehicular Environments (WAVE) - Multi-Channel Operation. IEEE Std 1609.4-2016 (Revision of IEEE Std 1609.4-2010), pp. 1–94 (2016)

24. Li, X., et al.: PAPU: pseudonym swap with provable unlinkability based on differential privacy in vanets. IEEE Internet Things J. **7**(12), 11789–11802 (2020)

25. Koblitz, N., Menezes, A.: Pairing-based cryptography at high security levels. In: Smart, N.P. (ed.) Cryptography and Coding 2005. LNCS, vol. 3796, pp. 13–36. Springer, Heidelberg (2005). https://doi.org/10.1007/11586821_2

26. Boneh, D., Lynn, B., Shacham, H.: Short signatures from the weil pairing. In: Boyd, C. (ed.) ASIACRYPT 2001. LNCS, vol. 2248, pp. 514–532. Springer, Heidelberg (2001). https://doi.org/10.1007/3-540-45682-1_30

27. Diffie, W., Hellman, M.: New directions in cryptography. IEEE Trans. Inf. Theory **22**(6), 644–654 (1976)

28. European Telecommunications Standards Institute. ETSI EN 302 636-6-1 V1.2.0: Intelligent Transport Systems (ITS); Vehicular Communications; GeoNetworking; Part 6: Internet Integration; Sub-part 1: Transmission of IPv6 Packets over GeoNetworking Protocol (2022)

29. IEEE standard for wireless access in vehicular environments-security services for applications and management messages. IEEE Std 1609.2-2016 (Revision of IEEE Std 1609.2-2013), pp. 1–240, (2016)

30. European Telecommunications Standards Institute. ETSI TS 103 097: Intelligent Transport Systems (ITS); Security; Security header and certificate formats. https://www.etsi.org/standards (2020). Accessed: 02 Jun 2022

31. piotrszyma. "MCL-python". https://github.com/piotrszyma/mcl-python (2020)

32. Arena, F., Pau, G., Severino, A.: A review on IEEE 802.11p for intelligent transportation systems. J. Sens. Actuator Netw. **9**(2), (2020)

33. Sedar, R., et al.: Standards-compliant multi-protocol on-board unit for the evaluation of connected and automated mobility services in multi-vendor environments. Sensors **21**(6), (2021)

Benchmark Performance
of the Multivariate Polynomial Public Key
Encapsulation Mechanism

Randy Kuang[1]($\boxtimes$), Maria Perepechaenko[1], Ryan Toth[1],
and Michel Barbeau[2]

[1] Quantropi Inc., Ottawa, Canada
{randy.kuang,maria.perepechaenko,ryan.toth}@quantropi.com
[2] School of Computer Science, Carleton University, Ottawa, Canada
barbeau@scs.carleton.ca,
https://www.quantropi.com/, https://carleton.ca/scs/

Abstract. This paper presents the results of benchmarking the quantum-safe Multivariate Public Key Cryptosystem (MPPK) key encapsulation mechanism for quadratic solvable univariate polynomials. We used a benchmarking tool containing implementations of the four NIST Post-Quantum Cryptography (PQC) finalists: Kyber, McEliece, NTRU, and Saber. The benchmark demonstrates that the performance of MPPK is comparable with that of the four PQC algorithms, offering relatively fast key generation and small key sizes. Key encapsulation and decapsulation performance are comparable with the PQC schemes, with room for improvement.

Keywords: Post-Quantum Cryptography · Public-Key Cryptography · PQC · Key Encapsulation Mechanism · KEM · Multivariate Polynomials · PQC Performance

1   Introduction

To address the advances in quantum computing, National Institute of Standards and Technology (NIST) began a Post-Quantum Cryptography (PQC) standardization project in 2017. In 2021, four Key Encapsulation Mechanism (KEM) finalists were announced: Kyber, McEliece, NTRU, and Saber [13]. Besides, a novel quantum-resistant KEM algorithm, called Multivariate Polynomial Public Key (MPPK) KEM has been introduced by Kuang and Barbeau [9]. McEliece falls under the category of code-based algorithms, Kyber, NTRU, and Saber fall under the category of lattice-based algorithms, and MPPK falls under a multivariate algorithm category. We present the results of benchmarking MPPK in a framework common with the four NIST finalists. We report on the performance of MPPK KEM when the security parameter λ is set to the value two, the quadratic case.

Related work is reviewed in Sect. 2. MPPK is summarized in Sect. 3. The results of benchmarking MPPK against the four NIST finalists are presented in Sect. 4. We conclude with Sect. 5.

© The Author(s), under exclusive license to Springer Nature Switzerland AG 2023
S. Kallel et al. (Eds.): CRiSIS 2022, LNCS 13857, pp. 239–255, 2023.
https://doi.org/10.1007/978-3-031-31108-6_18

2   Related Work

PQC refers to cryptosystems that can withstand quantum computing attacks, including KEMs [12]. There are two different KEM algorithm types that deserve special attention: code-based and lattice-based. The algorithm proposed by McEliece relies on the hardness of decoding a general linear code [11]. Its security has been demonstrated by Berlekemp et al. [2]. The other KEM finalists for PQC standardization, Kyber [1], Nth degree Truncated polynomial Ring Units (NTRU) [6], Saber [18] are lattice-based, with security arising from the hardness of solving the Shortest Vector Problem (SVP).

Kuang [7] proposed DPPK, a public key algorithm building on: i) the deterministic complexity $\mathcal{O}\left(p^2\right)$ of cracking the private key from a public key and ii) the deterministic complexity $\mathcal{O}\left(np^{1/2}\right)$ of solving the polynomial root finding problem [3,14,16] for breaking intercept ciphertext. Kuang and Barbeau [8,9] proposed an improvement of DPPK from a univariate to a multivariate base polynomial case to enhance the security of ciphertext with one multivariate noise function associated with the constant term in the public key. This improvement hardens the security of ciphers from a univariate root-finding problem to a problem of solving multivariate polynomial equation systems, which generally is NP-Hard [4,5]. This paper presents an updated multivariate public-key cryptography MPPK introducing a new hidden ring over which the new noise functions are defined.

3   Summary of MPPK KEM

Unless explicitly stated otherwise, all mathematical operations are modulo a prime number p, over the finite field $GF(p)$.

3.1   Key Generation

For key pair construction, three polynomials are generated, namely, a base multivariate polynomial $\beta(x_0, x_1, \ldots, x_m)$, of degree n concerning the variable x_0, and two solvable univariate polynomials $f(x_0)$ and $h(x_0)$, both of degree λ. Coefficients are chosen at random over $GF(p)$. The base polynomial has the following general format:

$$\beta(x_0, x_1, \ldots, x_m) = \sum_{i=0}^{n} \beta_i(x_1, \ldots, x_m)x_0^i \tag{1}$$

for $i = 0, \ldots, n$, where every $\beta_i(x_1, \ldots, x_m)$ is a polynomial in the following general form

$$\beta_i(x_1, \ldots, x_m) = \sum_{j_1=0}^{\ell_1} \cdots \sum_{j_m=0}^{\ell_m} c_{ij_1 \ldots j_m} x_1^{j_1} \cdots x_m^{j_m}. \tag{2}$$

The upper limits $\ell_1, \ldots, \ell_m$ are positive integers. The coefficients $c_{ij_1 \ldots j_m}$ are elements of $GF(p)$. Equation (2) can be simply rewritten as a sum of monomials:

$$\beta_i(x_1, \ldots, x_m) = \sum_{j=0}^{L} c_{ij} X_j \text{ with } X_j = x_1^{j_1} \cdots x_m^{j_m} \tag{3}$$

L is the total number of monomials. The product of the multiplicand polynomial $\beta(x_0, x_1, \ldots, x_m)$ and multiplier polynomial $f(x_0)$ yields a multivariate polynomial $\phi(x_0, x_1 \ldots, x_m)$ of degree $n + \lambda$, that is, a polynomial of the form

$$\phi(x_0, x_1, \ldots, x_m) = \sum_{i=0}^{n+\lambda} \phi_i(x_1, \ldots, x_m) x_0^i \tag{4}$$

with $\phi_i(x_1, \ldots, x_m) = \sum_{j+k=i} f_j \beta_k(x_1, \ldots, x_m)$. The same construction applies to the product between the multiplicand polynomial $\beta(x_0, x_1, \ldots, x_m)$ and multiplier polynomial $h(x_0)$ that result is the polynomial

$$\psi(x_0, x_1, \ldots, x_m) = \sum_{i=0}^{n+\lambda} \psi_i(x_1, \ldots, x_m) x_0^i \tag{5}$$

with $\psi_i(x_1, \ldots, x_m) = \sum_{j+k=i} h_j \beta_k(x_1, \ldots, x_m)$.

The positive integers λ and n, and the prime number p, are security parameters. Directly publishing the product polynomials $\phi(.)$ and $\psi(.)$ with all their coefficients would enable adversaries to perpetrate a variety of attacks leading to the extraction of the coefficients of $\beta(x_0, x_1, \ldots, x_m)$, $f(x_0)$, and $h(x_0)$. We set aside the first and last terms from the product polynomials $\phi(.)$ and $\psi(.)$ to prevent these attacks. To build the public key, we define the polynomials

$$\Phi(x_0, x_1, \ldots, x_m) = \sum_{i=1}^{n+\lambda-1} \phi_i(x_1, \ldots, x_m) x_0^i \text{ and} \tag{6}$$

$$\Psi(x_0, x_1, \ldots, x_m) = \sum_{i=1}^{n+\lambda-1} \psi_i(x_1, \ldots, x_m) x_0^i. \tag{7}$$

The first term and last terms in $\phi(.)$ and $\psi(.)$ share the first and last terms of the base polynomial $\beta(.)$. We introduce two noise functions with coefficients over a ring $\mathbb{Z}/t\mathbb{Z}$ as follows

$$N_0(x_1, \ldots, x_m) = \sum_{j=1}^{L} (R_0 c_{0j} \mod t) X_j$$

$$N_n(x_1, \ldots, x_m) = \sum_{j=1}^{L} (R_n c_{nj} \mod t) x_0^{n+\lambda} X_j$$

where R_0 and R_n are randomly chosen from the ring $\mathbb{Z}/t\mathbb{Z}$ with a condition that $GCD(R_0, t) = 1$ and $GCD(R_n, t) = 1$. The bit length of the ring $\mathbb{Z}/t\mathbb{Z}$

must be larger than $2\log_2 p + \log_2 L$ to make sure the calculation of polynomial values fall inside the ring. Moreover, we recommend picking values such that the coefficients of the noise functions are a few bits smaller than the bit-length of t. By introducing two noise functions over a ring structure, we overcome the security weakness in the previous version of MPPK where the noise functions are defined in the same prime field $GF(p)$ as the public key polynomials $\Phi(.)$ and $\Psi(.)$ [8,9]. We can keep all the parameters R_0, R_n, t as well as the results of the operations over the ring $\mathbb{Z}/t\mathbb{Z}$ as a part of the private key to address a security weakness of the previous MPPK.

Now, let us summarize the key pair construction of MPPK. Th public key consists of coefficients of $\Phi(x_0, x_1, \ldots, x_m)$ and $\Psi(x_0, x_1, \ldots, x_m)$ and coefficients of $N_0(x_1, \ldots, x_m)$ and $N_n(x'_1, \ldots, x'_m)$, with $x'_j = x_j x_0^{n+\lambda} \bmod p$. The private key is made of the coefficients of $f(x_0)$ and $h(x_0)$ and values R_0, R_n, and t.

3.2   Encryption

For our benchmarking, we focus on quadratic polynomials $g(x_0)$ and $h(x_0)$, i.e. $\lambda = 2$. Although we can mathematically use radicals for cubic polynomials, the decryption with modular cube roots is much more complicated than with modular square roots. For quadratic polynomials, decryption will produce two roots, requiring one to make a decision to choose the correct root. Considering NIST's requirement of a secret session key size of 32 bytes for all security levels, we suggest having one extra GF(p) field element, just like a message authentication code or MAC appended to the 32-byte key. Considering the results from our security analysis, we will choose the GF(p) field to be 64 bits. So we will hash a 32-byte secret and create a MAC of 64 bits. Therefore, MPPK cipher has five quadruples.

Let us define the variable x_0 with the secret $s \in GF(p)$ that is to be encrypted and decrypted. Let us define the noise variables $x_1, \ldots, x_m$ with randomly picked values $r_1, \ldots, r_m \in GF(p)$. The secret s is encrypted by evaluating the two polynomials

$$\Phi = \Phi(s, r_1, \ldots, r_m) \text{ and } \Psi = \Psi(s, r_1, \ldots, r_m). \tag{8}$$

and calculated values from the two noise functions

$$\bar{N}_0 = N_0(r_1, \ldots, r_m) \text{ and } \bar{N}_n = N_n(r'_1, \ldots, r'_m), \tag{9}$$

with $r'_j = (r_j s^{n+\lambda} \bmod p)$. We obtain the ciphertext quadruple $C[5] = \{\Phi[5], \Psi[5], \bar{N}_0[5], \bar{N}_n[5]\}$.

3.3   Decryption

To decrypt the secret s from the ciphertext quadruple $C[5] = \{\Phi[5], \Psi[5], \bar{N}_0[5], \bar{N}_n[5]\}$, we use the private key and compute for each segment $C[i]$ with $i \in$

$\{0, \ldots, 4\}$

$$\begin{cases} \bar{\beta}_0 = \left(\frac{\bar{N}_0[i]}{R_0} \mod t \right) \mod p \\ \bar{\beta}_n = \left(\frac{\bar{N}_n[i]}{R_n} \mod t \right) \mod p \\ \phi(s, r_1, \ldots, r_m) = \bar{\beta}_0 f_0 + \Phi[i] + f_\lambda \bar{\beta}_n \\ \psi(s, r_1, \ldots, r_m) = \bar{\beta}_0 h_0 + \Psi[i] + h_\lambda \bar{\beta}_n. \end{cases} \quad (10)$$

To cancel the base polynomial $f(x_0, x_1, \ldots, x_m)$ using the random noise, the following ratio is calculated

$$k = \frac{\phi(s, r_1, \ldots, r_m)}{\psi(s, r_1, \ldots, r_m)} = \frac{\beta(s, r_1, \ldots, r_m) f(s)}{\beta(s, r_1, \ldots, r_m) h(s)} = \frac{f(s)}{h(s)}. \quad (11)$$

This division cancels the random noise. When $\psi(s, r_1, \ldots, r_m) = 0$, decryption fails. The decryption with modular square root produces two roots r[i][2] for each $C[i]$. A verification process is required by concatenating them together and then comparing MAC from decryption with r[4][0] and r[4][1].

4   Benchmarking MPPK

The MPPK KEM described in [10] focuses on the case $\lambda = 1$. The security analysis is developed for any λ and applies directly to the case $\lambda = 2$ described in this work. The best complexity is at least $\mathcal{O}(p^{\lambda+3})$ for cracking the entire private key and $\mathcal{O}(p^{m-3})$ for ciphertext only attack respectively. Then configurations $(log\ p, n, \lambda, m)$ are $(64, 3, 2, 5)$ for security level I, $(64, 3, 2, 6)$ for level III, and $(64, 3, 2, 7)$ for level V, respectively.

We present performance data for key generation, encapsulation and decapsulation for the four NIST PQC finalists, namely, McEliece, Kyber, NTRU and Saber as well as RSA-2048, for the purpose of comparison with a currently widely used public key cryptosystem. We use a benchmarking toolkit called the SUPERCOP [17] on a 16-core Intel Core i7-10700 CPU system, at 2.90 GHz. SUPERCOP has been run on the four quantum-safe cryptosystems with parameter sets providing NIST security Levels I, III, and V. They respectively correspond to the hardness of breaking Advanced Encryption Standard (AES) 128, 192, and 256 bits. Note that the results presented correspond to the reference implementation; we have not configured an AVX solution.

4.1   NIST Level I

The configuration of MPPK KEM to meet the NIST security level I is as follows: $\log_2 p = 64, n = 3, \lambda = 2, m = 5$. As required by NIST, the secret to be encrypted and decrypted, also called the Session Key Bytes, is 32 bytes for all the measured primitives. Box plots in Figs. 1, 2 and 3 provide performance data for the NIST PQC algorithms: McEliece, Kyber, NTRU, and Saber, as well as MPPK KEM configured to provide security Level I, and RSA-2048. Note that we only illustrate the performance of RSA-2048 for security Level I. That is because RSA-2048

Table 1. NIST Level I parameter set.

Crypto system	Size (Bytes)			
	Public key	*Private Key*	*Ciphertext*	*Secret*
McEliece	261,120	6,492	128	32
Kyber	800	1,632	768	32
NTRU	699	935	699	32
Saber	672	1,568	736	32
MPPK-325	490	99	340	32
RSA-2048	256	384	256	32

provides 112 bits of entropy [15]. We point out that it is a little shy of the 128 its required by the NIST Level I.

Table 1 contains the public key, private key, and ciphertext sizes of the NIST PQC algorithms, MPPK KEM, and RSA-2048. The formula used to calculate MPPK KEM public key sizes in bits is

$$2\,m(n + \lambda - 1)\log_2 p + 2m\log_2 t$$

and private keys are calculated using the following formula

$$2(\lambda + 1)\log_2 p + 3\log_2 t.$$

Being 490 bytes, the public key size of MPPK KEM is relatively small. It is, however, larger than the RSA 256 byte public key. Among the four NIST PQC algorithms, McEliece has the largest public key with 261,120 bytes, followed by Kyber at 800 bytes. MPPK KEM also offers a rather small private key size of just 99 bytes. McEliece, Kyber and Saber have private keys over 1,500 bytes. NTRU's private key is 935 bytes. RSA private key is also larger than MPPK, at 384 bytes. The ciphertext sizes for all the primitives measured have the same order of magnitude, with McEliece, MPPK, and RSA ciphertext sizes falling into the interval of $[128, 340]$ bytes, and Kyber, NTRU, and Saber ciphertext sizes being in the interval of $[699, 768]$ bytes.

In measuring the performance of any KEM algorithm, there are three procedures to focus on: key generation, key encapsulation, and key decapsulation. Figure 1 illustrates the key generation performance of MPPK and the NIST PQC algorithms and RSA. The key generation performance values of MPPK primitive estimated in clock cycles tend to fall in the interval $[37000, 40000]$, with a median value being $37,906$ clock cycles. The fastest among the NIST PQC finalists, Saber, offers key generation performance values that fall in the interval of $[39000, 43000]$ clock cycles, with a median value at $39,654$ clock cycles. Meanwhile, the corresponding values for NTRU and McEliece have the general form $x = a \times 10^6$ and $x = a \times 10^8$, respectively, with median values being $6,554,031$ clock cycles for NTRU and $152,424,455$ clock cycles for McEliece. Key generation estimated in clock cycles for the Kyber primitive has the same order of

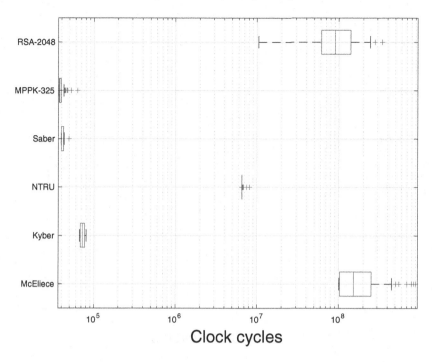

Fig. 1. NIST Level I - Key generation time in clock cycles, by cryptosystem. For every box, the central mark indicates the median, and the bottom and top edges of the box indicate the 25th and 75th percentiles. The whiskers extend to the most extreme data points not considered outliers. The outliers are individually represented by the marker '+'.

magnitude as MPPK and Saber. Indeed, the values for Kyber fall into the interval [68000, 78000], with a median value equal to 72, 403 clock cycles. RSA key generation is the next slowest after McEliece, with a median value of 91, 049, 514 clock cycles, majorly due to searching for two large prime numbers to create its public key.

A similar account can be observed in the Fig. 2 depicting key encapsulation performance in clock cycles. NTRU shows the longest time for encapsulation with values estimated in clock cycles that fall in the interval [418000, 422000], and a median value of 418, 622 clock cycles. Better performance is achieved by the McEliece scheme, with key encapsulation values estimated in clock cycles being in the interval [106000, 123000] clock cycles, with a median value of 108, 741 clock cycles. Kyber, Saber, and MPPK primitives all have key encapsulation values of the same magnitude. However, the median values for Kyber, Saber, and MPPK are 95, 466, 62, 154, and 99, 010 clock cycles. These three algorithms display comparable key encapsulation performance. The RSA algorithm has the fastest key encapsulation procedure with a median value of 13, 254 clock cycles thanks to its small encryption key. Much like with key encapsulation, the key decapsulation performance of MPPK is better than some of the primitives measured.

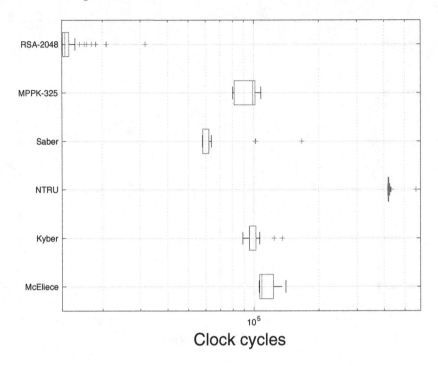

Clock cycles

Fig. 2. NIST Level I - Encapsulation time in cycles, by cryptosystem.

However, it does not offer the best performance. Figure 3 illustrates key decapsulation performance of the MPPK primitive and the NIST PQC primitives. The presented data shows that Saber has the fastest decapsulation performance with values estimated in clock cycles falling in the interval of [63000, 68000] clock cycles. The Saber key decapsulation performance's median value is 67, 165 clock cycles. The next best key decapsulation performance is achieved by Kyber with a median value of 117, 407 clock cycles, with upper and lower quartile values being 125, 684 and 117, 245 clock cycles, respectively. MPPK follows with key decapsulation performance estimated in clock cycles generally falling in the interval [460000, 496000], with a median value of 484, 344 clock cycles. The NTRU key decapsulation performance has a median value of 1, 246, 861 clock cycles. The described primitives perform better than RSA for key decapsulation. Indeed, values for RSA tend to be over 1.67 million and under 1.7 million, with the median value being 1, 676, 246 clock cycles. McEliece offers the slowest key decapsulation procedure with a median value of over 44 million clock cycles.

Note that such a difference in performance is due to different mathematical operations used for each procedure. For instance, performing arithmetical operations over a finite field is very fast. However, taking square roots over a finite field is expensive and requires a clever algorithm to guarantee efficient performance. The latter is precisely what is causing slower key decapsulation performance for MPPK. Similarly, calculating inverse functions over a finite field is costly, which

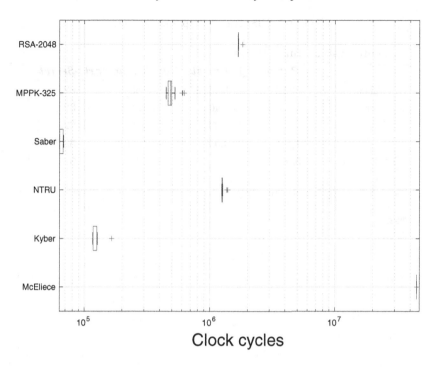

Fig. 3. NIST Level I - Decapsulation time in clock cycles, by cryptosystem.

affects NTRU key generation procedure performance. Thus, the differences in the performance come from unique ways to generate keys, encrypt and decrypt messages. Some constructions are more mathematically involved and result in performance challenges. However, one must consider that such constructions might be more resistant to attacks or perhaps easier to implement than others.

4.2 NIST Level III

We discuss the performance of the MPPK KEM algorithm and the four NIST PQC finalists, all configured to provide NIST security Level III. The configuration of MPPK KEM to meet the NIST security level III is as follows: $\log_2 p = 64, n = 3, \lambda = 2, m = 6$.

The parameter set is in Table 2. As with Level I, the secret size is 32 bytes, as NIST requires. The smallest public and secret key sizes displayed in Table 2 correspond to the MPPK primitive, followed by the NTRU scheme with a public key size of 930 bytes, and a secret key size of 1,234 bytes. Public key sizes for Kyber and Saber are over 1,000 bytes. The public key size for the McEliece algorithm is 524,160 bytes, the largest among the compared primitives. The secret key size for McEliece is also the largest among the values displayed, being

Table 2. NIST Level III parameter set.

Crypto system	Size (Bytes)			
	Public key	*Private Key*	*Ciphertext*	*Secret*
McEliece	524,160	13,608	188	32
Kyber	1,184	2,400	1,088	32
NTRU	930	1,234	930	32
Saber	1,312	3,040	1,472	32
MPPK-326	588	99	340	32

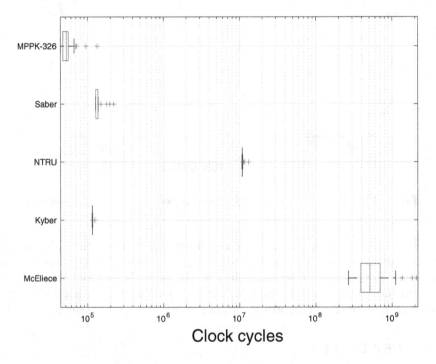

Fig. 4. NIST Level III - Key generation time, by cryptosystem.

13, 608 bytes. However, they offer the smallest ciphertext at 188 bytes. MPPK offers a rather small ciphertext with 340 bytes, followed by NTRU with 930 bytes. Ciphertexts corresponding to Kyber and Saber are over 1, 000 bytes.

Figure 4 illustrates the key generation performance of MPPK and NIST PQC algorithms providing security Level III. According to the table data, the MPPK KEM algorithm offers the fastest key generation procedure with a median value

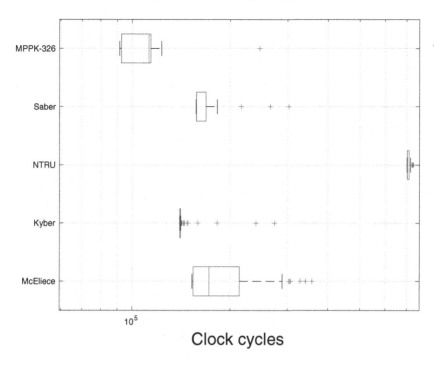

Clock cycles

Fig. 5. NIST Level III - Encapsulation time, by cryptosystem.

of $51,439$ clock cycles. The most efficient performance among the NIST PQC finalists is displayed by the Kyber and Saber primitives, with values for both schemes falling into the interval $[115000, 138000]$. McEliece has a rather slow key generation procedure with a median being over 387 million clock cycles.

Figure 5 illustrates the key encapsulation performance of MPPK and the four NIST PQC algorithms. As with key generation, MPPK offers fast key encapsulation performance for the Level III security configuration, with a median value of $112,607$ clock cycles. The values for the NIST PQC finalists are over $137,000$ with median values being $172538, 140376, 703046$, and 157554 clock cycles for the McEliece, Kyber, NTRU, and Saber primitives, respectively.

Decapsulation data as given in Fig. 6 illustrates that the McEliece primitive has the slowest performance with a median value at over 93 million clock cycles. NTRU follows at values over 2 million clock cycles. The fastest among the measured NIST PQC primitives is Saber, with values falling in the interval of $[173000, 200000]$ clock cycles. MPPK KEM displays results with a median value of $477,922$ clock cycles.

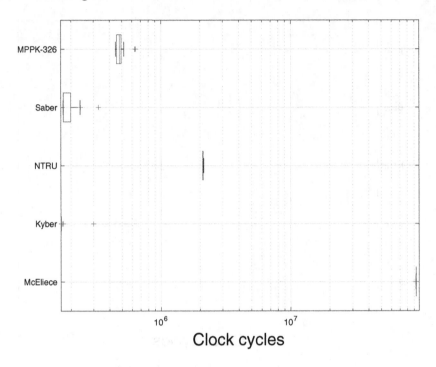

Fig. 6. NIST Level III - Decapsulation time, by cryptosystem.

Table 3. NIST Level V parameter set.

Crypto system	Size (Bytes)			
	Public key	*Private Key*	*Ciphertext*	*Secret*
McEliece	1,044,992	13,932	240	32
Kyber	1,568	3,168	1,568	32
NTRU	1,230	1,590	1,230	32
Saber	1,312	3,040	1,472	32
MPPK-327	686	99	340	32

4.3   NIST Level V

Figures 7, 8 and 9 explore the performance of MPPK together with the NIST PQC primitives at security Level V. The configuration of MPPK KEM to meet the NIST security level V is as follows: $\log_2 p = 64, n = 3, \lambda = 2, m = 7$. The secret remains 32 bytes, as required by NIST. The ciphertext sizes for the

McEliece and MPPK primitives are rather small concerning the other NIST PQC primitives. Indeed, the ciphertexts for McEliece and MPPK are less than 350 bytes, whereas the Kyber, Saber, and NTRU ciphertext sizes are over 1,200 bytes. MPPK also displays a small secret key of 99 bytes. Corresponding sizes for the Saber, Kyber, and McEliece algorithms are 3040, 3168, and 13932 bytes, respectively. The NTRU primitive has a relatively small secret key size of 1,590 bytes. The same observations apply to the public keys. That is, MPPK offers a small public key of 686 bytes. The public key sizes of the NIST PQC finalists are 1230, 1312, 1568, and 1044992 bytes for NTRU, Saber, Kyber, and McEliece, respectively.

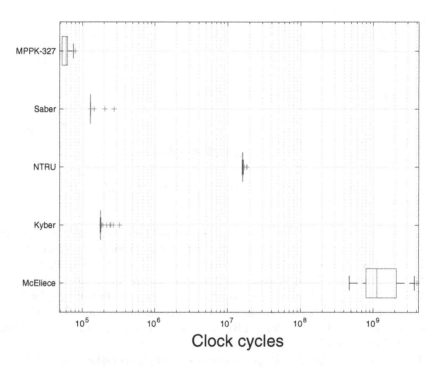

Fig. 7. NIST Level V - Key generation time, by cryptosystem.

Figure 7, Saber displays the best key generation performance among the NIST PQC finalists, with a median value of 128,412 clock cycles. McEliece, on the other hand, offers the slowest key generation performance with values over 800 million clock cycles. MPPK displays fast key generation performance with a median value of 59,566 clock cycles.

Figure 8, moving on to key encapsulation performance, NTRU has the slowest encapsulation procedure with values over 1 million clock cycles. McEliece and

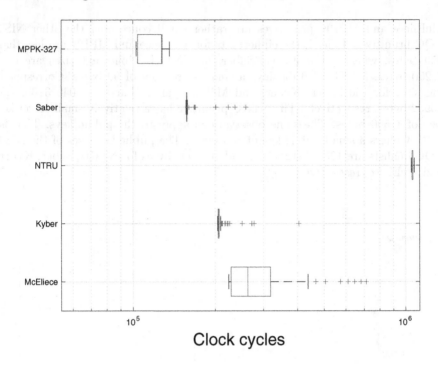

Fig. 8. NIST Level V - Encapsulation time, by cryptosystem.

Kyber offer better performance with cycles over 200, 000. Saber displays the best performance among the NIST PQC primitives with values below 160, 000 clock cycles. MPPK, too, offers fast performance with values under 130, 000 clock cycles. The best key decapsulation performance among all primitives measured is offered by Saber. Indeed, Fig. 9 show that key decapsulation values for Saber are under 190, 000 clock cycles, whereas the corresponding values for Kyber are over 235, 000, over 3 million for NTRU, over 179 million for McEliece, and over 460, 000 clock cycles for MPPK KEM.

Figure 10 plots the MPPK performances of key generation, encapsulation, and decapsulation for all three levels. Cycles of key generation and encapsulation slightly increase as the security level changes from level I to V. However, the decapsulation performance remains the same for all three levels. This behavior reflects the MPPK decryption mechanism. Basically, the same modular square root over the same prime filed $GF(p)$ for all security levels. It is also noticeable that this modular square root computation significantly contributes to the clock cycles of decapsulation. Although this relatively low performance in decapsulation compared with Kyber and Saber, MPPK still demonstrates much better than RSA-2048.

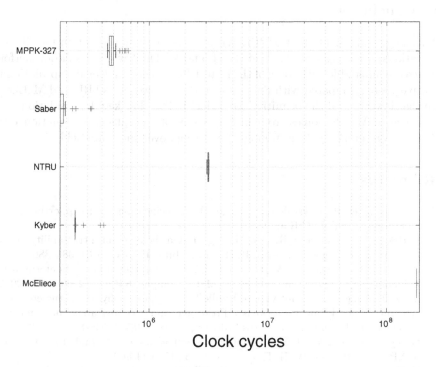

Fig. 9. NIST Level V - Decapsulation time, by cryptosystem.

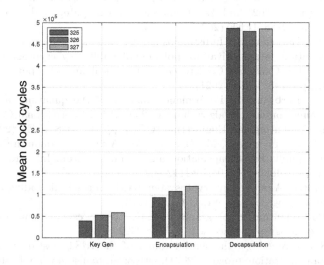

Fig. 10. Key generation, encapsulation and decapsulation means (clock cycles) for MPPK $(3, 2, 4)$, $(3, 2, 5)$ and $(3, 2, 6)$.

5   Conclusion

Our analysis highlights that MPPK KEM offers fast key generation for all configurations providing security levels I, III, and V. The key encapsulation performance is comparable with some of the fastest PQC schemes. Key decapsulation is relatively slow compared with Saber and Kyber. However, NTRU and McEliece are the slowest of all the primitives considered. The slow key decapsulation performance of MPPK comes from finding roots of the quadratic equation over $GF(p)$, more precisely, from taking square roots over the finite field.

References

1. Avanzi, R., et al.: Crystals-Kyber algorithm specifications and supporting documentation. NIST PQC Round **2**, 4 (2017)
2. Berlekamp, E., McEliece, R., van Tilborg, H.: On the inherent intractability of certain coding problems (corresp.). IEEE Trans. Info. Theory **24**(3), 384–386 (1978)
3. Bourgain, J., Konyagin, S.V., Shparlinski, I.E.: Character sums and deterministic polynomial root finding in finite fields. Math. Comput. **84**(296), 2969–2977 (2015)
4. Ding, J., Yang, B.Y.: Multivariate Public Key Cryptography. In: Bernstein, D.J., Buchmann, J., Dahmen, E. (eds.) Post-Quantum Cryptography, pp. 193–241. Springer, Heidelberg (2009). https://doi.org/10.1007/978-3-540-88702-7_6
5. Garey, M.R., Johnson, D.S.: Computers and intractability. A Guide to the Theory of NP-Completeness. W. H. Freeman and Co., USA (1990)
6. Hoffstein, J., Pipher, J., Silverman, J.H.: NTRU: a ring-based public key cryptosystem. In: Buhler, J.P. (ed.) ANTS 1998. LNCS, vol. 1423, pp. 267–288. Springer, Heidelberg (1998). https://doi.org/10.1007/BFb0054868
7. Kuang, R.: A deterministic polynomial public key algorithm over a prime Galois Field GF (p). In: 2021 2nd Asia Conference on Computers and Communications (ACCC), pp. 79–88. IEEE (2021)
8. Kuang, R., Barbeau, M.: Indistinguishability and non-deterministic encryption of the quantum safe multivariate polynomial public key cryptographic system. In: 2021 IEEE Canadian Conference on Electrical and Computer Engineering (CCECE), pp. 1–5. IEEE (2021)
9. Kuang, R., Barbeau, M.: Performance analysis of the quantum safe multivariate polynomial public key algorithm. In: 2021 IEEE International Conference on Quantum Computing and Engineering (QCE), pp. 351–358. IEEE (2021)
10. Kuang, R., Perepechaenko, M., Barbeau, M.: A new post-quantum multivariate polynomial public key encapsulation algorithm. Quantum Inf. Process. **21**, 360 (2022). https://doi.org/10.1007/s11128-022-03712-5
11. McEliece, R.J.: A public-key cryptosystem based on algebraic coding theory. Deep Space Netw. Progress Rep. **44**, 114–116 (1978)
12. NIST: Post-quantum cryptography (2021). https://csrc.nist.gov/projects/post-quantum-cryptography. Accessed 22 June 2022
13. NIST: Status report on the second round of the NIST post-quantum cryptography standardization process (2021). https://csrc.nist.gov/publications/detail/nistir/8309/final. Accessed 22 June 2022
14. Shoup, V.: On the deterministic complexity of factoring polynomials over finite fields. Inf. Process. Lett. **33**(5), 261–267 (1990)

15. Redpine Signals, Inc. – RS9113 FIPS 140–2 Module Non-proprietary Security Policy Version 1.0 (2016). https://csrc.nist.rip/groups/STM/cmvp/documents/140-1/140sp/140sp2548.pdf. Accessed 22 Apr 2022
16. Sun, G., Su, S., Xu, M.: Quantum algorithm for polynomial root finding problem. In: 2014 Tenth International Conference on Computational Intelligence and Security, pp. 469–473 (2014)
17. VAMPIRE: eBACS: ECRYPT Benchmarking of Cryptographic Systems - SUPERCOP. https://bench.cr.yp.to/supercop.html. Accessed: 2022-40-10
18. Vercauteren, I.F.: SABER: Mod-LWR based KEM (Round 3 Submission) (2017). https://www.esat.kuleuven.be/cosic/pqcrypto/saber/files/saberspecround3.pdf. Accessed 21 June 2022

Author Index

© The Editor(s) (if applicable) and The Author(s), under exclusive license
to Springer Nature Switzerland AG 2023
S. Kallel et al. (Eds.): CRiSIS 2022, LNCS 13857, pp. 257–258, 2023.
https://doi.org/10.1007/978-3-031-31108-6

Printed in the United States
by Baker & Taylor Publisher Services

Printed in the United States
by Baker & Taylor Publisher Services